Alcohol in the
Writings of
Herman Melville

Alcohol in the Writings of Herman Melville
"The Ever-Devilish God of Grog"

Corey Evan Thompson

McFarland & Company, Inc., Publishers
Jefferson, North Carolina

LIBRARY OF CONGRESS CATALOGUING-IN-PUBLICATION DATA

Thompson, Corey Evan.
    Alcohol in the writings of Herman Melville : "the ever-devilish god of grog" / Corey Evan Thompson.
        p.   cm.
    Includes bibliographical references and index.

    ISBN 978-0-7864-9960-1 (softcover : acid free paper) ∞
    ISBN 978-1-4766-2120-3 (ebook)

    1. Melville, Herman, 1819–1891—Criticism and interpretation. 2. Drinking of alcoholic beverages in literature. 3. Alcoholic beverages in literature. 4. Temperance in literature. I. Title.

PS2388.D75T46 2015
813'.3—dc23   2015011467

BRITISH LIBRARY CATALOGUING DATA ARE AVAILABLE

© 2015 Corey Evan Thompson. All rights reserved

No part of this book may be reproduced or transmitted in any form or by any means, electronic or mechanical, including photocopying or recording, or by any information storage and retrieval system, without permission in writing from the publisher.

Cover image of glass of whiskey and a bottle © 2015 iStock/Thinkstock

Printed in the United States of America

McFarland & Company, Inc., Publishers
  Box 611, Jefferson, North Carolina 28640
    www.mcfarlandpub.com

To those with whom I
have lifted a glass over the years

The conflict between man and alcohol is as old as civilization, more destructive than any other form of warfare, and as fierce today as at any time since the beginning.—Senator Henry William Blair of New Hampshire. Preface to *The Temperance Movement: Or, the Conflict Between Man and Alcohol*, 1888

Table of Contents

Acknowledgments	ix
Preface	1
Introduction	5
1. Melville's Temperance Fiction	17
2. The Prodromal Phase of Alcoholism	30
3. Melville's Supposedly Social Drinkers	43
4. Unscrupulous Sippers, Smugglers and Servers	52
5. Alcohol, Deception and Melville's Confidence Men	64
6. Loss of Rank, Loss of Reputation	79
7. Alcohol, Ill Health and Penury	88
8. Of Grog and Monsters: Melville's Addiction Narratives	101
9. Melville's Dark Temperance	111
Conclusion	120
Afterword: Melville and the Bottle	136
Appendix: A Concordance of Melville's Characters and Alcohol	151
Chapter Notes	163
Bibliography	189
Index	199

Acknowledgments

Portions of the Introduction and of Chapter 1 originally appeared in "Herman Melville's 'The Apple-Tree Table' as Temperance Fiction," *The Explicator* 71.2 (2013): 135–139. Copyright © 2013 Taylor and Francis. Published online 6 June 2013. Available online at http://tandfonline.com/10.1080/00144940.2013.781009

A small part of Chapter 1 and certain portions of Chapter 2 appeared in "The Prodromal Phase of Alcoholism in Herman Melville's 'Bartleby, the Scrivener' and 'Cock-A-Doodle-Doo!,'" *The Explicator* 71.4 (2013): 275–280. Copyright © 2013 Taylor and Francis. Published online 4 October 2013. Available online at http://tandfonline.com/10.1080/00144940.2013.842146

***

This book, as most academic studies are, is the result of many years of reading and writing, and of re-reading and re-writing. I am therefore thankful that my old Toshiba laptop held on until the last. All facetiousness aside, apart naturally from Herman Melville himself I am thankful to the countless scholars and critics whose work enabled me to complete mine. While there are far too many literary and historical scholars to thank, certain names come easily to mind. As it relates to biographical and factual matters concerning Melville including his drinking, I am indebted to the late Jay Leyda, whose *The Melville Log* is still an invaluable and necessary resource for any Melville scholar, and to Howard C. Horsford and Lynn Horth for their diligent work on and unrelenting dedication to their Northwestern-Newberry editions of *The Writings of*

Herman Melville: Journals (volume 15) and *Correspondence* (volume 14). Also to Hershel Parker, whose exhaustive—yet by no means exhausting—two-volume work *Herman Melville: A Biography* will continue to be the standard Melville biography no doubt for years if not decades to come, and to Laurie Robertson-Lorant. To David S. Reynolds, Paul McCarthy, and Robert S. Levine, whose work planted the seed for me to undertake this project, and to all of the social critics and historians who gave me a better understanding of the alcohol-fueled world of the early United States of America. A toast of thanks goes to you all.

I both need and want to thank former professors who piqued and then maintained my interest in literature and literary studies. Without most of them and in one way or another, this study would most certainly never have been even started. To A. W. Plumstead from Nipissing University in North Bay, Ontario, Canada, who introduced me intensely to Herman Melville in an undergraduate honors seminar in the fall of 1998 and who set me on the path to graduate school (I am unsure whether I should thank him for that). Many decades before I met him (many years before I was even born, in fact) he along with renowned American scholars William H. Gilman, Harrison Hayford, and Ruth H. Bennett did integral editorial work on two volumes of *The Journals and Miscellaneous Notebooks of Ralph Waldo Emerson* (Cambridge: Harvard University Press; volumes 7 [1969] and 11 [1975]) and independently edited *The Wall and the Garden: Selected Massachusetts Election Sermons, 1670–1775* (Minneapolis: University of Minnesota Press, 1968). Not strictly an accomplished scholar and academic, his creative works include his 1992 novel *Loon* (Cobalt, Ontario: Highway Book Shop), which was adapted into a motion picture under the title *That Beautiful Somewhere* in 2006 (Lumanity). Also due immense thanks are all of the professors at the University of Windsor from my time there as a graduate student. There are three, however, who deserve special mention. To Thomas Dilworth: Killam Fellow, Fellow of the Royal Society of Canada, and author of books including *The Shape of Meaning in the Poetry of David Jones* (Toronto: University of Toronto Press, 1988) and *David Jones in the Great War* (London: Enitharmon Press, 2012). His graduate seminars on James Joyce and twentieth-century poetry (the mid-length modern poem, more specifically) were both entertaining and educational beyond belief and he did what all teachers at any level of education should encourage their students to do: think. Also, to prolific Gothic and Victorian scholar Carol Margaret Davison, whose publications include *History of the Gothic: Gothic Literature, 1764–1824* (Wales: University of Wales Press, 2009), *Anti-Semitism and British Gothic Literature* (New York: Palgrave MacMillan, 2004), and the edited *Bram Stoker's "Dracula": Sucking Through the Century, 1897–1997* (Toronto: Dundurn, 1997). Her graduate seminars were nothing short of intense but like all good things in life they were—and trust that they still are—entirely worth the effort. In more ways than one, thank you, Carol. Finally to the late Alistair MacLeod, who passed away in 2014 after many decades teaching creative writing at the University of Windsor. His short stories are among the best written and most vivid in Canadian literature and his 1999 novel *No Great Mischief* (Toronto: McClelland and Stewart), which received many accolades including the Trillium Book Award (2000) and the International IMPAC Dublin Literary Award (2001), rightfully stands among very few other worthy contenders for the title of the Great Canadian Novel. Although I never took a class with him I was nevertheless afforded the opportunity and honor to converse with him relatively frequently and to see that he was a man who truly exemplified and made one feel the meaning of his lone novel's resonating final line: "All of us are better when we're loved." A *cheers* goes out to all of you for your academic guidance, harsh yet constructive criticism, and unwavering encouragement and support from what has quickly become so many years ago.

Thanks are also due to those with whom I had the privilege of studying at both Nipissing University and the University of Windsor. First and foremost to Eric Peysar: my Hawthorne. A few years my senior, he courageously left the world of automotive manufacturing and the financial security that at the time accompanied it to return to school and pursue a degree in environmental science and geography. Despite our differing areas of academic study and schedules at Nipissing, together we always found time to grab a few pints of ale or drams of Southern Comfort, hold the pool table all night, and discuss our own "ontological heroics" in the tobacco smoke-filled air at the seedy Library Lounge in the Sands Hotel during those frigid and early dark winter nights in North Bay. While at the University of Windsor, a two-minute drive from Detroit, I met fellow graduate students Nasser Hussain, Kaley Kramer, Kim Brown, and the eclectic Stephen Braund. We together talked and attempted to "settle the affairs of the universe" over many a glass—ok, pitcher—of ale at the Grad House Pub. Each of you, our far-from-temperate times, and intellectual discussions are all dearly missed.

I would like to raise a glass to those who offered insight and expressed interest in this project. Special thanks go out to Melville biographer and literary scholar *extraordinaire* Hershel Parker, who graciously provided me with invaluable direction concerning textual interpretation and general insight in our enlightening email conversations, and to my colleagues Tami Kroon, Lisa Zeran, and Angel Brant from the Akwesasne Mohawk Board of Education, each of whom offered me the inspiration and encouragement needed to get this book finished and to get back to my real job: teaching.

On a more personal note and as always with anything to do with my life, my biggest debt goes to my family: my parents Ron and Maureen, siblings Trevor and Angela, and daughters Jerika and Jordan. The influence that all of you have had on every aspect of my life is far too profound for words, so I will leave it at that. And now that this book is completed, the gin is finally here.

Preface

This book is about alcohol and intoxication in the works of the nineteenth-century American fiction writer and poet Herman Melville (1819–1891). Melville was born in an era when drinking and drunkenness were accepted and expected rituals of daily life for American men, and he came of age during a time when the temperance movement—a crusade against alcohol and intoxication that would, to use Richard Worth's words, "change the history of America"[1]—had already gained significant momentum and was a momentous social and literary force. This study will show how Melville through his literature and much like many of his contemporary authors resoundingly entered into the debate surrounding alcohol and inebriation in mid- to late nineteenth-century America.[2] It will illustrate how he wrote both fictional and poetical works in which he consistently supported a social movement—temperance—whose overwhelming significance and presence in the nineteenth century has now largely been lost in the shadow of the era's other and, in retrospect, perhaps more pressing social concerns including the Peculiar Institution and the Woman Question.[3]

Considering the fact that library shelves are already groaning due to the weight that they bear from texts of Melville criticism,[4] one may rightfully question the need for yet another book devoted to him and his works. The justification for this study, though, is simple: it has yet to be done. Granted, simply because this work enters into uncharted waters does not on its own make it a valid and necessary contribution to Melville studies, yet given the extensive and at times controversial

• Preface •

commentary that Melville biographers including Edwin Haviland Miller, Laurie Robertson-Lorant, and Hershel Parker have provided on the frequency of drinking by both Melville and those in his extended family,[5] and taking into account the overwhelming role that alcohol played in his society at large,[6] one may erroneously yet understandably assume that drinking and drunkenness in his novels, short fiction, and poetry would have also garnered significant critical attention. Curiously, however, this is not the case. While I concede that brief discussions of alcohol's presence in some of Melville's novels and short stories have appeared in a few concise essays and in select parts of certain book chapters,[7] there is to date no single extended study that examines the overwhelming presence and implications of alcohol in the full body of Melville's works. When one recognizes the consistency with which imbibing and intoxication permeate his writings—there are far too many instances of them in Melville's fiction and poetry for us to ignore them—and the intense debates surrounding alcohol and inebriation that occurred in the society in which he lived, this is, indeed, a serious deficiency in both Melville and nineteenth-century American cultural studies. *Alcohol in the Writings of Herman Melville: "The Ever-Devilish God of Grog,"* then, is a valuable and necessary contribution to Melville criticism because it is the first full-length investigation that will discuss in detail Melville's views on alcohol and inebriation in a society where liquor was running like a river and where the temperance movement was seeking to stop its flow.

The book's subtitle—*"The Ever-Devilish God of Grog"*—is taken from two different chapters in Melville's fifth novel *White-Jacket*. The first occurrence is found at the beginning of Chapter 43, "Smuggling in a Man-of-War," when the titular narrator discusses the temptation that alcohol has for the sailors on board the man-of-war *Neversink* who are anchored a good distance from land:

> It is in a good degree owing to the idleness just described, that, while lying in harbor, the man-of-war's man is exposed to the most temptations, and gets into his saddest scrapes. For though his vessel be anchored a mile from the shore, and her sides are patrolled by sentries night and day, yet these things can not entirely prevent the seductions of the land from reaching him. The prime agent in working his calamities in port is his old arch-enemy, the ever-devilish god of grog.[8]

Preface

The second instance is in Chapter 91 when White-Jacket talks about, in part, the sailors' inability to resist the lure of libations: "But, alas for the man-of-war's man, who, though he may take a Hannibal oath against the service; yet, cruise after cruise, and after forswearing it again and again, he is driven back to the spirit-tub and the gun-deck by his old hereditary foe, the ever-devilish god of grog" (390). I have chosen this phrase as a part of the book's title because it exemplifies everything that I am attempting to argue throughout this study. In Melville's view and as will be discussed more thoroughly in the Introduction and illustrated in the chapters that follow, alcohol was something that tempted people to consume it for the sake of inebriation despite the countless inherent dangers that existed surrounding and associated with it. Alcohol, like the Devil, was without question and for a variety of reasons diabolical and evil. At the same time, however, it was worshipped like a god by countless late-eighteenth and early to mid-nineteenth-century American men through their excessive consumption of it. It was revered by the men in his society, but as Melville consistently shows in his writings from the 1840s and onward, it was for many damning reasons certainly not worthy of any such reverence. It was, therefore, something that should be avoided under all circumstances.

The organization of this study is thematic rather than chronological and as much as possible it is void of the esoteric language and at times inaccessible critical theory that has, in my mind, plagued literary studies for both undergraduate students and those general lay-readers who might have an interest in a variety of topics, in this case Herman Melville, nineteenth-century American literature, or the temperance movement. If theory must be applied to appease those with a penchant for such academic classifications, then I have written the book as much as possible from a Historical Critical perspective, a theoretical approach that examines the respective writers' works within the cultural context of the society in which they lived. Contrary to the views of the staunch supporters of New Criticism—a critical stance that looks at the text and only the text for meaning—authors do not write in a social vacuum; their art is always influenced by their own experiences, by that of those around them, and by the overall societal forces to which they are subjected.[9] Firmly believing this, I have therefore chosen the route of Historical Criticism and as cogently and as clearly as possible I have attempted to allow all lovers of Melville and those with even a mere

• Preface •

interest in nineteenth-century debates surrounding temperance to see precisely the role that alcohol played in Melville's life and society and, more importantly, to show how he lambasted the pastime that he apparently loved.

Initial references to a work, whether in the text or in the notes, will appear in the notes. Subsequent references to the same work will be from the same edition and will be cited parenthetically in the text.

Introduction

According to the nineteenth-century American Transcendentalist Ralph Waldo Emerson, literary artists relish the intoxicating effects of drugs, alcohol, and other stimulants: they "love wine, mead, narcotics, coffee, tea, opium, the fumes of sandalwood and tobacco, or whatever other procurers of animal exhilaration" they can find.[1] The American fiction writer and poet Herman Melville (1819–1891) is certainly no exception; it is no secret among scholars and critics of nineteenth-century American literature that Melville liked—loved, in fact—to drink. As Emerson suggests, this does not make him unique among other notable men of American letters including Edgar Allan Poe, Ernest Hemingway, F. Scott Fitzgerald, William Faulkner, or Jack Kerouac, whose issues with or addictions to alcohol and other narcotics have been well documented.[2] Yet what is different in Melville's case is that biographers and critics alike have been unable to come to a consensus on the precise extent and nature of his drinking; there is no unanimously accepted view in academic circles concerning the type of drinker that Melville was.

The number of differing theories that critics, scholars, and biographers have presented about Melville's drinking habits is enough to make one's head spin worse than it would from a night of over-indulgence at a frat-house keg party. To some, Melville was merely a social drinker who imbibed with acquaintances and when discussing matters of metaphysics and philosophy at his farmhouse Arrowhead with his friends including his fellow American author Nathaniel Hawthorne.[3] To others, he was a man of the opposite extreme who drank heavily whenever he wanted for decades and whose supposedly monstrous drunken rampages resulted in physical and emotional abuse directed toward his children and wife, Elizabeth.[4] There are those who believe that he drank medicinally, strictly as a way to seek physical relief "from his tightened muscles,"[5] while others maintain that he imbibed during a midlife crisis in order to numb himself mentally from depression stemming from his failing literary career and from the growing stresses of his financial and familial responsibilities (Rollyson and Paddock 117, 119).[6] For some he was certainly and without question a heavy drinker whose family maintained "a conspiracy of silence" about his drunken stupors, but he "was not an alcoholic" (E. H. Miller 321), while for others he was undoubtedly a heavy drinker and possibly was an alcoholic from the 1850s onward,[7] and for still others he was without question an alcoholic and a man whose addiction "plagued" him his entire adult life.[8] Some have argued that perhaps his drinking got progressively worse over time,[9] while others conversely believe that it likely subsided as he got older (Robertson-Lorant, *Melville* 559). Which of these assessments is the most accurate? While the debate will all but certainly continue, the question about Melville's drinking and whether or not he was an alcoholic, as Robert Milder accurately states in his 2006 book *Exiled Royalties: Melville and the Life We Imagine*, is—and always will be— "unanswerable."[10]

I wholeheartedly agree with Milder and therefore the aim of this study is not to address, arrive at, or even attempt to answer what I classify as the Melville Question—whether or not Melville was an unequivocal alcoholic. We know from his own descriptions of drinking in his letters and some of his journals that he loved to imbibe, but that is all that can be said for certain: anything more would be mere speculation fueled by personal opinion or agenda.[11] Rather, the primary focus in these pages will be on Melville's works and on the alcohol and alcoholics that are contained therein.

Despite the frequency with which Melvilleans have cast their lenses on and debated Melville's own drinking, the presence of alcohol and intoxication in his fiction and poetry has garnered from the majority of critics scant attention at best. Two notable exceptions, however, are Paul McCarthy and David S. Reynolds. Both McCarthy—in a few pages of his pioneering 1990 study on mental abnormality in Melville's

• Introduction •

prose works *"The Twisted Mind": Madness in Herman Melville's Fiction*—and Reynolds—in parts of various publications including his classic 1988 book *Beneath the American Renaissance*—provide some insightful commentary on alcohol's role in some of Melville's fiction (his poetry, typically, is curiously and consistently exempt from such alcohol-related analysis). Without question, McCarthy and Reynolds are owed a debt of gratitude from the academic community for their efforts in identifying and (limitedly) discussing the presence of alcohol in some of Melville's writings, yet even they underestimate just how frequent an occurrence it is. According to McCarthy, for instance, alcohol abuse is merely present in *"most* of [Melville's] novels and *a few* short stories" (38, emphasis added), and Reynolds' focus on intoxication in Melville's works consistently rests on only a select few of his extended narratives, thereby suggesting that they are the only works in which alcohol plays a role.[12] While I concede that alcohol and its consumption are indeed absent in works including the traditionally–British Gothic short story "The Bell Tower" (1855),[13] "The Happy Failure" (1854), and "The Piazza" (1856), and are only mentioned in passing and with little-to-no significance in other shorter works including "The Fiddler" (1854), when the failed poet Helmstone and his friends go to Taylor's pub to drink their punch,[14] and "I and My Chimney" (1856), when the narrator refers to his appreciation of "old wine" (337),[15] alcohol is far more common in Melville's writings than both McCarthy and Reynolds suggest.

Throughout the course of this study I will illustrate that alcohol has a significant and purposeful if not always an extended presence in all nine of Melville's novels—*Typee: A Peep at Polynesian Life* (1846), *Omoo: A Narrative of Adventures in the South Seas* (1847), *Mardi: And a Voyage Thither* (1849), *Redburn: His First Voyage, Being the Sailor-Boy Confessions and Reminiscences of the Son-of-a-Gentleman, in the Merchant Service* (1849), *White-Jacket; or, The World in a Man-of-War* (1850), *Moby-Dick; or, the Whale* (1851), *Pierre; or, The Ambiguities* (1852), *Israel Potter: His Fifty Years of Exile* (1855), and *The Confidence-Man: His Masquerade* (1857)—both of his novellas—"Benito Cereno" (1855) and the posthumously-published *Billy Budd, Sailor (An Inside Narrative)* (1924)—a significant number (more than a half dozen) of his shorter works—"Bartleby, the Scrivener: A Story of Wall Street" (1853), "Cock-A-Doodle-Doo!, or the Crowing of the Noble Cock Beneventano" (1853), "The Encantadas, or Enchanted Isles" (1854), "The

• INTRODUCTION •

Paradise of Bachelors and the Tartarus of Maids" (1855), "Jimmy Rose" (1855), "The Apple-Tree Table, or Original Spiritual Manifestations" (1856), "The Two Temples" (1924; published posthumously),[16] and "Under the Rose" (1924; published posthumously)—and in various sections of his poems "The Scout Toward Aldie" from the collection *Battle Pieces and Aspects of the War: Civil War Poems* (1866), the religious epic *Clarel: A Poem and Pilgrimage to the Holy Land* (1876), and "Bridegroom Dick," which was published as a part of *John Marr and Other Sailors, With Some Sea Pieces* in 1888. Given the prevalence of alcohol and its consumption in both Melville's fiction and poetry—he essentially created a world of drunks—one could rightfully say that they are insistent themes and, therefore, are surely worthy subjects for an intense and focussed examination.

Although this study, in part, seeks to illustrate more accurately and conclusively than critics including McCarthy and Reynolds just how common alcohol is in Melville's novels, short fiction, and poetry, its main objective extends far beyond that. Its purpose is not simply to identify the myriad of drinkers in Melville's writings; rather, and of far more importance, it is to consider the implications of alcohol's consistent presence in Melville's fictional and poetical worlds. There are two central questions that I pose here and that I seek to answer over the course of this study: why does alcohol have such a prominent occurrence in Melville's works, and what is he trying to relate about alcohol and inebriation to his mid- to late nineteenth-century American audience? The answer to the first of these queries is straightforward: as will be shown in great detail in the Afterword, alcohol had such an immense presence in Melville's life and society at large that it is only natural that it would be so common in his writings. Just as he had done by writing works about a trans–Atlantic crossing to and life in Liverpool (*Redburn*), the experiences of those who are employed on a whaling vessel (*Moby-Dick*), and the harsh realities of life on board a man-of-war (*White-Jacket*), Melville is adhering to the writers' old adage of writing about what you know best.[17] The answer to the latter and more important of these questions, however, is in stark contrast, as I will show, to what many critics of nineteenth-century American literature would assume about Melville and alcohol.

The enterprise I seek to undertake was initiated in part yet by no means completed by Robert S. Levine in his 1991 contribution to *The*

• *Introduction* •

Columbia History of the American Novel. In his thorough essay on literature and social reform during the American Renaissance, the period now generally marked by the years 1830–1860,[18] Levine accurately notes that Melville viewed alcohol and drinking as a "considerable social problem."[19] While Levine is certainly correct in this view, there are certain aspects of his argument that are nonetheless problematic. For one, he fails to specify or describe precisely how severe a "considerable" social problem is; moreover, he curiously neglects to demonstrate exactly how or why Melville views alcohol thus. In fact, he provides nearly no clear or specific extended examples directly from Melville's fiction or poetry to illustrate his otherwise valuable insight, and by neglecting to do so his argument becomes mere conjecture and, therefore, its force is tragically all but lost. I intend to continue from where Levine accurately yet vaguely left off.

Numerous critics have rightfully noted that Melville wrote with enthusiasm about drinking and intoxication in many of his correspondences and some of his journals. Robert Milder, for instance, properly observes that Melville frequently celebrates drunkenness in many of his personal writings as "festive and, at its best, conducive to philosophical talk" (*Exiled* 277n32), while Elizabeth Renker accurately notices that Melville describes imbibing in his letters with a passionate form of writing—"orgiastically" as she sexually describes it (143n12)[20]—that even I would argue is unequalled anywhere in his fiction or poetry. Yet Milder's and Renker's respective views on alcohol in Melville's personal writings are, despite their accuracy, misleading and perhaps misconstrue what Melville is actually saying in his novels, short fiction, and poetry about it and its consumption. In such latter writings and in contrast to his correspondences and journals, Melville consistently illustrates that alcohol was not simply a social inconvenience, as Levine suggests, or something that caused mere raucous drunken importunity. For Melville and in opposition to how he presents it in his letters and journals, alcohol was something far more nefarious. It was, quite literally, diabolical, evil, and therefore something best to be avoided. All one has to do to see the truth in this statement is casually browse his works and consider the rhetoric that he uses to depict alcohol, imbibing, and drunkenness. Taking just a few descriptions of alcohol from his fiction and poetry that point to its wickedness, Melville classifies it as "the ever-devilish god" (*White-Jacket* 176, 390), "the devil's drugged stuff,"[21] "poison," a "fiend," "death,"[22] and as an evil that was unleashed by the "civilized" missionaries onto the pure islanders of the South Pacific.[23] Being equally condemned by Melville, the act of drinking is regarded as a "sad habit," a sin (*White-Jacket* 241, 242),[24] a "failing" (*Omoo* 7), and a vice.[25] These are clearly not complimentary terms and certainly not ones that would be associated with mere social inconvenience; rather, they point to a deeply-rooted degenerative influence that, in Melville's mind, was controlling and contributing to the deterioration of nineteenth-century American society.

Put quite simply, Melville in many episodes from all of his novels, much of his short fiction, and some of his poetry does not describe drinking with "a kind of nostalgic or sentimental idealizing of tippling," as Robert Ryan curiously believes[26]; rather, he presents numerous characters who are always adversely affected by alcohol either through their own consumption of it (past or present), their association with those who do, or even merely their close proximity to it.[27] Melville's works illustrate that he was distrustful of those who drank and he shows in a variety of ways why. He thought that alcohol would bring ruin to those who imbibed, and he provides graphic demonstrations of how. He urges his readers to give up the bottle and to adopt a life of sobriety and he frequently exposes the variously harsh—in some cases deadly—fates that will ultimately be theirs if they continue to drink or associate with those who do. As a result of writing so consistently works that urge the avoidance of alcohol, Herman Melville is—and should be but has yet to be regarded as—one of the most staunch supporters of temperance, if not prohibition, of all nineteenth-century American male authors.

This study's first chapter will examine three of Melville's works—the historical novel *Israel Potter* and the short stories "Cock-A-Doodle-Doo!" and "The Apple-Tree Table"—through the lenses of temperance fiction (a very brief episode from Chapter 72 of *Moby-Dick* will also be considered). As will be shown in the beginning of this opening chapter, by the 1820s many American women had grown tired of and become frustrated with the amount of alcohol that their husbands and (male) family members were consuming. The end result was the birth of the temperance movement, a social crusade that called for the reduction or even elimination of alcohol consumption altogether. Looking to promote the cause, or simply to capitalize on its popularity for financial success as some did, many authors began to write works of temperance fiction, or literature that encouraged people to quit drinking. Although he has yet to be given much credit for doing so,[28] Melville indeed did write works that support temperance and that offer the drunkards hope that their addiction to alcohol can be overcome. In *Israel Potter* Melville offers frequent temperance advice to the titular character through one of the Founding Fathers of the United States—Benjamin Franklin—and in "Cock-A-Doodle-Doo!" and "The Apple-Tree Table" Melville presents alcoholics who have ("Cock-A-Doodle-Doo!") and who eventually do ("The Apple-Tree Table") successfully give up the bottle with the assistance of their loving wives. In these works, Melville is optimistic for his readers that the abandonment of the bottle is certainly possible and that a liquor-free life is unquestionably attainable.

Whereas Melville offers encouragement and hope to his readers in the moments from the works considered in Chapter 1 that chronic drunkenness can be overcome, the remaining chapters of this study will illustrate the various fates that will inevitably await those who continue to imbibe or associate with those who do. In the works considered in Chapter 2, Melville chronicles the stories of those who use alcohol as a means of escaping their life's difficulties—drinkers who are in what Dr. E. M. Jellinek in 1960 coined as the prodromal phase of alcoholism—and illustrates that using alcohol for such purposes for an extended period of time will ultimately make the drinkers' situation worse. Such potential and stereotypical alcoholics are found to varying degrees in *Pierre*, "Bartleby, the Scrivener," "Cock-A-Doodle-Doo!" and *White-Jacket*.

In the short stories and novels examined in Chapters 3 and 4 Melville variously shows how drinkers are selfish and self-centered individuals, unscrupulous and devious people who will, in a variety of ways, take advantage of others for the sake of alcohol. In "The Paradise of Bachelors" and "Jimmy Rose" (Chapter 3) alcoholics use and abuse their supposed friends simply to feed, or drink in such cases, their addictions. They mask their alcoholism under the guise of friendship, and such so-called friendships are forged and maintained merely for the sake of alcohol. They are the proverbial wolves in sheep's clothing who appear to have the strongest dedication to and the deepest reverence for others when in reality their thirst for liquor is all that they truly value. In *Billy Budd, Sailor, Redburn, Omoo, White-Jacket,* and

• INTRODUCTION •

Moby-Dick (Chapter 4), people are in a variety of ways taken advantage of or cheated, betrayed, and again abused by others who are associated with alcohol. Even those who refrain from drinking, as is illustrated in certain instances in Chapter 4, are negatively affected by alcohol through the actions of those who do not.

While the characters from the stories discussed in Chapters 3 and 4 are taken advantage of by drinkers *for* alcohol, those from the works considered in Chapter 5 of this study are taken advantage of by drinkers *with* liquor. This chapter is a detailed examination of Melville's most notorious character: the confidence man. Melville's writings are rife with con men who use alcohol as a type of tool or weapon against others for the sake of obtaining something of value from their victims. The item of value ranges from money, to privileged information, to even the drinkers themselves: alcohol in these final instances is used to kidnap the characters who are enticed into drinking. In addition to episodes from the most obvious example of Melville's con men—those found in the novel *The Confidence-Man*—con artists who use alcohol against others, whether they are successful or not, appear in the poems "Bridegroom Dick" and "The Scout Toward Aldie," the novels *Omoo* and *Israel Potter*, and in the ninth sketch of "The Encantadas" ("Hood's Isle and the Hermit Oberlus").

Melville was well aware of how rare employment opportunities were during the early to mid-nineteenth century; he himself searched for work unsuccessfully and spent time holding various jobs that he despised until he ultimately accepted a full-time and permanent position as an inspector of customs at the port of New York in 1866, a post that earned him approximately $4 a day ($1,200 per annum) and that he would hold until the end of 1885. Since he was so aware of the scant employment opportunities other than those to be found on board whaling vessels or in the navy, Melville in the novels *Typee*, *White-Jacket*, and *Omoo*, and in the novella *Billy Budd, Sailor*, urges his readers to abandon the bottle for the sake of their careers. In these narratives from Chapter 6 and as Melville himself had witnessed during his own time at sea on a number of ships from 1841 to 1844, we see characters whose employment or professional character on board various whalers and man-of-wars is destroyed by their alcoholism or conversely those whose careers are advanced due to their sobriety.

As investigations into alcohol consumption progressed during the

• Introduction •

early to mid-nineteenth century, it was becoming evident that frequent drinking did not have, as was long believed during the early republic, medicinal benefits. Rather, it was becoming known that chronic alcohol consumption was in fact detrimental to one's health; excessive drinking could cause harmful medical conditions and exacerbate existing ones. In addition to having ill effects on one's physical well-being, it was also known that the money people were spending on alcohol was equally leading to financial ruin. It will be shown in Chapter 7 how Melville clearly illustrates each of these emerging facts. Through certain characters in "Benito Cereno," *Redburn, White-Jacket,* and *The Confidence-Man* Melville illustrates that alcohol truly has no medicinal benefits; some in *White-Jacket, Omoo,* and *Mardi* have their health negatively affected by frequent or excessive consumption of alcohol; others in "Cock-A-Doodle-Doo!," *Redburn,* and *Omoo* lose their financial security due to alcoholism (either their own or that of others). These characters who have physical and financial difficulties, however, continue to drink and thereby exacerbate their health and monetary problems.

Chapter 8 and the works considered therein delve into the dramatic and horrific alterations that drinkers can experience once they become intoxicated. Looking at parts of *Pierre, Clarel,* "Cock-A-Doodle-Doo!," "Bartleby," *Omoo,* and "Bridegroom Dick" through the lenses of the literary tradition of addiction narratives, drinkers in these works are drastically transformed into the Gothic character of the *other* or *Doppelgänger* once they become intoxicated. When they are sober, most of the characters are typically caring and well-meaning individuals who to varying degrees genuinely care about others. Once they are inebriated, however, they become devilish monsters whose actions and emotions range and escalate from anger to violence to mass murder. Alcohol, Melville shows in these works, is the root cause of such devilish behavior.

The chapters up to this point in the study will have shown how Melville in the majority of his works illustrates the various detrimental effects that alcohol can have on people's lives and on that of those around them. In the ninth and final chapter, Melville progresses and provides the ultimate warning to those who continue to drink excessively: drinking will ultimately bring either a horrific and early death or unimaginable personal ruin. Episodes in *Redburn* and *Moby-Dick* are graphic examples of dark temperance, or works that demonstrate what the most terrifying of all consequences will be for those who refuse or who are unable to give up the bottle.

The central question and concern for this study's conclusion surround the discrepancy between Melville's own seemingly enjoyable experiences with alcohol and the negative ones that affect the characters that he presents in his fiction and poetry. Why does Melville revere drinking so fervently in his personal writings, yet urge his readers in his novels, short fiction, and poetry to avoid alcohol and abstain from drinking? The conclusion will demonstrate that the differences between Melville's own drinking experiences and those of his characters are not necessarily as distant and different as one may think. Melville implores his readers to abstain from drinking because he was aware of the various deceits and dangers that alcohol and its excessive consumption could cause as he or those around him experienced them first-hand. Throughout his novels, short stories, and poems, Herman Melville is trying to save his readers from the various fates to which his characters are subjected and from ones that he or his family had gone through themselves. He is urging his audience for their own benefit, as did those who initiated and promoted the temperance movement in the first place, to give up the bottle and to live an alcohol-free life, and in turn avoid the various horrors that inevitably accompany it. That Melville would use his writings to offer such advice to his readers based on his own experiences concerning alcohol is certainly plausible; after all, as Jay Leyda astutely observes in the outset of his 1952 anthology *The Portable Melville*, "there is a link between Melville's experiences and his works, which are all a transmutation, to some degree, of a reality he had observed or lived."[29]

Despite not seeking to answer or even contemplate the Melville Question—was he an alcoholic—specific discussion of his own drinking is required, especially since I posit that it is one of the reasons for alcohol's persistent recurrence in his works. As noted at the beginning of this Introduction, speculation about Melville's drinking is rampant in Melville studies; there have been countless varying theories concerning the type of drinker that Melville was. In the Afterword I will do what past scholars have not: chronicle all of the known factual documents—letters and journal entries—either by or about Melville that discuss his relationship with alcohol without offering opinion or making inferences, no matter how likely they may be. It will be, to the best of my

• Introduction •

knowledge, the first attempt to gather such information in one place. While my aim in doing so is not to deal with the Melville Question, what other critics choose to do with this accumulated knowledge is their prerogative. The Afterword, then, is a type of biography that is specifically focused on alcohol and inebriation and that will offer factual insight into the extent and nature of alcohol's role in the life of Herman Melville.

The Appendix is a concordance in which I present the most notable examples of individuals from Melville's novels, short fiction, and poetry who are in one way or another involved or associated with alcohol. It includes characters who offer temperance advice to those who imbibe, those who are drinkers or alcoholics themselves, those who abuse and betray others with or for the sake of liquor, and those who are taken advantage of by those who drink. Without including the number of individuals from large groups of characters (the *Neversink*'s crew in *White-Jacket*, the French army from *Omoo*, and Liverpool's destitute from *Redburn*, among others, are listed in the Appendix but since they are all of an indeterminate number it is impossible for them to be accurately included in the overall count) there are more than 80 individuals from more than 20 of Melville's works included in this Appendix who fit one of the aforementioned associations with alcohol. If we include those from the groups mentioned above, then the number of characters from Melville's writings who are involved with or affected by alcohol in some way would number in the hundreds. Each entry also contains a brief description of how the character is affected by or associated with alcohol. To reiterate what I stated earlier in this Introduction and as this Appendix will show more glaringly and immediately than the chapters, then, there clearly is a myriad of individuals from Melville's writings who are associated with and negatively affected by alcohol in one way or another, and given their overwhelming presence, therefore, they certainly cannot be ignored.

Chapter 1

Melville's Temperance Fiction

It has been well documented by historians that a love for if not an addiction to alcohol and drunkenness in the United States is as old as the country itself. In fact, in the nation's formative decades of the late eighteenth century simply questioning drinking and inebriation in America was unheard of. To "condemn liquor" in the early republic, to use Debra Rosenthal and David Reynolds' words, "was to denounce the very structure of early society. The tavern and church stood as twin pillars of community life in the eighteenth century, suggesting townfolk's equal devotion to spirits and the Spirit."[1] Such veneration of and ultimate addiction to alcohol in America continued on into the early nineteenth century to such a degree that by the 1830s the average American was downing the equivalent of certainly over four—some estimates say likely over five and, almost unbelievably, possibly near seven—gallons of pure alcohol a year (Rosenthal and Reynolds 2; Rorabaugh 8).[2] To put that astounding number in perspective, a 2014 report by the World Health Organization found that Americans in the opening decade of the twenty-first century were drinking on average far less than their national predecessors: they were consuming on average far less than 2.5 gallons of pure alcohol, per person, per year.[3] Given the inconceivable amount of booze that Americans drank for the better part of their nation's first century, the United States was clearly a liquor-loving, alcohol-guzzling nation. It should come as no surprise, therefore, that Melville himself and those around him were such frequent imbibers as well.

Excessive drinking, as Klaus P. Stich has stated and as the above figures clearly show, "was part of the decorum of life" in Melville's society.[4] Yet based on the amount of liquor that Americans were consuming in the late-eighteenth and early-to-mid-nineteenth centuries, drunkenness was increasingly being regarded around the world as "the American disease,"[5] and the United States itself was negatively becoming known, even among its own citizens and as illustrated in an 1831 publication by the Boston Society for the Suppression of Intemperance, as "*a nation of drunkards*."[6] It appears that Melville himself was well-aware of such derogatory views directed toward his nation and its citizens and that he, more importantly, actually agreed with and supported them. He calls attention to the world-renowned drunken Yankee / American in both *Israel Potter* and in the second part of his short story "The Two Temples," which despite its posthumously-published 1924 status was written like *Israel Potter* during the temperance crusade of the early-to-mid 1850s.[7] In Chapter 3 of *Israel Potter* the titular character has escaped incarceration as a prisoner of war only to be again quickly apprehended. After being taken back to the inn by his captors, where two soldiers are appointed to guard him all night, the landlord observes that Israel "must needs be a true-blooded Yankee." In the process he thereby stereotypes Potter and his assumed Yankee love of or addiction to alcohol and "calls for liquors to refresh Israel after his run."[8] In "The Two Temples" the narrator is at a pub in London and declines what he believes to be coffee. As the narrator says, "'Thank you,' said I, 'I won't take any coffee, I guess'" (163). The young English boy who offers it to him, completely astounded that the narrator would refuse what is actually alcohol, replies: "'Coffee?—I guess?—ain't you a Yankee?'" (163). The narrator subsequently confirms the boy's impression of Americans and ultimately accepts a free glass of ale. In these two works, then, Melville clearly demonstrates his knowledge of and even promotes the condescending views toward alcohol consumption by the citizens of the New World.

As a result of such disparaging remarks and views directed toward America and Americans, public opinion in the United States concerning inebriation for many began to change. A significant portion of American society had had enough of constant drinking and public intoxication and wives were growing even more frustrated with having their husbands imbibing frequently at the local tavern, arriving home late (Worth 44), and in certain cases becoming abusive. Instead of being viewed as

1. Melville's Temperance Fiction

something that went hand-in-hand with the country's formation and being considered as a type of birth-right for American men, drunkenness was increasingly being associated with the "undisciplined, ungodly, or degenerate" (Rorabaugh 241). Women—wives and otherwise—took action and initiated what would become known as the temperance movement, "the largest single organizing force for women in U.S. history, moving women to take action in unprecedented numbers" against alcohol and intoxication.[9] The temperance movement was officially born in the 1820s and the achievement of its goals was highly successful.

Once the wheels of alcohol reform and social change were set in motion and the temperance movement had gained momentum, it seemed that there was little, if anything, that could stop it. Within the first decade of its establishment the temperance movement had enlisted the support of more than a million Americans (Worth 40), which was an astounding ten percent of the free population, and by the mid–1850s it was a "well established, thriving reform movement" (Cordell 3) that had reduced the per capita consumption of alcohol in the United States by a factor of four.[10] Despite such success, however, temperance was not enough for some citizens. In 1840, a group of tradesmen and recovering alcoholics founded the Washingtonians—named after George Washington—who were committed not just to temperance but to absolute abstinence. In a more impressive fashion than the temperance movement, the group had attracted one million people who had taken the pledge within its first three years (Worth 42). As quickly as the Washingtonian movement began, however, it ended. Within a few years of its formation and as a result of its expanding focus on other social causes, the Washingtonian movement was over. It fizzled out just as quickly as it had ignited. The issue of temperance and the continued push for it in America, however, did not disappear with it.

It was not simply society's teetotalers, wives, and Washingtonians who were screaming for temperance or outright prohibition. Writers of the American Renaissance also had a profound voice in the movement and they began to write what has become known as temperance fiction. As world renowned expert on the subject David Reynolds describes it, temperance literature contains "straightforward, didactic expositions or exempla against drinking, with emphasis on the benign rewards of the virtue rather than the brutal results of the vice" ("Black" 22). In other words, it encourages abstinence from drinking and provides hope to the reader / drinker that sobriety is attainable. Considering the force with which wives and women supported the temperance movement, it should come as no surprise that female writers including Harriet Beecher Stowe, Lydia Howard Huntley Sigourney, Louisa May Alcott, and Elizabeth Cady Stanton were all such significant contributors to the genre. Yet it was not simply the female writers of the era who contributed to the temperance movement and its associated literature. "All of the major American Renaissance authors," according to Reynolds, "were influenced by the temperance movement" ("Black" 32), men included.[11] More than a decade before *Leaves of Grass* (1855) was published, for instance, Walt Whitman wrote his temperance novel *Franklin Evans* (1842),[12] and long before Nathaniel Hawthorne gained notoriety from his novels *The Scarlet Letter* (1850) and *The House of the Seven Gables* (1851) he preached temperance in "A Rill from the Town Pump" (1835), a short story from his collection *Twice Told Tales*.[13] Even Timothy Shay Arthur, who some have regarded as "perhaps the most prolific and popular [American] writer of the nineteenth century,"[14] voiced his views in overwhelming support of the temperance movement and alcohol avoidance in his renowned 1854 work *Ten Nights in a Barroom*. Despite not having been given credit for writing works of traditional temperance fiction, Melville's *Moby-Dick* and to a greater extent *Israel Potter* without question contain, to varying degrees, episodes that clearly promote the cause, whereas other works such as "Cock-A-Doodle-Doo!" and, more notably, "The Apple-Tree Table" are, indeed, clear and, with regard most specifically to the latter, traditional examples of temperance fiction.

Melville offers a brief piece of temperance advice to his readers in *Moby-Dick*. This instance occurs in Chapter 72 when Aunt Charity advises Dough-Boy to give the sailors only the ginger water to drink that he has smuggled on board the *Pequod* for her (256–257). That being said, Melville provides more thorough discussions of the theme in other works. In portions of *Israel Potter*, Melville's historical novel that chronicles the titular character's fall from Revolutionary War hero to London peddler, Melville encourages his readers to abstain from consuming alcohol, and in the short stories "Cock-A-Doodle-Doo!" and "The Apple-Tree Table" he offers hope and encouragement to heavy drinkers or alcoholics that overcoming their addiction is certainly possible.

• *1. Melville's Temperance Fiction* •

Although it is by no means a full-length temperance novel, the theme of alcohol avoidance is found throughout much of *Israel Potter*'s seventh chapter. In this part of the novel, Potter has at the request of the country squire John Woodcock arrived in Paris from England to deliver secret papers and information to Dr. Benjamin Franklin, who was at the time the American ambassador to France. The real-life Benjamin Franklin was without question a temperate man. In fact, based on the advice he gave to others in the eighteenth century, one would think him a teetotaler. He pleaded with his friends to abstain from drinking, thought that the money that people spent on liquor would be better donated to charity,[15] and even did the unthinkable for his time by urging his coworkers to stop drinking while on the job. As Franklin Parks writes,

> Benjamin Franklin, a reputed teetotaler and water guzzler, during his time at John Watt's print shop, fall 1725 to summer 1726, opposed this practice of beer consumption during working hours, resisted making a contribution to the beer fund, and succeeded in getting his fellow workers to substitute cheaper and non-intoxicating gruel for brew.[16]

In Melville's novel, the fictionalized Franklin holds and promotes the same views, and through Melville they are passed on to his mid–nineteenth-century audience.

After Israel finally arrives at Franklin's estate in France from England in Chapter 7 and sits down to dinner with him, "a decanter-like bottle of uncolored glass, filled with some uncolored beverage" (44) is on the table. Potter thinks it to be white wine but after tasting it he realizes that it is just water. He then expresses to Franklin his hope that he would have been offered something much stronger. As he tells his host about his prior drinking engagements with the country squire and his acquaintances, "Woodcock gave me perry, and the other gentlemen at White Waltham gave me port, and some other friends have given me brandy" (44). In response and as one would expect, the wise Franklin calmly informs Potter that he will not tolerate any liquor drinking: "Very good, my honest friend; if you like perry and port and brandy, wait till you get back to Squire Woodcock, and the gentleman at White Waltham, and your other friends, and you shall drink perry and port and brandy. But while you are with me, you will drink plain water" (44). Israel is not the only person who Franklin urges to refrain from drinking in this episode. In further association with temperance fiction, he wants all people from all castes to view alcohol as something negative and as something to be avoided. As Franklin says to Potter, "My honest friend, if you are poor, avoid wine as a costly luxury; if you are rich, shun it as a fatal indulgence. Stick to plain water" (45).[17] As we shall see in Chapter 5 of this study, Israel should have been listening more carefully to and taken more seriously Franklin's advice.

Although the theme of temperance is evident in *Moby-Dick* and to a greater degree in *Israel Potter*, there are far more extensive examples of it in Melville's works. Both "Cock-A-Doodle-Doo!" and "The Apple-Tree Table" contain characters who have been or who are in the process of being urged by their loved ones to abstain from the use of alcohol. In "Cock-A-Doodle-Doo!" the drinker has already given up the habit, while in "The Apple-Tree Table" the imbiber eventually does adopt sobriety. In both cases, the character who implores the drinker to abstain is female: the drinkers' wives. Having a female presence play this significant role for the respective alcoholics in these works is something that aligns these stories in direct relation to temperance fiction because, as Karen Sanchez-Eppler argues in her essay on the topic, moral suasion is woman's work because it "depends upon women's presumed skill at nurturing the good."[18]

"Cock-A-Doodle-Doo!" is a symbolically rich and complex tale that has received countless varying interpretations with nearly every subtle aspect of the story having been examined.[19] That being said, the presence of alcohol in the work remains almost entirely unexplored.[20] "Cock-A-Doodle-Doo!" is about an unnamed narrator who is depressed for a variety of legitimate reasons. As the story progresses and the narrator becomes more frustrated and depressed, he begins to hear the crowing of a noble rooster, which goes by the names Signor Beneventano and Trumpet, that apparently restores his happiness and positive frame of mind. The rooster's crowing appears to invigorate the depressed narrator so much throughout the beginning of the story that it causes him to seek its location out and attempt to purchase it. The narrator eventually finds the rooster, which brings him into contact with its owner, Merrymusk the wood-sawyer. The narrator pleads with Merrymusk to sell him the rooster, but the request is continually denied. At the end of the story, Merrymusk, his family, and Signor Beneventano all die, prompting the narrator to bury them.

1. Melville's Temperance Fiction

Throughout "Cock-A-Doodle-Doo!," Merrymusk is consistently described as a man who works diligently for his sickly family despite the constant hardships with which he is presented. As the narrator relates about the wood sawyer,

> His wife was become a perfect invalid; one child had the white-swelling, and the rest were rickety. He and his family lived in a shanty on a lonely barren patch nigh the railway track, where it passed close to the base of a mountain. He had bought a fine cow to have plenty of wholesome milk for his children; but the cow died during an accouchement, and he could not afford to buy another. Still, his family never suffered for lack of food. He worked hard and brought it to them [89].

The narrator indirectly emphasizes Merrymusk's dedication to his family further when he describes that the narrator will not sell the family's rooster to the narrator, not even for offers progressing in value from $50 to $500, because it provides solace and comfort for his family.[21] The spiritual and emotional well-being of his family, it is implied, is more important and beneficial to his wife and children than any of the material comforts that Merrymusk could purchase for them with the money that would be acquired by selling the rooster. Based on his actions it is safe to say that Merrymusk is an individual whose sole interest in the story is his family's well-being.

Merrymusk was not always the sober and diligent type of individual that we see throughout the narrative. Before getting married and having children he was an intermittent yet nonetheless wild partier who "would work hard a month with surprising soberness" strictly for the purpose of letting loose and "spend[ing] all his wages in one riotous night" (89). He was a man who saved his money only so that he would be able to partake in his blacked-out binges. Why is this no longer the case? What, we must ask, prompted him to adopt his sober lifestyle? Despite his wife's apparent insignificance throughout the narrative—she is nameless, speaks and is spoken to infrequently, and dies in the end[22]—there would seem to be no other reasonable explanation for Merrymusk's change in lifestyle other than her. She is a figure of temperance for Merrymusk, which as noted earlier is certainly in accordance with much of temperance literature in nineteenth-century America, and it is likely her influence that has persuaded him to give up the bottle.

The timeline surrounding Merrymusk's abandonment of an alcoholic (at least heavy partying) lifestyle clearly suggests that his wife played a significant role in his decision to adopt sobriety. As the narrator was informed by a townsman, the wood sawyer gave up the bottle roughly ten years before the story begins; he was a "wandering man" who drank "until within some ten years ago" (89). A decade is also the approximate length of time it has been since Merrymusk married his wife; as the narrator is told by other townsfolk, the two were married "nine years back" (89). Granted, temporal coincidence between Merrymusk's abandonment of alcohol and his courtship with and subsequent marriage to his current wife may not conclusively demonstrate causality for his adoption of sobriety, but considering the lengths to which he goes to ensure his family's well-being and happiness after a decade of marriage, it is highly probable and understanding that he would have given up the bottle for her. Thanks to his wife, we can safely say, Merrymusk is a successfully-recovered binge-drinker.

Melville's most notable and traditional piece of temperance fiction is his 1856 short story "The Apple-Tree Table." His specific use of an apple tree—more importantly one that has been turned into a table—in this story is no coincidence; Melville cleverly uses this particular type of tree in his tale to emphasize the theme of temperance as the crusaders against drinking and drunkenness in New England actually chopped down apple trees and rebelled against the sale of their seedlings due to the apple cider alcohol that could be made from them.[23] By using this important symbol and naming the story after it, Melville places temperance in this work front and center.

Melville's story is an American Gothic satire that concerns the narrator who finds the titular table, a "satanic-looking little old table" as he describes it (362), in the supposedly-haunted garret of his "very old home [that is situated] in an old-fashioned quarter of one of the oldest towns in America" (362).[24] After he brings the table downstairs, has it refurbished at the cabinet maker's shop, and subsequently brings it back home, the narrator's wife places the table on display in the cedar-parlor. Night after night the narrator sits by the table and reads until late one evening he hears a mysterious sound emanating from it, a sound that he believes to be caused by spirits. His wife scoffs at his conclusion and, in the end and as the naturalist Professor Johnson ultimately deduces, there is a logical explanation for the mystifying sounds. The ticking is caused by bugs that had hatched from eggs that had been "laid inside the bark of the living tree in the orchard" (381) prior to the apple

• *1. Melville's Temperance Fiction* •

tree being made into the table. The eggs then hatched and the bugs from within them began to make the noise that so terrifies the narrator.

It has been illustrated in a brief 2005 essay concerning Melville's commentary on the Woman Question in "The Apple-Tree Table" that the narrator's wife in the tale is arguably

> the most progressive female character in the Melville canon [as she] eschews many of the ideals of domesticity [that permeated mid-nineteenth-century America] by portraying more masculine characteristics than her narrator-husband and by refusing to exhibit the supposedly inherent virtues prescribed by them [Thompson, "Melville's 'The Apple-Tree Table'" 38–39].

Despite her above-mentioned rebellion against the ideals of domesticity, or her refusal to enter into and to adhere to what Barbara Welter coined in 1966 as the Cult of True Womanhood,[25] there is one area in which the narrator's wife is a mirror image of many nineteenth-century American wives. Namely, she is aggravated by and frustrated with her husband's drinking and she lovingly urges him to give up his habit.

The unnamed narrator of "The Apple-Tree Table"[26] does not appear to have as severe an addiction to alcohol as some of Melville's other characters that will be examined—he is certainly not as addicted to drink as the alcoholic sailors on board the *Neversink* in *White-Jacket* that will be considered throughout this study, for instance—yet his so-called "occasional tippling," as Marvin Fisher recklessly describes it in a curious attempt to minimize the narrator's drinking, is not simply "exaggerated into addiction" by his "domineering wife."[27] She undoubtedly has a legitimate gripe. Her husband clearly has a drinking ritual in which he partakes weekly, thereby making his imbibing more than merely an occasional or irregular activity as Fisher suggests. As the narrator himself admits, he has grown accustomed to treating himself to drinking his alcoholic punch "every Saturday night" (367). His wife, on the other hand, does not imbibe at all (367). She is a teetotaler and pretty much a prohibitionist and, as would be expected, his punch drinking is a habit against which she "had long remonstrated" (367). Throughout the story it is clear that the narrator's wife is accustomed to his weekly tradition and the irritating drunken behavior that accompanies it, and she shows frustration with and expresses her desire for her husband to refrain from consuming alcohol. By the end of the story, the narrator does just that and becomes another example of hope that

Melville offers to his readers who may, like the narrator, imbibe too frequently and to excess.

Without calling attention to any specific event, the narrator relates to his wife's hatred toward his drinking by alluding to what she interprets as his hangovers. On days following his imbibing, the narrator is aware that he must not demonstrate any irritability whatsoever or else he will be subjected to his wife's disapproval concerning his excessive consumption of alcohol. She reminds him that his hangovers are the result of his overindulgence from the previous night: "Indeed, I may here mention that, on the Sunday mornings following my Saturday nights, I had to be exceedingly cautious how I gave way to the slightest impatience at any accidental annoyance; because such impatience was sure to be quoted against me as evidence of the melancholy consequences of over-night indulgence" (367). While this statement clearly illustrates the teetotaler wife's disapproval of his drinking, there are more specific examples of her attempts to persuade her husband to not only reduce the frequency of his alcohol consumption but to abstain from imbibing altogether.

As noted earlier, after the apple-tree table is brought down from the garret early in the story and placed in the cedar parlor, the narrator begins spending his nights reading at it. On one particular Saturday he extends his drinking late into the night. Accompanying him in his weekly ritual is a copy of Cotton Mather's *Magnalia Christi Americana*, which traces the religious development of Massachusetts and other New England colonies throughout the seventeenth century. The narrator becomes so petrified by his reading of "doleful, ghostly, ghastly Cotton Mather" that he wishes that instead of his usual punch mixture he had "concocted some potent draught" (367), something stronger to both quench his thirst for liquor and calm his nerves. After drinking his punch and reading Mather for an extended period of time—his wife had taken his pocket watch upstairs so he is unaware of the hour (368)—the narrator begins to hear a ticking sound emanating from the apple-tree table. He is terrified by the mysterious sound and hurries upstairs and into his bedroom to tell his wife about it. In the process he possibly illustrates the extent of his intoxication as he "stumbled against a chair" (368) on his way to see her.

Once the narrator finally arrives in the bedroom he begins to tell his wife about the frightening sound that is coming from the table. As

1. Melville's Temperance Fiction

opposed to listening attentively to her husband's supposed tale of terror and subsequently shrieking and running out of the house as would have been expected if the story was a true work of Gothic fiction,[28] she instead notices and focuses her attention on his intoxication. She calmly tries to get him to come to bed without incident as if she is used to such drunkenness and irrational behavior: "'Do try and make less noise, my dear,' said my wife from the bed. 'You have been taking too much of that punch, I fear. That sad habit grows on you. Ah, that I should ever see you thus staggering at night in your chamber'" (368). The narrator, still in fear of the supposed spirits in the table, continues to try and get his wife's attention and for her to take his concerns more seriously: "'Wife, wife,' hoarsely whispered I, 'there is—is something tick—ticking in the cedar-parlor'" (368). Again as if accustomed to such behavior, the wife again simply attributes his fears and actions to his intoxication and prompts him to sober-up by sleeping: "'Poor old man—quite out of his mind—I knew it would be so. Come to bed; come and sleep it off'" (368). After the narrator attempts to get his wife's attention once more, she yet again shows no interest in his fears and lovingly expresses her hope that he would give up drinking and join her in bed: "'Do, come to bed. I forgive you. I won't remind you of it to-morrow. But you must give up the punch-drinking, my dear. It quite gets the better of you'" (368). Whether through actual intoxication or mere frustration at his wife's disbelief and indifference to his fears, the narrator threatens to leave the house. Even when presented with her husband's alcohol-induced disrespectful attitude, she continues to urge him lovingly to return to bed: "'No, no! not in that state. Come to bed my dear. I won't say another word'" (369). Considering that the narrator provides no further commentary on the night's excitement and is finally silenced about the ghostly terrors that he thinks he has experienced, it appears that he has heeded his wife's desire for him to go to bed and, quite likely, has simply passed out as a result of his excessive imbibing.

The next morning the narrator does his best to impress his wife in a clear attempt to distract her from his prior night's behavior by cleaning himself thoroughly and dressing impeccably. Upon seeing him, the narrator's wife keeps her promise to her husband from the night before and says nothing to him about his drunken behavior. She does not need to say anything to him because he is fully aware, as is likely always the case on their Sunday mornings, that she believes that his actions were cause by the alcohol: "The next morning, upon waking, my wife said nothing about the past night's affair, and, feeling no little embarrassment myself, especially at having been thrown into such a panic, I also was silent. Consequently, my wife must still have ascribed my singular conduct to a mind disordered, not by ghosts, but by punch" (369). This is the last reference to the narrator's drinking in the story. Perhaps his wife's requests have finally been heeded and he has finally given up his punch drinking. This is highly possible.

As the narrator says while still in bed suffering from the after-effects of his excessive drinking, he has decided to give up on reading Cotton Mather's works: "For my own part, as I lay in bed watching the sun in the panes, I began to think that much midnight reading of Cotton Mather was not good for a man; that it had a morbid influence upon the nerves, and gave rise to hallucinations. I resolved to put Cotton Mather permanently aside" (369). Does he truly mean that he will refrain from reading Cotton Mather? Possibly, but there is, I would argue, another possibility that accompanies his decision to cease reading Mather's works.

Although he despised drinking to excess and drunkenness, Cotton Mather nonetheless viewed alcohol, as did his father Increase, as "a creature of God" that had "nutritional and medical value" and that could be consumed in moderation in order for people to gain strength (Rorabaugh 30). It had for the Mathers, in other words, certain positive effects and benefits. By deciding to put down Mather's writings, then, the narrator is also putting down Mather's appreciation of alcohol and whatever positives he believed it had. The "morbid influence upon the nerves" to which the narrator refers is not simply Mather's "doleful, ghostly, ghastly" writings, but the alcohol that Mather reveres and the "hallucinations" that it causes. Deciding to put down Mather, and thereby his veneration for alcohol, is a type of synecdoche for the narrator to put down all alcohol and quit drinking entirely. The narrator is not just putting down Mather forever, but is also doing the same with his punch and in the process becomes with the assistance of his wife another successfully-recovered alcoholic.

It is important to note that in "The Apple-Tree Table" the narrator's wife does not urge her husband to quit drinking in the story simply to harass or nag him, as Marvin Fisher seems to suggest (*Going Under* 124); rather, she is genuinely concerned about the effects that imbibing

• *1. Melville's Temperance Fiction* •

will eventually have on him. She wants him to give up drinking because she genuinely loves him and does not want alcohol to end up causing his death (367). This is precisely the rationale and attitude that accompanied the temperance movement and its accompanying literature in nineteenth-century America, and in the process "The Apple-Tree Table" becomes another yet more profound example of a work in which Melville demonstrates his sympathy and support for the cause.

In keeping with traditional temperance fiction, Melville does not condemn his drinkers in the end of these stories to a horrific fate, nor does he judge them harshly for their addiction prior to their acceptance of sobriety. In *Israel Potter* he offers temperance advice to his readers through Benjamin Franklin, while in "Cock-A-Doodle-Doo!" and "The Apple-Tree Table" he illustrates to his readers that temperance and total abstinence are beneficial and attainable even for those who are severely addicted to drink. This is the only chapter and these are the only works, however, in which Melville offers hope to his readers. If temperance is not adopted, then the drinkers will experience one of the variously negative fates that will be illustrated in the remaining chapters of this study.

Chapter 2

The Prodromal Phase of Alcoholism

As noted in Chapter 1, temperance as an official movement in the United States was born in the 1820s out of a belief that drunkenness was contributing to the deterioration of society at large and that it was causing the destruction of the domestic home atmosphere. It was not just in the United States where such opinions were held, however. The view that alcohol was socially destructive had gained immense support around the world by the middle of the nineteenth century. In 1847 in England, for example, Peter Burne's *The Teetotaler's Companion; or, A Plea for Temperance* identified drunkenness as a habit and made causal connections between alcohol and a variety of social issues including crime, poverty, and secularism.[1] Two years later, the Swedish physician Dr. Magnus Huss in his continued study into alcohol's damning effects on individuals and on societies at large classified chronic drinking not simply as a habit that could be easily kicked, as certain temperance proponents believed (most thought that drinking was entirely a choice), but as something far more complex. It was, in his view, an addiction and a disease and one over which those afflicted with it had no control. In his *Alcoholismus Chronicus, or Chronic Alcohol Illness: A Contribution to the Study of Dyscrasias based on My Personal Experience and the Experience of Others*, Huss coined the term *alcoholism* and classified it as a disease in which there existed "a state of chronic alcohol intoxication that was characterized by severe physical pathology and disrup-

2. The Prodromal Phase of Alcoholism

tion of social functioning."[2] Detailed investigations into alcohol addiction and alcohol as a disease continued over the next century, and in 1960 the American physician Dr. E. M. Jellinek identified four progressive phases of alcoholism: pre-alcoholic, prodromal, crucial, and chronic.

Of particular interest in this chapter is what Jellinek describes as the prodromal phase of alcoholism, a designation that many of us would likely associate with those who drink chronically; these are the stereotypical alcoholics. According to Jellinek, prodromal phase alcoholics have "identified alcohol as an essential means for escaping life's problems."[3] Although it would have been impossible for Melville to be cognizant of the classification or designation *prodromal phase alcoholism* as it is a twentieth-century term, it appears that he was well aware of the condition itself and of how people used alcohol as a means of masking the harsh realities of their existence. This is what we see in the drinkers from the works considered in this chapter. For this group of Melville's drinkers, alcohol is used to varying degrees as an escape mechanism, something that they rely on in order to alleviate the various stresses in their lives. Such unremitting imbibers adamantly yet incorrectly believe that alcohol is, as the Cypriote says in Part III of *Clarel*, "care-killing" (III iv 3). For those who are true prodromal phase alcoholics, however, their alcohol consumption does nothing to improve the quality of their lives. For many, in fact, it only makes their various problems—and thereby their reliance on alcohol—worse.

Characters who appear susceptible to becoming prodromal phase alcoholics are found in *Pierre*, Melville's 1852 novel that was panned by critics and urged by them to be left "unbought on the shelves of the bookseller" (Leyda, *Log* 1: 460). The first example occurs in Book 3, Part 3, when Mary Glendinning, Pierre's overbearing mother, is scolding her titular son for what she views as his neglect of her. If he ever were to leave her, she tells him in a type of guilt-trip manner, then she would deal with the loss by seeking solace in drink. As Mrs. Glendinning says to her son,

> Do you know, Pierre, that if you continue these irregular meals of yours, and deprive me so entirely almost of your company, that I shall run fearful risk of getting to be a terrible wine-bibber;—yes, could you unalarmed see me sitting all alone here with this decanter, like any old nurse, Pierre; some solitary, forlorn old nurse, Pierre, deserted by her last friend, and therefore forced to embrace her flask? [55].

Mary's fear of losing her son eventually becomes a reality; Pierre ultimately decides to leave her and the Saddle Meadows estate at the beginning of Book 12, Part 2. After informing her of his intention, Mary Glendinning then disowns Pierre and reduces him to a mere object, referring to him with the generic and in this situation degrading pronoun *it*. Her words during this episode oscillate between hatred and despair, leaving us to realistically image her sitting alone, distraught, and relying on alcohol in order to cope with the loss of her son:

> See the vile boy of Mary Glendinning!—Deceitful! thick with guilt, where I thought it was all guilelessness and gentlest docility to me. It has not happened! It is not day! Were this thing so, I should go mad, and be shut up, and not walk here where every door is open to me.— My own son married to an unknown—thing! My own only son, false to his holiest plight public vow—and the wide world knowing to it! He bears my name—Glendinning. I will disown it; were it like this dress, I would tear my name off from me, and burn it till it shrivelled to a crisp!—Pierre! Pierre! come back, come back, and swear it not so! [193].

Pierre never does return to his mother and in a near replay of the series of events to the conclusion of William Shakespeare's *Romeo and Juliet* he ultimately commits suicide at the novel's end, resulting in Isabel's subsequent decision to do the same.[4]

Mary Glendinning is not the only character in *Pierre* who (possibly) comes to rely on alcohol as a type of crutch for a time in order to deal with various ordeals. Her son, it appears, is also susceptible to alcohol abuse.[5] This further and more detailed episode occurs in Book 25, Part 3, after Pierre and Isabel Banford, his putative and orphaned half-sister, have left Mrs. Glendinning and the Saddle Meadows estate in upstate New York for New York City. At this point in the story, Pierre is frustrated, as Melville himself was during the composition of *Moby-Dick*, over the writing of his novel; more specifically, he is overwhelmed with the difficulties that he is experiencing in writing anything of worth at all: "As every evening, after his day's writing was done, the proofs of the beginning of his work came home for correction, Isabel would read them to him. They were replete with errors" (340). In order to alleviate his stress and frustration, he initially takes solace in walking the city streets at night. As the narrator relates, "In the earlier progress of his book, he had found some relief in making his regular evening walk through the greatest thoroughfare of the city; that so, the utter isolation

2. The Prodromal Phase of Alcoholism

of his soul, might feel itself the more intensely from the incessant joggings of his body against the bodies of the hurrying thousands" (340). As time goes on he becomes aggravated even by the crowd that he walks among. In a further attempt to lessen his burden, he begins walking the city streets alone during thunder-storms while the others have sought shelter in their homes:

> Stemming from such tempests through the deserted streets, Pierre felt a dark, triumphant joy; that while others had crawled in fear to their kennels, he along defied the storm-admiral, whose most vindictive peltings of hail-stones,—striking his iron-framed fiery furnace of a body,— melted into soft dew, and so, harmlessly trickled from off him [340].

Eventually, even this loses its calming effects for Pierre, and he progresses into further depression. Although he, unlike certain characters from later in this chapter (Turkey from "Bartleby," for instance, is overcome by alcoholism in New York City), is not completely "undone by the usual urban temptations of alcohol,"[6] he nonetheless for a time uses liquor as a means of escaping his growing frustrations:

> By-and-by, of such howling, pelting nights, he began to bend his steps down the dark, narrow side-streets, in question of the more secluded and mysterious tap-rooms. There he would feel a singular satisfaction, in sitting down all dripping in a chair, ordering his half-pint of brown ale before him, and drawing over his cap to protect his eyes from the light, eye the varied faces of the social castaways, who here had their haunts from the bitterest midnights [340–341].

Pierre, it would seem, is well on his way to becoming a stereotypical alcoholic, or one who imbibes simply to escape his life's difficulties.

The depression that Pierre experiences is something that could have caused him to continue to drink excessively, developing into a form of alcoholism that would ostensibly mask the pain associated with the depressing state of his writing. For whatever reason, he is somehow able to separate himself from such indulgence in his times of depression and despair: "But at last he began to feel a distaste for even those; and now nothing but the utter night-desolation of the obscurest warehousing lanes would content him, or be at all sufferable to him" (341). This is not the case, however, for all of Melville's drinkers who seek relief in the bottle. For the true prodromal phase alcoholics in the following works, drinking does nothing to ease their respective plights.

"Bartleby, the Scrivener: A Story of Wall Street" is Melville's famous tale of an unnamed Wall Street lawyer who tells the story of his newly-hired scrivener, Bartleby. Bartleby is employed to work alongside and assist the other law copyists Turkey and Nippers and the office boy Ginger Nut. Although Bartleby begins working at an incredibly impressive pace—"Bartleby did an extraordinary quantity of writing. As if long famishing for something to copy, he seemed to gorge himself on [the narrator's] documents" (46)—he eventually prefers not to do anything that his boss asks of him. Every request, even those that are entirely within the parameters of his job, is passive-aggressively refused by Bartleby, causing enormous stress and anxiety for all of those who work in the office. Even after Bartleby is fired by his boss, albeit unsuccessfully as it ultimately turns out, he continues to show up unwanted at the narrator's place of business, thereby forcing the lawyer-narrator to move his law office to another location in the city. Bartleby, who still refuses to leave his boss's prior premises, is placed in jail for vagrancy by the subsequent tenant, where he goes on a hunger strike and in the process thereby commits suicide.

It has been frequently suggested by critics that the aging scrivener Turkey is an alcoholic.[7] Although he is never formally referred to as such in the story and his drinking is never directly mentioned or explicitly condemned by the narrator or any other character, and while some critics have offered different explanations for his actions,[8] Melville's description of the aging scrivener's behavior leaves little room for any other valid interpretation. Turkey is a "most valuable person" to the narrator who, in the morning hours of business, is "the quickest, steadiest creature" who accomplishes "a great deal of work in a style not easily to be matched" (41). Yet in the afternoon he and his work ethic are entirely different. It would appear that his lunches consist of alcohol and that he returns to work heavily intoxicated. After his lunch breaks he becomes boisterous, careless with his work, and shows various characteristics of his inebriation. As the narrator informs us, Turkey

> would be incautious in dipping his pen into his inkstand. All his blots upon my documents were dropped there after twelve o'clock, meridian. Indeed, not only would he be reckless, and sadly given to making blots in the afternoon, but, some days, he went further, and was rather noisy. At such times, too, his face flamed with augmented blazonry, as if cannel coal had been heaped on anthracite. He made an unpleasant racket

2. The Prodromal Phase of Alcoholism

with his chair; spilled his sandbox; in mending his pens, impatiently split them all to pieces, and threw them on the floor in a sudden passion; stood up, and leaned over his table, boxing his papers about in a most indecorous manner, very sad to behold in an elderly man like him [41–42].

The consistent difference in Turkey's emotional state between the mornings and afternoons is also indicative of drinking. While Turkey is "the civilest, nay, the blandest and most reverential of men in the morning, yet in the afternoon, he was disposed, upon provocation, to be slightly rash with his tongue—in fact, insolent" (42). When he is drunk and without even noticing it he also has a propensity for violence, which also illustrates the transformative effects of drunkenness that will be discussed in Chapter 8. As he says to the narrator with regard to Bartleby: "'All beer,' cried Turkey; 'gentleness is effects of beer—Nippers and I dined together to-day. You see how gentle I am, sir. Shall I go and black his eyes?'" (51).

Like many alcoholics, Turkey is in total denial about his drinking problem.[9] When the narrator goes to see Turkey on a Saturday afternoon (when Turkey is undoubtedly hung-over; "he was always worse on Saturdays" the narrator says [42]) and suggests to him that he should just go home after lunch during the work week due to the shoddiness of his work, which undoubtedly stems from his intoxication, Turkey refuses and offers only excuses for his poor post-lunch performance: "'True; but, with submission, sir, behold these hairs! I am getting old. Surely, sir, a blot or two of a warm afternoon is not to be severely urged against gray hairs. Old age—even if it blot the page—is honorable. With submission, sir, we *both* are getting old'" (42). In addition to not realizing or admitting that he has an alcohol problem, he also refuses to view his drinking as something that impedes the quality of his work; in fact, he touts alcohol and its supposed positive effects when he suggests that it would actually be beneficial for Bartleby and perhaps restore his prior incredible work ethic: "'With submission, sir,' said he, 'yesterday I was thinking about Bartleby here, and I think that if he would but prefer to take a quart of good ale every day it would do much towards mending him, and enabling him to assist in examining his papers" (58). These episodes clearly demonstrate that Turkey is unequivocally a full-fledged alcoholic. The question that must be but has yet to be asked, though, is "why does Turkey drink?" Again, his drinking is the drug that he uses to escape the cruel realities of his existence.

With the undeniable and possible exceptions of *Moby-Dick* and "Benito Cereno" respectively, "Bartleby" has received arguably the most frequent attention from critics. Despite such constant examination, however, the exact focus in Melville's tale—who or what it is about—remains a point of debate. J. Hillis Miller and Michael Paul Rogin have examined the story as if, and understandably so based on its primary title, the focus in "Bartleby" *is* Bartleby,[10] while other critics including Thomas Dilworth have taken an opposite view, arguing that the central figure in the story "is not Bartleby but the anonymous lawyer who is the narrator."[11] Still others, focusing on the story's sub-title "A Story of Wall Street," read "Bartleby" as a parable of "a commercial society, dominated by a concern with property and finance."[12] While each of these three frequent interpretations could be viewed as valid, and to varying degrees are, there is at least a fourth possibility concerning the exact focus in Melville's tale, one that provides a much clearer insight into the reason behind Turkey's alcoholism.[13]

As opposed to being about a character or a specific type of society, the focus in "Bartleby," as David Kirby writes, "is on work: not the dangerous or unethical variety, just ordinary, mind-numbing, soul-destroying work."[14] It is about such alienating work, as Andrew Delbanco also suggests, in "a commercial society that depended increasingly on multiple copies of many kinds of documents, but in which no technology for copying yet existed beyond the handheld pen" (214); Melville's story takes place in a world long before type-writers or spirit machines (or the Ditto machine), computerized word processors or photocopiers. More importantly, it is about such work where there is no end in sight; being a law copyist is a dead-end job that makes a *lifer*, for lack of a better term, of the employee. It is a depressing career as "apprenticeship in a law office was more likely to be a dead-end job than a stepping stone to a legal career, and so the law office in 'Bartleby' is a dungeon where broken men grown old, fidgeting away their vitality until the last sparks of life go out" (Delbanco 214). So this is Turkey's existence: working in a monotonous job for a significant period of time, garnering no advancement, in an environment that is reminiscent of a catacomb and from which he receives very little remuneration for his work (44).[15] These are the reasons why Turkey drinks, but where does his drinking ultimately lead him? The answer to this rhetorical question is *nowhere*. His alcoholism does nothing to improve the quality of his life as he, at the story's conclusion, remains a mere copyist surrounded by the depression that prompted him to drink in the first place.

It was shown in Chapter 1 that Merrymusk the wood sawyer from "Cock-A-Doodle-Doo!" was a binge-drinker who overcame his addiction to alcohol roughly ten years prior to the story for the sake and love of his likely teetotaler and temperate wife. Yet Merrymusk is not the only drinker, reformed or otherwise, in the story. The unnamed narrator also drinks, but unlike Merrymusk he continues to suffer from his addiction to alcohol. Like some of the other drinkers examined in this chapter, the narrator of "Cock-A-Doodle-Doo!" is an alcoholic who uses liquor consistently as a futile way to mask the various hardships that he experiences.

Without question and to a greater extent than the Glendinnings (Mary and Pierre) and possibly Turkey, the narrator of "Cock-A-Doodle-Doo!" lives a life of such genuine extreme turmoil that it legitimately warrants a need for escape. He is a man who lives in "[a] miserable world" (77), a "divided empire" (76) that "call[s] the facilitation of death and murder an improvement" (77). The town's children are plagued with "measles, mumps, croup, scarlet fever, chicken-pox, cholera morbus" and he himself suffers from rheumatics and dyspepsia (78). His "own private affairs were also full of despotisms, casualties, and knockings on the head" (75) and he is constantly hounded by his creditor throughout the story. Even the climate in which he lives, "the cool and misty, damp, disagreeable air" (75), would be conducive to a depressed mindset. The narrator's situation weighs so heavily on him, in fact, that it thrusts him into an existential crisis in which he contemplates humans' very existence: "My eyes ranged over the capacious rolling country, and over the mountains, and over the streams, rocks, fells—and I thought to myself, what a slight mark, after all, does man make on this huge earth. Yet the earth makes a mark on him" (76). Based on these factors, it is certainly understandable that the narrator is depressed— and justifiably so—and that he would be in search of some type of relief. Like Turkey, the narrator chooses alcohol as his supposed coping mechanism. Yet as is also the case with Turkey, his drinking does nothing to improve his situation. In fact, in this case it only makes it worse.

Despite being a part of the decorum of nineteenth-century America, morning drinking is nonetheless a telling sign of alcohol abuse and of alcohol being used as a means of escape.[16] The narrator affirms this and demonstrates his alcoholism early in the story when he decides on having "brown-stout and a beef steak" for breakfast and on drinking until he feels "about as stout as Samson" (80). Not only does the narrator indulge in drink during breakfast but he continues to imbibe afterwards and is seemingly already intoxicated by eleven in the morning. He does so in order to avoid his impending problems because he thinks that the bill collector or dun may be paying him a visit. His creditor, indeed, does arrive:

> I felt in rare spirits the whole morning. The dun called about eleven. I had the boy Jake send the dun up. I was reading *Tristram Shandy*, and could not go down under the circumstances. The lean rascal ... entered, and found me seated in an armchair, with my feet on the table, and the second bottle of brown-stout handy, and the book under eye [80].[17]

When the bill collector comes up to meet him, the narrator is unconcerned with the severity of his financial situation and offers the dun a drink, which illustrates his use of alcohol as something that he uses to distract himself from his financial hardships. His positive outlook and welcoming language to a man he detests attests further to the narrator's inebriation: "'My friend,' said I, 'what a charming morning! How sweet the country looks! Pray, did you hear that extraordinary cock-crow this morning? Take a glass of my stout!'" (81). The dun, who *is* fully cognizant of the severity of the narrator's debt, replies: "'*Yours?* First pay your debts before you offer folks *your* stout!'" (81). Perhaps becoming infuriated and again trying to forget about his debt, the narrator then demonstrates both his possession and knowledge of fine stout: "'You think then, that, properly speaking, I have no *stout*,' said I, deliberately rising, 'I'll undeceive you. I'll show you stout of a superior brand to Barclay and Perkins'" (81).[18]

Later in the story the narrator continues to show that he uses alcohol in order to distract him from his various hardships. After going even further in debt and while experiencing the death of his relatives, all that the narrator does is drink: "I saw another mortgage piled on my plantation; but only bought another dozen of stout, and a dozen dozen of Philadelphia Porter. Some of my relatives died; I wore no mourning, but for three days drank stout in preference to porter, stout

2. The Prodromal Phase of Alcoholism

being the darker color" (95).[19] Little does the narrator seem to realize, his drinking is only contributing to his financial difficulties, and alcohol will not bring back his relatives. His drinking is only exacerbating his problems.

The final moments of Melville's story contain even more hardships for the narrator: Merrymusk, his family, and the rooster all die. As the narrator says, "The wood sawyer and his family, with the Signor Beneventano, lie in that spot; and I buried them, and planted the stone, which was a stone made to order; and never since then have I felt the doleful dumps" (97). The narrator's remark of never feeling depressed again does not necessarily mean, as Robert Milder optimistically suggests, that he has been "redeemed through the life-affirming crow of a marvellous cock."[20] Rather, it is quite likely that the narrator, when presented with these deaths and as he had done when his relatives died, has not felt the doleful dumps because he has been drinking constantly and is numbed by liquor. This would explain his final actions. After learning about the deaths, the narrator does not feel his doleful dumps, but "under all circumstances crow[s] late and early with a continual crow. COCK-A-DOODLE-DOO!—OO!—OO!—OO!—OO!" (97). He no longer feels the doleful dumps because he cannot feel them due to his intoxication, and his boisterous and cacophonous imitation of the rooster is nothing more than juvenile drunken behavior. His use of alcohol as a coping mechanism has had no positive benefits; rather, it has only made his situation worse as it appears that he has been consumed by his alcoholism to the proverbial point of no return, trapped in his addiction to drink and leaving him to forever and with futility rely on alcohol to "solve" his problems.

Of all Melville's characters there is no better example of the prodromal phase of alcoholism than is found among the sailors on board the *Neversink* in *White-Jacket*,[21] Melville's novel that received a favorable review from the temperance journal the Honolulu *Friend* (Reynolds, "Black Cats" 37). As Charles Nordhoff chronicles in his 1856 memoir *Man of War Life: A Boy's Experience in the United States Navy*, and as Melville himself recounts in *White-Jacket* stemming from his own experiences on board the *United States*, life on board a man-of-war was certainly not easy. It was difficult, life threatening work and the voyages could last upwards of, as was the case for Nordhoff, nine years.[22] Recognizing just how difficult, demanding, "monotonous and restrictive" the work on board man-of-wars was during the nineteenth century, the American government allotted sailors "one gill, or quarter-pint" of whiskey per day (McCarthy 46). This, in fact, is why many men remain in the navy: "It is hardly to be doubted," White-Jacket says, "that the controlling inducement which keeps many men in the Navy, is the unbounded confidence they have in the ability of the United States government to supply them, regularly and unfailingly, with their daily allowance of [alcohol]" (53). As other sailors freely admit, alcohol is all that the sailors care about. Landless, or Happy Jack, for instance, claims that "Rum and tobacco" are all that sailors including himself want (383) and, complementing this viewpoint, "an old toper of a top-man" tells White-Jacket that he will not give up his drinking, despite knowing full-well that it is destroying him, and he uses the Christian virtue of loving your enemy from Matthew 5.44 as justification for his continued alcoholism: "'Give up my grog? And why? Because it is ruining me? No, no; I am a good Christian, White-Jacket, and love my enemy too much to drop his acquaintance'" (54).[23] The sailors are so displeased with their lives on board the ship and are so accustomed to heavy drinking that the daily allowance provided to them by their government had "almost no palliating effect" on them (McCarthy 46), causing them to take advantage of any opportunity they have to drink, as is the case in Chapter 54 when the sailors are given their "liberty" to go ashore and return drunk and are then unable to perform their required duties (225–229). Their addiction to liquor is the reason that the sailors also risk floggings by smuggling liquor on board because without their alcohol their lives possess "no further charms for them" (53).[24] A clear example of this occurs in Chapter 14 of *White-Jacket*.

Shortly after the *Neversink* has left port, the sailors are informed that the ship's supply of alcohol—grog—is nearly gone. This throws the crew members into a state of total panic. They recognize that without their liquor they will be unable to cope with their duties:

> "The grog gone!" roared an old Sheet-anchor man.
> "Oh! Lord! what a pain in my stomach!" cried a
>   main-top man.
> "It's worse than the Cholera! Cried a man of the
>   After-guard.
> "I'd sooner the water-casks would give out!" said a
>   Captain of the Hold.

2. The Prodromal Phase of Alcoholism

> "Are we ganders and geese, that we can live without grog?" asked a Corporal of Marines.
> "Ay, we must now drink with the ducks!" cried a Quarter-master.
> "Not a tot left?" groaned a Waister.
> Not a toothful!" sighed a Holder, from the bottom of his boots [54].

It is during this alcoholic drought on board the ship that the sailors truly show just how severe their alcohol addictions are and of how unable they are to perform their duties without their grog.[25]

Although the *Neversink* has no liquor on board, "ten men" were nonetheless "reported by the master-at-arms to be intoxicated." Due to the supposed absence of alcohol on board the ship, some doubted whether or not such allegations were true. Drunk, however, they clearly are: "They were brought up to the mast, and at their appearance the doubts of the most skeptical were dissipated; but whence they had obtained their liquor no one could tell. It was observed, however, at the time, that the tarry knaves all smelled of lavender, like so many dandies" (54). Where, the question remains, did they get their liquor? The source is ultimately revealed at the chapter's conclusion.

Since the sailors are unable to function without their alcohol, they devise a scheme that will allow them to satisfy their addiction and to mask their harsh reality. As White-Jacket relates again in Chapter 14, the alcoholic sailors resort to making and drinking a cologne-based beverage in order to get intoxicated. White-Jacket explains the process:

> It had come to his knowledge that the purser's steward was supplied with a large quantity of *Eau-de-Cologne*, clandestinely brought out in the ship, for the purpose of selling it, on his own account, to the people of the coast.... With brown sugar, taken from the mess-chests, and hot water begged from the galley-cooks, the men made all manner of punches, toddies, and cocktails, letting fall therein a small drop of tar, like a bit of brown toast, by way of imparting flavour [54–55].

Such extreme actions are of those who clearly have an uncontrollable dependency on alcohol and who are the modern-day equivalent of people who use hand sanitizers and other alcohol-based personal hygiene products to satisfy their addiction.[26]

Numerous characters from Melville's works live lives that for various reasons are depressing and mundane and they use alcohol as a means of numbing themselves. They are alcoholics in the prodromal phase of the disease, which will ultimately not aid the quality of their lives. It will lead to the chronic level of alcoholism, the phase in which the addict drinks "compulsively and continuously ... the bottle comes before friends, relatives, employment, and self-esteem" (Coon 248). They will become alcoholics, as it appears Turkey, the narrator of "Cock-A-Doodle-Doo!," and the sailors on board the *Neversink* have become, individuals whose lives are totally and forever controlled by their compulsion to drink. Such characters serve as distinct warnings to Melville's readers to abandon the bottle or suffer a similar fate,[27] and that destiny will be to continually rely on alcohol for alleviation of daily stresses, a reliance that will in the end provide no true assistance in the battle against personal demons. If they continue drinking to such an extent, then they will likely—inevitably, actually—be subjected in one way or another to one of the horrific fates that await the chronic drinkers who are examined in this study's ninth and final chapter.

CHAPTER 3

Melville's Supposedly Social Drinkers

Throughout their respective 1979 and 2002 books *The Alcoholic Republic: An American Tradition* and *Taverns and Drinking in Early America*, W. J. Rorabaugh and Sharon Sallinger outline the quantity of alcohol that was consumed during late eighteenth- and early nineteenth-century America and examine how frequently American men in the early decades of the new republic ventured out into social settings to drink and fraternize with other men in the spirit of genuine friendship. For those of the middle-class to the financially-elite, the group of individuals with whom Melville associated, "men gathered on a regular basis [at the urban tavern] to transact business, argue over issues of local politics, or share a convivial pint with friends" (Sallinger 1). Such studies chronicle what Sallinger has just described and detail the activities of what I classify as social drinkers. Naturally, many of the men that Rorabaugh and Sallinger discuss undoubtedly had dependencies on alcohol, but regardless of whether or not they may have been alcoholics, the time that they sought at the tavern (or any other social setting for that matter) was to be filled with enjoyable company and camaraderie. Alcohol for these men enhanced the jovial and social atmosphere and enriched their friendships with each other.

As his biographers have long noted, Melville seems to have been no different from those early-republic men whom Rorabaugh and Sallinger discuss in their respective studies. It is certain, as will be shown in greater detail in the Afterword, that Melville shared in his fellow countrymen's constant indulgence of liquor in seemingly friendly and social settings. Whether it be drinking till late at night, or early in the morning depending on one's perspective, on board the *Southampton* with George Adler and Frank Taylor during an Atlantic Ocean crossing from New York to a final destination of London in 1849,[1] or imbibing copious amounts of champagne with other giants of American letters on Monument Mountain in 1850,[2] or having various types and at times excessive amounts of alcohol at Arrowhead with, among others, Nathaniel Hawthorne and Evert Duyckinck,[3] it does not seem to matter who Melville drank with as long as he had cherished, or at least agreeable, people with whom to share in the experience. In some of his works it appears that Melville celebrates his apparent reverence for this social bond between drinkers. Appearances, however, can be deceiving. The truth is, in Melville's writings there is no such thing as an honest social drinker. A drinker who truly enjoys imbibing with friends or even general acquaintances strictly for moments of authentic camaraderie at various social events simply does not exist.

In his 1857 novel *The Confidence-Man* Melville writes about a seemingly friendly and cordial drinking experience between two new and supposed friends who have just met on board the *Fidèle*: Francis Goodman (the confidence man) and Charles Arnold Noble.[4] As will be discussed in greater detail in Chapter 5 of this book, however, the meeting between these two men (for one of them, anyway) is anything but one of true friendship. For one of these drinkers, true friendship is not what is sought. Although I am putting off my analysis of this episode in *The Confidence-Man* until later, my rationale will hopefully be clear when the time comes. I will, though, examine here other supposedly-social drinkers in two of Melville's shorter works in which social gatherings and frequent drinking are central, but in which true and genuine friendship is not.

In two of his shorter works Melville demonstrates his belief that those who imbibe in the company of apparent friends are in reality only distrustful and dishonest, self-centered and selfish individuals whose only concern is their addiction to alcohol and how they can and what schemes they can use to get more liquor. As far as the research from the early twentieth century and later illustrates, Melville was prophetic and spot-on in his assessment. Selfishness and alcoholism, as George

3. Melville's Supposedly Social Drinkers

Barton Cutton details in his 1907 book *The Psychology of Alcoholism*, go hand-in-hand. Being the "embodiment of selfishness," alcoholics have no regard for anyone or anything except for themselves and where and how they will get their next drink.[5] This is precisely what we see in Melville's stories that contain supposedly social drinkers. In the first half of his diptych "The Paradise of Bachelors and the Tartarus of Maids" and in the rarely-considered short story "Jimmy Rose,"[6] Melville demonstrates that there are those who drink under the guise of sociality and who are, therefore, only selfish alcoholics who take advantage of those with whom they drink. The drinkers' only concern is the alcohol that is offered to them, thereby suggesting that there is no loyalty or true friendship whatsoever among heavy drinkers or alcoholics.

During "The Paradise of Bachelors," the narrator is in London and is taken by his host, a gentleman known only by the initials R. F. C.,[7] to the Temple Cloisters, a club for unmarried and seemingly satisfied lawyers, for a sumptuous banquet and excessive amounts of alcohol. As is typically the case in most of Melville's writings, the full extent and implications of alcohol's presence in "The Paradise of Bachelors" has been largely overlooked by critics. Particularly in this story, such a blind-eye toward drinking is curious indeed as alcohol is of such significance in this story that the narrator even refers to R.F.C. in comical yet nonetheless liquor-related terms: "At the core he was a right bluff, care-free, right comfortable and most companionable Englishman. If on a first acquaintance he seemed reserved, quite icy in his air—patience; this Champagne will thaw. And if it never do, better frozen Champagne than liquid vinegar" (207). As this description suggests and as we shall see, alcohol is central to Melville's tale.

The party that the narrator attends with R.F.C. is nothing but a posh drunk-fest, a more sophisticated yet nonetheless equally intoxicating experience that the lowbrow, crass sailors from "The Spouter Inn" chapter from *Moby-Dick* experience once they have arrived back in New Bedford.[8] The narrator describes the nine bachelors' festivities as follows and in the process illustrates just how important alcohol is for the party and for those who are in attendance:

> I have above endeavored to give some slight schedule of the general plan of operations. But any one knows that a good, genial dinner is a sort of pell-mell, indiscriminate affair, quite baffling to detail in all particulars. Thus, I spoke of taking a glass of claret, and a glass of sherry,

and a glass of port, and a mug of ale—all at certain specific periods and times. But those were merely the state bumpers, so to speak. Innumerable impromptu glasses were drained between the period of those grand imposing ones.... And so the evening slipped along, the hours told, not by a water-clock, like King Alfred's, but a wine-chronometer.... For fear one decanter should not with sufficient speed reach his destination, another was sent express after him to hurry him; and then a third to hurry the second; and so on with a fourth and fifth [207–208].

The narrator also relates in this initial observation of the party that the nine bachelors appear to care for each other's well-being; they "seemed," as the narrator says, "to have the most tender concern for each other's health" (207). The key word in this description, though, is *seemed*. In stark contrast to what the narrator thinks he observes and interprets as camaraderie, or "homoerotic fraternalism" as David Serlin describes it,[9] and in opposition to what critics have long maintained,[10] the bachelors do not truly or genuinely care about each other or their well-being.

In his compelling 1997 book *The Selfish Brain: Learning from Addiction*, Robert L. DuPont states that "drug using friends are not friends; they are allies and accomplices in drug use. They help provide the drug, and they sustain the environment in which drug use takes place. They help the addict rationalize the drug use with the view that 'everyone is doing it, not just me.'"[11] This exact rationale or scenario can be applied to the bachelors in Melville's tale. The reality is, the bachelors are co-dependent alcoholics—alcohol, remember, is a drug—and selfish enablers who urge their companions to continue drinking, preying on each other's alcoholism essentially, so that they themselves will be able to continue imbibing and feeding their own addiction as well. The bachelors are not true friends; their only true concern is alcohol and their intoxication and they will go to great lengths to ensure that their thirsts are satisfied for as long as possible.

There are various reasons that suggest that the bachelors are merely selfish drunkards with no sincere regard for their drinking companions. For one, the well-wishes that the nine bachelors extend to each other are always and only accompanied by alcohol. The men show gratitude to each other only once the wine flows and they become intoxicated. It is only "in flowing wine" that "they most earnestly expressed their sincerest wishes for the entire well-being and lasting

3. Melville's Supposedly Social Drinkers

hygiene of the gentlemen on the right and on the left" (207). As the men continue to drink and become more heavily inebriated, their apparent appreciation for each other grows: "Meantime, as the wine ran apace, the spirits of the company grew more and more to perfect genialness" (208). While they are enjoying their time getting inebriated with each other, the truth is, they would enjoy doing so with anyone; the only true bond these men share is alcohol.

The nine bachelors use a variety of ploys against each other in order to ensure that the party, and in turn their drinking, lasts as long as possible. One is to make certain that they fill the others' glasses prior to their own. They all refuse to drink unless they are accompanied in their imbibing by one of their fellow bachelors. While this may appear to be well-intentioned politeness, it is actually a deceptive ploy that ensures that the party continues. By filling others' glasses first, each drinker will also be afforded the opportunity to fill up the glass in front of them. As long as the others' glasses are full, none of the bachelors will leave:

> I noticed that when one of these kind bachelors desired a little more wine ... he would not help himself to it unless some other bachelor would join him. It seemed held something indelicate, selfish, and unfraternal, to be seen taking a lonely, unparticipated glass.... Pass the sherry, sir.—Pooh, pooh! Can't be!—The port, sir, if you please. Nonsense; don't tell me so.—The decanter stops with you, sir, I believe. And so it went [207–209].

As went the alcohol, so continued the party.

A second technique that the seemingly-refined gentlemen employ in order to ensure that the festivities continue late into the night occurs when they begin regaling each other with their drunken and never-before-heard stories, tales in which truths may or may not exist: "They related all sorts of pleasant stories. Choice experiences in their private lives were brought out, like choice brands of Moselle or Rhenish, only kept for particular company" (208). These stories are told simply to maintain the interest of the others and to ensure that, as long as the stories are told, the alcohol will continue to be passed around in copious amounts and in the process ensuring that the drinking will not cease.

The nine bachelors in Melville's story are clearly and simply co-dependent alcoholics who, in reality, have no regard for anyone or anything but their addiction. They selfishly appease one another in a variety of ways simply to ensure that they are able to continue satisfying their alcohol addiction. Yet they are not the only selfish, self-centered drinkers in Melville's writings; more shameful illustrations of characters whose only interest is quenching their thirst for alcohol and who will also do so at the expense of their supposed friends are found in Melville's 1855 short story "Jimmy Rose."

The outset of "Jimmy Rose" chronicles the titular character's fall from affluence to penury. As the narrator of the story William Ford relates, Jimmy—much like F. Scott Fitzgerald's Jay (Jimmy) Gatsby from his 1925 novel *The Great Gatsby*[12]—was a rich and "uncommonly handsome person: large and manly, with bright eyes of blue, brown curling hair, and cheeks that seemed painted with carmine" (318). Despite being "a great ladies' man," or perhaps because of being such, he never married, "never tied up his freedom of general worship by making one willful sacrifice of himself at the altar" (318). Rather, he spent his efforts—and his money—on hosting extravagant "dinners, suppers, and balls," parties that "were not to be surpassed by any given in the party-giving city of New York" (319). Jimmy, naturally, was a popular man and his parties were talked and raved about all over the city.

On the surface it appears that the people who attend these parties are genuinely appreciative of Rose's hospitality and of his "uncommon cheeriness; the splendour of his dress; his sparking wit; radiant chandeliers; infinite fund of small-talk; French furniture; glowing welcomes to his guests; his bounteous heart and board; his noble graces and his glorious wine" (319). This apparent gratitude is demonstrated in a stirring toast by one of Jimmy's female guests: "Our noble host; the bloom on his cheek, may it last long as the bloom in his heart!" (319–320). This adoration for Jimmy, however, does not last. In reality and as is clearly demonstrated subsequent to his financial ruin, the "glorious wine" that he freely supplied is all that was ever truly appreciated by his supposed friends; he is merely an afterthought.

Jimmy eventually becomes a "ruined man" (319) and his affluent lifestyle is reduced to bankruptcy first as a result of poor business handlings and then by a fierce storm that sinks two ships carrying his business's merchandise:

> Sudden and terrible reverses in business were made mortal by mad prodigality on all hands. When his affairs came to be scrutinized, it was found that Jimmy could not pay more than fifteen shillings in the

pound. And yet in time the deficiency might have been made up—of course, leaving Jimmy penniless—had it not been that in one winter gale two vessels of his from China perished off Sandy Hook, perished at the threshold of their port [319].

Once this happens Rose is no longer regarded in as high esteem as he was previously. With the exception of Ford, he is abandoned by his "friends" and is merely an afterthought at best. After hearing of Jimmy's misfortune, for instance, Ford tries to find and comfort him. Although everyone the narrator meets in his search for Rose is aware of his downfall, they are unaware of and more importantly uninterested in his whereabouts. "No man could tell where Jimmy was," Ford tells us after learning about Rose's downfall, "and no one seemed to care" (320). Such people are clearly not, nor have they ever been, Jimmy's true friends, and as the story continues this becomes even more abundantly clear.

One question that has yet to be considered seriously in the scant criticism that exists on Melville's story is "why do Rose's supposed friends abandon him?" Why, in other words, is this man who had given his so-called friends so much and so frequently forgotten so quickly and easily? To date, critics have been satisfied with accepting the general and seemingly obvious view that these so-called friends abandon Jimmy simply because he lost his money and is no longer able to host opulent parties of high social standing; they used him to appear more important than they actually are and, in the process, lived vicariously through him.[13] While this is true in part, there is a more specific and selfish reason for their abandonment of him. In reality, these individuals' primary reason for deserting Rose is not strictly the loss of his parties, but more specifically the loss of free liquor that will inevitably accompany the formerly-affluent Rose's demise. Like the drinkers from "The Paradise of Bachelors," the people who attend Rose's parties are alcoholics who demonstrate the selfishness associated with alcoholism and whose only concern was the spirits that they mooched from their noble host.

As noted earlier, selfishness and alcoholism are one-and-the-same. Alcoholics are the "embodiment of selfishness" and they have no regard for anyone or anything except for themselves and their quest to find alcohol and satisfy their addiction to it. This is precisely what we see with some of the individuals who Ford meets subsequent to Jimmy's ruin. While Ford is genuinely concerned about Rose, the alcoholic guests and their dependency on and addiction to alcohol has deprived them of the most basic of human sympathy and compassion.

Subsequent to Jimmy Rose's downfall Ford encounters various selfish and alcoholic individuals who show their indifference for or anger toward the narrator's now-ruined friend. The first alcoholic Ford meets is the man who informs him of Jimmy's demise. He is the party-goer who had "been the first to spring to his feet in eager response to the lady's toast" (320) that praised Jimmy's generosity. As a typical selfish alcoholic, however, this man did not truly appreciate Rose's hospitality, nor does he have any sympathy or compassion for Rose's hardships. Rather, the drinker's sole focus is on alcohol. He laments that he will no longer get wine from Rose but anticipates future drinking, likely at some else's expense. As he smugly says to Ford: "Ah, lad, that was rare wine Jimmy gave us the other night. Shan't get any more, though. Heard the news? Jimmy's burst. Clean smash, I assure you.... And if you say so, we'll arrange over a bottle of claret for a sleighing party to Cato's tonight, Come along" (320). It makes no difference to this drinker that Ford will not be attending the party at Cato's, which is a reference to an actual nineteenth-century New York City tavern (the Oyster Saloon) that was owned by Alexander Cato at 566 Broadway,[14] or suffering from whatever hardships that his new-found poverty will bring him. There will likely be someone else at Cato's off of whom this selfish alcoholic will mooch his liquor.

The second selfish and self-centered alcoholic that Ford meets in his ongoing quest to find his ruined friend is infuriated because he lost $75.75 indirectly as a result of Jimmy's misfortune, causing him to refer to Rose as a "rascal" and a "regular scamp" (320). Considering that he lost such a paltry sum in relation to Jimmy, why is his frustration so extreme? Rose is, after all, apparently his friend. The more logical reason behind his infuriation with and hostility toward Rose is not because of the financial loss but due to the loss of liquor that will inevitably accompany Jimmy's demise. He had consistently and deceitfully used Jimmy for his seemingly-endless supply of liquor, yet no longer will he be able to do so. He was never truly interested in being regaled by Jimmy's tales: like the nine bachelors at the Temple Cloisters who listen to each other's heroic stories while imbibing, this selfish drunkard only wanted to drink. He tolerated Rose and his tales of adventure in order to continue getting intoxicated for free; the longer Jimmy spoke, the more time this drunk had to drink. This fact is not lost on Ford:

> And yet I dare say the share of the dinners he had eaten at Jimmy's might more than have balanced that sum considering that he was something of a wine-bibber, and such wines as Jimmy imported cost a plum or two. Indeed, now that I bethink me, I recall how I had more than once observed this same middle-aged gentleman, and how that toward the close of one of Jimmy's dinners he would sit at the table pretending to be earnestly talking with beaming Jimmy, but all the while, with a half-furtive sort of tremulous eagerness and hastiness, pour down glass after glass of noble wine, as if now, while Jimmy's bounteous sun was at meridian, was the time to make his selfish hay [321].

This character, more than any other in either "The Paradise of Bachelors" or "Jimmy Rose," embodies the alcoholic's selfishness.

When Jimmy dies, which occurs about twenty-five years after his financial ruin (322), his funeral is attended by only three people, including the narrator. Considering how quickly his so-called friends abandoned him after his financial collapse, it is not surprising that his funeral was so poorly attended. Rose had been long forgotten and in reading his obituary it is likely that they, much like the readers in Melville's time who thought that he had died long before his actual death in 1891, would have thought him long dead.[15] It is equally likely, however, that they continued to remember and lament the loss of the free-flowing alcohol that was ever-present at Rose's parties.

Throughout "The Paradise of Bachelors" and "Jimmy Rose" Melville consistently demonstrates that there is no such thing as a social drinker. There are only heavy drinkers or alcoholics who are selfish and whose only concern is to obtain alcohol and to become inebriated, no matter the manner or cost of doing so. Social relationships will be falsely forged and ultimately sacrificed for the sake of inebriation. Avoiding alcoholics and those who drink excessively should be the goal for everyone who does not wish to be subjected to the selfish and self-centered nature of the alcoholic. Alcoholics, Melville shows in these works, have no loyalty to anything but the bottle. He continues to show this but to a further and more despicable extent in works including *Redburn*, *White-Jacket*, *Billy Budd, Sailor*, and *Moby-Dick*.

Chapter 4

Unscrupulous Sippers, Smugglers and Servers

By the second half of 1856 Herman Melville was experiencing physical pain stemming from an array of health issues including sciatica, rheumatism, chronic back problems, and eye strain, and was mentally exhausted from completing his final novel—and his astounding ninth in roughly 12 years—*The Confidence-Man*.[1] Naturally, Melville's physical condition was an issue of tremendous concern for his entire immediate and extended family, yet his mental state was arguably the cause of more significant worry, especially since he had already been accused of being "crazy" by reviewers of *Pierre* roughly four years earlier.[2] On 1 September 1856, Melville's father-in-law and Chief Justice of Massachusetts Judge Lemuel Shaw wrote a letter to his son, Samuel Shaw, describing the extent of Melville's poor health and what possible remedy may exist:

> I suppose you have been informed by some of the family, how very ill, Herman has been. It is manifest to me from Elizabeth's letters, that she has felt great anxiety about him. When he is deeply engaged in one of his literary works, he confines him[self] to hard study many hours in the day, with little or no exercise, & this specifically in winter for a great many days together. He probably thus overworks himself & brings on severe nervous affections. He has been advised strongly to break off this labor for some time, & take a voyage or a journey, & endeavor to recruit. No definite plan is arranged, but I think it may result, in this that in the autumn he will go away for four or five

4. Unscrupulous Sippers, Smugglers and Servers

months, Elizabeth will come here with her younger children, Mrs. Griggs and Augusta will each take one of the boys, their house at Pittsfield will be shut up. I think he needs such a change & that it would be highly beneficial to him & probably restore him [Leyda, *Log* 2: 521].

Six weeks later Melville would somewhat selfishly yet nonetheless necessarily leave behind his wife and four children (Malcolm, Stanwix, Elizabeth, and eighteen-month-old Frances) to embark on a near seven-month tour that was funded by Judge Shaw of Europe and the Holy Land in an attempt to restore his physical health and alleviate his mental strain. He departed from New York City on the 11th of October and would arrive at his first destination, Glasgow, Scotland, on the 26th.

Unlike his 1849 voyage to Liverpool on board the *Southampton* (during which he drank heavily), Melville kept no journal chronicling his two-week journey across the Atlantic Ocean in 1856. Even so, there exists at least one document that recounts certain aspects of his voyage. On November 10, 1856, Melville wrote a letter to his brother, Allan, detailing his ocean crossing and, in one specific part of the letter, the fellow passengers who accompanied him on board the ship *Glasgow*. The picture that Melville paints of some of them, from his perspective at least, is not flattering:

> As for the voyage over, it was upon the whole not disagreeable, though the passengers were not all of a desirous sort. There was, I think, but one American beside myself. The rest were Scotch with a sprinkling of English. Among others there were six or seven "commercial travelers," a hard set who did little but drink and gamble the whole way over. With these fellows of course I had precious little to do [*Correspondence* 301].[3]

Melville's decision to avoid these unknown drinkers may come as somewhat of a surprise, especially when considering that he spent so much of his time on board the *Southampton* in 1849 drinking with, among others, George Adler and Frank Taylor; he also drank extensively at Arrowhead during the early 1850s. So why, it must be asked, was it different for Melville in 1856? As Melville makes clear in his letter to Allan concerning the other drunken passengers who drank the whole voyage, the reason for his sobriety was not due to a lack of available alcohol on the ship, as Howard Horsford suggests (Garner et al. 244),[4] so what was it about "these fellows" that prevented Melville from drinking with them? What was Melville so wary of? Although he does not state it explicitly, he surely must have found something so unscrupulous about them or their character that they would best be avoided.

Melville outright refused to associate with the drinkers on board the *Glasgow* in 1856. In his novella *Billy Budd, Sailor* and novels *Redburn, Omoo, White-Jacket,* and *Moby-Dick,* Melville urges his readers to do the same. In these works he illustrates that both drinkers and those merely associated with alcohol in any way are not worthy of anyone's acquaintance. The characters therein are not simply hypocritical and therefore questionable people like King Mehevi in *Typee,* who is a member of the Hawaiian Temperance Society despite being the "most inveterate dram drinker,"[5] and Dr. Jack Bunger in Chapter 100 of *Moby-Dick,* who proclaims that he is "a strict total abstinence man" (339) yet continues as his captain (and patient at one point) says to get drunk on the sly (339).[6] Nor are they like the self-centered supposedly social drinkers in "The Paradise of Bachelors" and "Jimmy Rose" who were discussed in the previous chapter: they are far worse. In these novels Melville illustrates more forcefully than he did in Chapter 3 of this study that drinkers and those merely associated with alcohol are all unscrupulous individuals. They are a "hard set" of men, to use Melville's words from his letter to his brother, with no moral fabric whatsoever who will take advantage of and betray others no matter what the situation or what consequences await those who fall victim to their unprincipled behavior.

Melville presents an example of an unscrupulous drinker in Chapter 23 of *Redburn*: the Greenlander. The Greenlander is a member of the *Highlander*'s crew who has no reservations about the manner in which he obtains money for his addiction to alcohol; at times he finances his drinking through extortion. In the scene in question Melville introduces "an extremely little man," a "solitary cabin-passenger" (107) with a severe stuttering problem who is sailing on the *Highlander*. He is harmless and has done nothing on the voyage, as Redburn admits, to inconvenience or even be noticed by anyone else on board the ship. He is, in fact, the antithesis to those passengers on board the *Glasgow* that Melville himself would avoid in 1856: "He was never seen reading; never took a hand at cards; never smoked; never drank wine; never conversed; and never staid to the dessert at dinner time" (108).[7] Despite being a teetotaler who tends to his own business while on the ship, this

4. Unscrupulous Sippers, Smugglers and Servers

passenger is terrified, subjected to harsh treatment, and taken advantage of by the Greenlander for the sole sake of alcohol.

There is a tradition of sorts on board merchant ships, Redburn relates, that is "still in vogue among some merchant sailors, of trying fast in the rigging any lubberly landsman of a passenger who may be detected taking excursions aloft, however moderate the flight of the awkward fowl." This process is called "'*making a spread eagle*' of the man; and before he is liberated, a promise is exacted, that before arriving in port, he shall furnish the ship's company with money enough for a treat all round" (108–109). This is the unfortunate fate that awaits the wandering passenger. On a "remarkably pleasant morning" the traveler wanders on deck and is later seen "half way up the mizzen rigging," which draws the attention of the ship's mate: "'Good heavens!' said the mate, who was a bit of a wag, 'you will surely fall, sir! Steward, spread a mattress on deck, under the gentleman!'" (109). While the mate is genuinely concerned for the man's safety, the Greenlander sees only opportunity: "But no sooner was our Greenland sailor's attention called to sight, than snatching up some rope-yarn, he ran softly up behind the passenger, and without speaking a word, began binding him hand and foot" (109). The passenger is terribly frightened and has no idea what is happening to him:

> "Wha-wha-what i-i-is this f-f-for?"
> "Spread-eagle, sir," said the Greenlander, thinking that those few words would at once make the matter plain.
> "Wha-wha-what that me-me-mean?"
> "Treats all around, sir," said the Greenlander,
> wondering at the other's obtusity, who, however, had never so much as heard of the thing before [109].

Ultimately and with no other option, the passenger gives the Greenlander the money that was sought for the booze and was released. The Greenlander cares not that the passenger was fearful for his life as he got the money he needed for his alcohol.

Melville provides arguably a harsher example of just how unscrupulous drinkers are in *Omoo*. Bungs, the *Julia*'s cooper, is a selfish alcoholic who goes to great lengths in order to satisfy his addiction to liquor and to keep the source of his alcohol a secret from the rest of the crew save Chips, Bungs' accomplice in the scheme and the ship's carpenter.[8] Yet there are more despicable aspects of his character than simply being a self-centered and secretive individual. Despite being well-respected among the *Julia*'s crew members and appearing to be a care-free individual with a jovial nature—he and Chips "rolled about the deck, day after day, in the merriest mood imaginable" (no doubt intoxicated from their stolen liquor) (50)—Bungs is nothing more than an untrustworthy scoundrel who will betray anyone as long as it serves his own purpose.

The extent of Bungs' unprincipled nature is demonstrated in the episodes concerning the Round Robin that is signed by many of the members of the *Julia*'s crew.[9] Drinkers, Melville illustrates through Bungs in this part of the novel, will deceive anyone in order to spare themselves from any dire consequence that may be impending, even in situations that do not involve alcohol. Drinkers, Melville suggests through Bungs, have moral and ethical defects that permeate every aspect of their character.

The safety of and living conditions on board the *Julia* are not sufficient for the sailors. As it relates to the ship's sea worthiness,

> she was a small barque of a beautiful model, something more than two hundred tons, Yankee-built and very old. Fitting for a privateer out of a New England port during the war of 1812, she had been captured at sea by a British cruiser, and, after seeing all sorts of service, was at last employed as a government packet in the Australian seas. Being condemned, however, about two years previous, she was purchased at auction by a house in Sydney, who, after some slight repairs, dispatched her on her present voyage. Notwithstanding the repairs, she was still in a miserable plight [5].

To place the crew at even more risk, the provisions that are brought on board are not much safer to eat than the ship is to sail:

> The Julia's provisions were very poor. When opened, the barrels of pork looked as if preserved in iron rust, and diffused an odour like a stale ragout. The beef was worse yet; a mahogany-coloured fibrous substance, so tough and tasteless, that I almost believed the cook's story of a horse's hoof with the shoe on having been fished up out of the pickle of one of the casks. Nor was the biscuit much better; nearly all of it was broken into hard, little gunflints, honeycombed through and through, as if the worms usually infesting this article in long tropical voyages had, in boring after nutriment, came out at the antipodes without finding anything [10].

In secretive response and rebellion, sixteen of the *Julia*'s sailors, including Bungs, opt to sign a circular petition or Round Robin to detail

• 4. Unscrupulous Sippers, Smugglers and Servers •

their concerns about the safety of the ship, the quality of the provisions thereon, and the actions of the despised Captain Guy himself, who the sailors refer to with various "undignified names" (6). The benefit of the Round Robin or list that includes all of the willing sailors' names is that they are all found in a ring so that no man can be picked out as the first signatory and therefore the likely leader of the rebellion (68). The petition is to be sent ashore with Baltimore, the ship's cook, and be given to Pritchard, the British consul. As a result of the hostilities between the English and French, however, Pritchard is in England at this time and his temporary replacement is Wilson, "an educated white man" who was born on the island but who was so "exceedingly unpopular" and who had "such an intolerable air of conceit about [him] that it was almost as much as one could do to refrain from running up and affronting him" (69). Once Baltimore gives Wilson the documents, he learns that Wilson and Captain Guy "were as sociable as could be—old acquaintances, in fact" (69). This, naturally, causes concern for the sailors who had signed the Round Robin. What would the ramifications be, they wonder, for what they wrote and signed? All Baltimore can say is that "in the morning the consul would pay us a visit, and settle everything" (69).

After the signed roundtable is given to Wilson and subsequently Captain Guy, the sailors are brought before the consul, overseen by Guy, to review their complaints. In the consul's reading of the documents, it is revealed that Bungs has betrayed his soon-to-be former shipmates. He has, it appears, singled out certain sailors and has decided to remain on board the *Julia*: "The third affidavit was that of the seamen remaining aboard the vessel, including the traitor Bungs, who, it seemed, had turned ship's evidence. It was an atrocious piece of exaggeration, from beginning to end" (129). Bungs ultimately remains on board and continues to sail on the *Julia*, leaving the supposed mutineers including Typee and Dr. Long Ghost in the lurch and incarcerated in the Calabooza Beretanee in Papeetee,[10] where their fate is, at the point of their jailing, uncertain yet nonetheless bleak. The so-called rebellious radicals are placed in this position solely by the actions of an untrustworthy drunk: Bungs.

Yet another unscrupulous drinker is found in one particular episode in *Billy Budd, Sailor*, the story of the titular character's execution for killing the master-at-arms John Claggart after Claggart had

57

falsely accused Billy Budd to Captain Vere of plotting a mutiny on board the *Bellipotent*. Right at the beginning of the novella Melville presents a gruff and rude alcoholic who is nothing but a thief: Lieutenant Ratcliffe. At the beginning of the novella, Ratcliffe boards the merchant ship *Rights of Man* in search of a sailor to join the English Navy and to come on board the H. M. S. *Bellipotent*. Despite the *Rights of Man*'s Captain Graveling's objection—Billy is Graveling's peacemaker whose loss would be devastating to the both the captain and his crew—the young sailor is nonetheless chosen by Ratcliffe. While Billy is down in the forecastle gathering his belongings for his transfer to the *Bellipotent*, Lieutenant Ratcliffe demonstrates his selfish, thievish, and unprincipled nature:

> Now while Billy Budd was down in the forecastle getting his kit together, the *Bellipotent*'s lieutenant, burly and bluff, no-wise disconcerted by Captain Graveling's omitting to proffer the customary hospitalities on an occasion so unwelcome to him, an omission simply caused by preoccupation of thought, unceremoniously invited himself into the cabin, and also to a flask from the spirit locker, a receptacle which his experienced eye instantly discovered [46].

Ratcliffe has no remorse for his rude and selfish actions; Captain Graveling is left to sit and watch him enjoy the liquor that was not offered to him: "[T]he unembarrassed officer deliberately diluting his grog a little, then tossing it off in three swallows, pushing the empty tumbler away, yet not so far as to be beyond easy reach, at the same time settling himself in his seat and smacking his lips with high satisfaction, looking straight at the host" (46). Lieutenant Ratcliffe is by no means the only thieving drinker from Melville's writings; there are others who steal liquor and in the process of doing so they demonstrate more clearly than Ratcliffe just how unscrupulous they are.

Just like those who strictly drink, those who smuggle alcohol (who may also be drinkers) are also devious and corrupt individuals. One excruciatingly despicable example of a scoundrel smuggler is found in Chapter 79 of *Omoo*: Captain Crash. This "foreigner," to which he is referred, "had lost a colonial armed brig on the coast of New Zealand; and since then, had been leading the life of a man about town among the islands of the Pacific" (281). During this time he had been making his living by smuggling French wine and brandy. At a late point in the novel (Chapter 79 out of 82), a ship—the *Leviathan*—enters the bay and drops anchor, and the following day "Captain Crash entertains the sailors in his grove. And rare times they have of it:—drinking and quarrelling together as sociably as you please" (282). Seeing this, the natives become infuriated at the sailors and their unruly behavior, so one-hundred of the islanders confront the drunken crew. A riot ensues and both Crash and the sailors are ultimately subdued and subsequently brought before a tribunal.

After the arrests everyone but Crash is dismissed as it is determined that he is the one who was in charge of and therefore the only one charged with inciting the riot. It is not simply for this riot that he is being tried, however. In a demonstration of his deplorable character, it also comes to light during the tribunal that he is responsible for corrupting a fourteen-year-old girl and assisting—and undoubtedly causing—her to participate in or commit various crimes. The narrator and others attend the trial, which is described as "that of a decayed naval officer, and a young girl of fourteen; the latter charged with having been very naughty on a particular occasion set forth in the pleadings; and the former with having aided and abetted her in her naughtiness" (281). Crash, who the court finds to be "incorrigible" and responsible for "manifold offences," is found guilty and banished from the island (283). Precisely what he convinced the young girl to do and how he assisted her in doing it is left unsaid in the narrative—a sexual encounter, consensual or otherwise, also for me seems to be lingering beneath the text—but nothing truly needs to be revealed. All that is needed to be known is that this smuggler and shamed former naval officer is responsible for in some way corrupting this fourteen-year-old girl.

Melville's novel *White-Jacket* is rife with unconscionable smugglers. Considering how small an amount of liquor man-of-war sailors were allotted by the American government in the mid-nineteenth-century, a quarter-pint per day (McCarthy 46), and taking into account the alcoholism that was rampant among them, it should come as no shock that attempts to smuggle alcohol on board military ships was a common occurrence. If caught participating in such activity, as many characters in *White-Jacket* are, then they were typically subjected to a flogging, a harsh form of corporal punishment in which sailors were bound with their hands above their head and lashed bare-backed resulting in ripped flesh and inevitable scars, unbelievable amounts of blood, and unimaginable pain. It was a harsh form of punishment that Melville himself would witness about 150 times during his fourteen-month service on board the *United States*.[11] Yet it was not just the threat of corporal punishment that the smugglers had to be wary of, however. As Melville writes in Chapter 43 of the novel, "there is little [honor] among man-of-war smugglers" (181); other drinkers and smugglers posed a more immediate threat. Just like being on a foundering ship, it is every man for himself when it comes to getting one's hands on smuggled alcohol.

Smuggling liquor on board a ship is easier for the forward officers than it is for the common seaman. One such officer who takes advantage of his rank in order to bring contraband liquor on board the *Neversink* in Chapter 43 is the boatswain Yarn. In this chapter and in some "inexplicable way," Yarn had "contrived to slip several skins of brandy through the air-port of his own state-room" (179). Although he is successful in getting the alcohol onto the ship and into his cabin, another alcoholic sailor witnesses Yarn's actions and sees him climbing back on board. Before he can get back into his stateroom and secure his contraband, however, the other cowardly drinker "stole in the boatswain's room, and made away with the prize, not three minutes before the rightful owner entered to claim it" (179). Honoring others' rank, it would seem, is irrelevant when it comes to alcohol and scruples.

White-Jacket's forty-third chapter contains more extreme examples of the "intertwisted villainy" (179) of drinkers and smugglers. In another episode, the Cockswain of the boat assembles what he believes to be reliable men who will smuggle liquor onto the *Neversink* for him. Although the alcohol is brought within close proximity of the ship and is in the process of being brought on board without initial notice, the Cockswain's smuggling racket is revealed by "a weak-pated fellow," a member of his own crew who selfishly "drank somewhat freely ashore" (180) and, due to his intoxication, offered "tipsy hints concerning some unutterable proceeding on the ship's anvil" (180). The crew member's drunken tongue enables a "knowing old sheet-anchor-man, an unprincipled fellow," to catch on to the Cockswain's activities. After he hears the drunken sailor talking about the smuggling, the old sailor "seeks [the Cockswain] out, takes him to one side, and addresses him thus":

> Cockswain, you have been smuggling off some *red-eye*, which at this moment is in your barge at the booms. Now, Cockswain, I have stationed two of my mess-mates at the port-holes, on that side of the ship; and if they report to me that you, or any of your bargemen, offer

4. Unscrupulous Sippers, Smugglers and Servers

to enter that barge before morning, I will immediately report you as a smuggler to the officer on the deck [180].

Naturally, the Cockswain does not want to be singled out as a smuggler and be flogged, so he agrees with the sheet-anchor-man's demands. In the process of doing so, the Cockswain is immediately taken advantage of—blackmailed for his liquor essentially—by the unscrupulous old sailor and there is nothing that he can do about it:

> This done, the sheet-anchor-man goes to his confidants, and arranges his plans. In a word he succeeds in introducing the six brandy bottles into the ship; five of which he sells at eight dollars a bottle; and then, with the sixth, between two buns, he secretly regales himself and confederates; while the helpless Cockswain, stifling with rage, bitterly eyes them from afar [180–181].

The Cockswain placed trust in his smuggling crew members, but the influence that alcohol has on them enables the sheet-anchor-man to take advantage of him. As is so often the case, Melville illustrates, there is no honor or scruples among those associated with alcohol.

Arguably the most notorious example of a character who betrays another's trust for the sake of alcohol in *White-Jacket* is seen in Chapter 44. In this chapter, Captain Claret is infuriated with the number of sailors who are intoxicated on board his ship. Rightfully suspecting smuggling, he instructs his master-at-arms Bland to inspect all cargo that is being brought on board. Eventually Bland discovers twenty-five brown jugs containing alcohol. Although Bland is unable to determine what type of liquor it is, "he was not used to liquor" he says (184), an officer identifies it as brandy. After some investigating, it is revealed that the smuggler is a sailor named Scriggs, a man whose appearance is just as detestable as his actions are for Claret: "He had always been noted for his personal uncleanliness, and among all hands, fore and aft, had the reputation of being a notorious old miser, who denied himself the few comforts, and many of the common necessaries of a man-of-war life" (184). Scriggs is questioned about a possible accomplice in his smuggling racket and after some pressing he ultimately identifies and thereby betrays his associate. His partner-in-crime is none other than the master-at-arms himself, Bland: the same man who had repeatedly flogged sailors for committing the same crime in which he had been participating. Scriggs clearly illustrates his disloyalty to Bland in this episode, yet Bland equally—perhaps more so—destroys the trust that Captain Claret had placed in him, which again illustrates Melville's belief of how untrustworthy drinkers and smugglers are.

Melville shows in other works that it is not only those who imbibe or smuggle alcohol—not simply the drinkers or smugglers themselves—who are callous individuals who seek to take advantage of those around them. Based on their mere association with or proximity to alcohol, as if they are affected by liquor through some sort of mystical scientific diffusion process, even those who sell it legally are unprincipled and therefore are also best to be avoided. Melville expresses his contempt for Liverpool's barkeepers in Chapter 29 of *Redburn* when he groups them along with "land-sharks, land-rats, and other vermin" that prey on innocent mariners and who metaphorically "devour" the sailors—both physically and financially—"limb by limb" with their liquor (139). Just as Timothy Shay Arthur does in his sketchbook *Ten Nights in a Barroom*,[12] Melville stresses with more detail in Chapter 3 of *Moby-Dick*, "The Spouter Inn," the devilish nature of taverns and of how devious bartenders are. In this chapter Ishmael describes how the inn's barkeep, a "withered old man" that the sailors call Jonah (27), takes advantage of both the sailors' insatiable penchant for alcohol and their excruciatingly hard-earned money. As Ishmael relates just prior to the return of "the Grampus's Crew" in New Bedford after four years at sea (28), Jonah is a devious and dishonest business man—or a highly adept one depending on one's ethics—who cunningly serves the sailors their drinks in tapered glasses that distort to his benefit the amount of alcohol that is being poured. It appears to the sailors that they are getting their money's worth when they are actually being served less liquor than what their money deserves. It is in these cheating mugs that the bartender swindles his unwitting clients out of their money and sells them, as Ishmael describes the alcohol, the poison that will inevitably cause death:

> Within are shabby shelves, ranged round with old decanters, bottles, and flasks; and in those jaws of swift destruction, like another cursed Jonah (by which name indeed they called him), bustles a little withered old man, who, for their money, dearly sells the sailors deliriums and death. Abominable are the tumblers into which he pours his poison. Tough true cylinders without—within, the green, villainous green goggling glasses deceitfully tapered downwards to a cheating bottom. Par-

4. Unscrupulous Sippers, Smugglers and Servers

allel meridians rudely pecked into the glasses, surround these footpads' goblets. Fill to *this* mark, and your charge is but a penny; to *this*, a penny more; and so on to the full glass—the Cape Horn measure, which you may gulph down for a shilling [27].[13]

As Melville suggests in *Redburn* and *Moby-Dick*, taverns are clearly best avoided as they are places where the devious bartenders will short-change the sailors out of their money. The sailors, more focussed on satisfying their thirst for liquor, are entirely unaware.

Melville avoided those certain passengers on board the ship *Glasgow* in 1856 without question because he found something out of sorts with or questionable about them. He illustrates consistently in *Redburn, Omoo, Billy Budd, Sailor, White-Jacket,* and *Moby-Dick* that he held this belief to be true even prior to sailing on board the *Glasgow* with them. Drinkers and those associated with alcohol seem to have been corrupted by alcohol, turning them into unscrupulous, immoral, and greedy individuals who will take advantage of others no matter what the cost, situation, or results may be for those who fall victim to their unethical ways. Such people and the product that they sip, smuggle, or serve, Melville is telling his readers in the episodes from these works, are not worthy of anyone's association.

CHAPTER 5

Alcohol, Deception and Melville's Confidence Men

In his 1982 study *The Confidence Man in American Literature*, Gary Lindberg traces the lineage of and illustrates that the confidence man, con man, or con artist, an individual who gains people's trust or confidence only to dupe them out of something of value, is a common and important albeit shameful and therefore somewhat marginalized figure in American literature and culture. As Lindberg writes, the confidence man "occupies a central place in our popular mythology; yet not many of us would want to acknowledge this fact when stated so bluntly, and that is why we don't notice his centrality."[1] Considering the origin of the term, which dates back to the middle of the nineteenth century, the hesitant, if not resistant, recognition of the confidence man—the likeable criminal—is certainly understandable.

The term *confidence man* was coined in the *New York Herald* in 1849 by a journalist during the press coverage of the arrest and subsequent trial of the swindler William Thompson. Thompson was notorious for robbing about one-hundred people, typically upper-class individuals. He would approach strangers and after conversing briefly with them Thompson asked his soon-to-be victims if they had the confidence or trust in him for them to lend him their watch until the following day. Once handed the watch, Thompson walked away with the valuable item and, with one notable instance other than at his trial, the victims never saw Thompson or their watches again.[2] This one exception occurred when Thompson was ultimately brought to justice when he was spotted one day by Thomas McDonald, one of Thompson's victims. McDonald, clearly not impressed with the ingenuity of and likely embarrassed about being duped by Thompson's game, had him arrested and placed in the Tombs.

In 1855, many years after his initial capture, there were reports that Thompson had resurfaced. This possible reappearance prompted a resurgence of interest in the confidence man and he immediately became a "common [character] in literary culture."[3] Melville's ninth and final novel *The Confidence-Man* significantly contributes to the literary tradition and cultural lore of the con artist and contains his most renowned example(s) of the character.[4] That being said and in contrast to what the absence of critical commentary seems to suggest,[5] *The Confidence-Man* is not his only work in which the con artist appears. Nor, I would argue, is the con man in that novel the most successful con artist in Melville's writings.

In his classic 1940 study *The Big Con*, David Maurer writes that confidence men are typically successful in their plots against their victims because they are "suave, slick, and capable."[6] In this chapter we will see that Melville's confidence men do that one better. In addition to possessing the characteristics valued by Maurer and employed by Thompson, Melville's con artists are fully aware of and recognize that the lure of libations is difficult for many people to resist. Armed with this vital knowledge, Melville's confidence men, much like Montresor and his use of alcohol in his plot to murder his fellow nobleman Fortunato in Edgar Allan Poe's "The Cask of Amontillado" (1846), complement their charisma by using alcohol as a type of tool or weapon against their victims. The items sought by the confidence men in Melville's works vary from privileged information, to money and property, to even the drinkers themselves. In the end, the works that will be examined herein become Melville's warning to his readers to be vigilant against and aware of those who come in the guise of seemingly well-meaning individuals, especially when offering alcohol.

Melville's "Bridegroom Dick," from his 1888 poetry collection *John Marr and Other Sailors, With Some Sea Pieces*, is a lengthy narrative poem in which the titular speaker, a retired sailor, relates to his wife Bonny Blue his various adventures at sea on board a man-of-war. Many of his tales, as will be shown here and in Chapter 8, involve sailors and their addictions to alcohol. In this episode, Dick is recounting to Blue stories involving Lieutenant Tom Tight, a man who was well-known for "boozing away at the well-brewed bowl" (214) and who is all but certainly based on Melville's cousin Guert Gansevoort.[7] The specific tale that Dick relates to Blue in this instance concerns the execution of a supposed mutineer that occurred on board the ship, an event that recalls the *Somers'* mutiny affair of 1842 in which Gansevoort participated and foreshadows the execution of the titular sailor Billy Budd from Melville's posthumously-published 1924 novella. After the death sentence in "Bridegroom Dick" is carried out, suspicions concerning the legitimacy of the sailor's execution arise:

> Tom was lieutenant in the brig-o'-war famed
> When an officer was hung for an arch mutineer,
> But a mystery cleaved, and the captain was blamed,
> And a rumpus, too, raised, though his honor was clear [216–219].

Subsequent to the execution the sailors seek to know the truth behind the condemned sailor's trial and of the supposed evidence against him, so they approach Tight for such insight when he is intoxicated. The sailors recognize that he in such a state of drunkenness may be more likely to divulge secret or privileged information. Although they supply him with even more alcohol, frequent cups of burgundy, their scheme is ultimately unsuccessful. As Dick relates and as his surname suggests, Lieutenant Tight is aware of and refuses to fall for their scheme and become loose-lipped about the sailor's trial and his accompanying execution:

> And Tom he would say, when the mousers would
>   try him,
> And with cup after cup o' Burgundy ply him:
> "Gentlemen, in vain with our wassail you beset,
> For the more I tipple, the tighter do I get."
> No blabber, no, not even with the can—
> True to himself and loyal to his clan [220–225].

In the end, the sailors do not get the information that they sought. Tom is one of a few, but not the only one of, Melville's characters who are able to see through the confidence man's plot using liquor.

Another brief example of alcohol being used as a potential weapon against a drinker occurs in the poem "The Scout Toward Aldie" from

• 5. Alcohol, Deception and Melville's Confidence Men •

Battle-Pieces and Aspects of the War: Civil War Poems. In "The Scout Toward Aldie," Melville creates a fictionalized version of an historical event of the Civil War that he experienced himself first-hand.[8] It concerns the story of a hundred-man cavalry seeking to find and eliminate the guerrilla fighter John Mosby and his men, Mosby's Raiders, who had staged commando raids on Union supply lines. From 18–20 April 1864 Melville himself was a member of the cavalry patrol as they headed toward Aldie, Virginia. Eventually, a handful of Mosby's men were captured and it is subsequent to the arrests that the episode of the poem in question takes place. Like the passage that was just related from "Bridegroom Dick," alcohol is intentionally given to a character by a type of confidence man for the purpose of gaining valuable information. The outcome, again, is the same.

During this part of the poem, ten of Mosby's men have been detained, one of whom is named Reb. Despite being a Confederate prisoner of the Colonel's men, Reb is offered a drink by his captors. It is not simply out of good nature that he is offered it, however; rather, the Colonel attempts to use alcohol as a type of weapon, a subtle tool of coercion that, he hopes, will cause Reb's tongue to figuratively loosen and thereby make him more likely to reveal information about the location and strategies of Mosby and his Raiders. Reb accepts the friendly offer, but the Colonel's trick is ultimately unsuccessful. Reb, like Lieutenant Tom Tight, is able to overcome the intended effects that the charismatic Colonel hopes the alcohol will have:

> Herewith he turned—"Reb, have a dram?"
>   Holding the surgeon's flask with a smile.
> To a young scapegoat from the glen.
> "Oh yes!" he eagerly replied,
>   And thank you, Colonel, but—any guile?
>   For if you think we'll blab—why, then
>   You don't know Mosby or his men."[9]

Although the Colonel's trick fails, like that of the sailors in "Bridegroom Dick," this episodes nonetheless again illustrates the potential that alcohol has to be used to take advantage of those who may not have either the ability or the will-power to resist.

The slyest and most deceptive use of alcohol, although not the most grotesque or, once again, successful, to obtain a valued possession occurs in Melville's final novel *The Confidence-Man*. *The Confidence-Man*, as some of its 1857 reviewers clearly observed, is a complex book whose meaning and plot is onerous to understand[10] and, as at least one of our contemporary critics have stated, it is difficult to make sense of what is even going on in the narrative (Lindberg 19). The same holds true for the use of alcohol between the confidence man, known as Francis Goodman in these episodes, and his new friend, Charles Arnold Noble. It is challenging at first to see precisely how Goodman is using alcohol against Noble. In fact, at first reading it appears that Goodman's use of liquor is counter-productive if not outright self-destructive. It is the confidence man, not Noble, who imbibes most of the alcohol. Yet Goodman uses alcohol in this manner in order to continue gaining Noble's trust and to increase the possibility that he will be successful in his con.

At the end of Chapter 28 and as mentioned earlier in Chapter 3 of this study, Goodman and Noble meet on board the *Fidèle*, which is steaming down the Mississippi River on April Fool's Day, and Goodman suggests that he and Noble have a drink together in order to celebrate their new friendship: "'No doubt they treated you to something strong; but wine—surely, that gentle creature, wine; come, let us have a little wine at one of these little tables here. Come, come'" (212). As the following chapter begins, the two commence drinking and talking about the nature of love and of friendship. As it is described and as Noble says,

> The wine, port, being called for, and the two seated at the little table, a natural pause of convivial expectancy ensued; the stranger's eyes turned toward the bar near by, watching the red-cheeked, white-aproned man there, blithely dusting the bottle, and invitingly arranging the salver and glasses; when, with a sudden impulse turning round his head toward his companion, he said, "Ours is friendship at first sight, ain't it?" [214].

Goodman, seeing an opening to instill confidence in Noble, replies in agreement and emphasizes that their friendship truly is like love: "'It is,' was the placidly pleased reply; 'and the same may be said of friendship at true sight as of love at first sight; it is the only true one, the only noble one. It bespeaks confidence. Who would go sounding his way into love or friendship, like a strange ship by night, into an enemy's harbour?'" (214). The confidence in this episode has been established and Noble is ready, in Goodman's mind, for the trick to begin.

From Chapters 29–35 inclusive, Goodman and Noble together

5. Alcohol, Deception and Melville's Confidence Men

drink alcohol. Yet it is the confidence man, Goodman, who is the only one who is urged to drink excessively by his potential victim, Charles Noble. Why would the con artist subject himself to intoxication and risk his plot failing or, even worse, backfiring? Goodman, basically, is simply going along with the game. Alcohol is being used as something to instill further confidence in Noble. For whatever reason, Goodman—without question knowing full-well of his drinking prowess—is able to drink a substantial amount of alcohol while still remaining sober[11]; he is a possible alcoholic who certainly knows his own limits of consumption. This seemingly obvious observation must not be overlooked. Goodman's ability to imbibe so much and remain sober is precisely his trick. He can consume such copious amounts of alcohol without getting inebriated over such a long period of time, hoping that Goodman will become intoxicated by the albeit lesser amount that he has consumed. He hopes, essentially, that Goodman is not accustomed to drinking and that he will ultimately become intoxicated over the course of their lengthy encounter.

In Chapter 30 Goodman recognizes that he is drinking more than his share while Noble has not seemed to imbibe much of anything at all. As Goodman says to Noble, "Freely drink? you haven't drunk the perfect measure of one glass yet. While for me, this must be my fourth or fifth, thanks to your importunity" (233). Noble then replies, "'Oh, I drink while you are talking,' laughed the other, 'have a queer way I learned from a sedate old uncle, who used to tip off his glass unperceived. Do you fill up, and my glass, too. There! Now away with that stump, and have a new cigar. Good fellowship forever!'" (233). By drinking to such an extent and talking about friendship with such passion, Goodman has formed in Noble even further trust and confidence.

At the end of Chapter 30, Noble notices that Goodman has something on his mind, something that he appears to want to ask. After a few moments of encouragement, Goodman admits what he has been thinking, and the purpose of him wanting Noble to drink, regardless of the amount, becomes clear. He wanted Noble to become intoxicated so that he would be more willing to give him money: "'Out it shall come, then' said the cosmopolitan. 'I am in want, urgent want, of money'" (239). Naturally, Noble becomes infuriated, calling Goodman a beggar and an impostor for being so deceived: "'none of your why, why, whys!' tossing out a foot, 'go to the devil, sir! Beggar, impostor!—

never so deceived in a man in my life" (240). After Noble reacts thus, Goodman takes "ten half eagles" (241) from his pocket and places them on the table, attempting to show Noble that it was all a sly joke. Noble accepts Goodman's explanation of the episode, calling him a "funny man" (241) and subsequently suggests to Goodman that they continue drinking: "But I relish a good joke too well to spoil it by letting on. Of course, I humoured the thing; and, on my side, put on all the cruel airs you would have me. Come, this little episode of fictitious estrangement will but enhance the delight reality. Let us sit down again, and finish our bottle" (242). Noble has clearly not learned his lesson as the invitation to continue drinking is accepted, subjecting himself to possible inebriation and further ploys from the confidence man that he will inevitably be unable to resist.

Thus far, the confidence men in Melville's writings have been unsuccessful in gaining the various items that they sought, yet the use of alcohol as a weapon is nonetheless clear. A more successful example of alcohol being used as a type of conning tool against less vigilant people occurs in Chapter 32 of *Omoo*. Tahiti was annexed to the French in 1843 and various battles were fought between the two for years thereafter. There is a minor episode in *Omoo* where Melville refers to these hostilities and the battle for land control that existed. After various fights between the French and the islanders, French soldiers are ambushed and slaughtered: "Shortly after the engagements at Hararparpi, three French were waylaid in a pass of the valleys, and murdered by the incensed natives" (115). After this event, the despised Armand-Joseph Bruat, the French governor who has total control and exerts draconian power over the recreant chief Kitoti,[12] tries his hand at being a confidence man. Kitoti is urged by Bruat to host a great feast in the Vale of Paree, to which all of Kitoti's islanders are invited. Bruat's goal in doing so "was to gain over all he could to his interests" and in his attempt to acquire total and uncontested control of the area, Bruat supplies the islanders with "an abundance of wine and brandy" (116). The drinking results in a "scene of bestial intoxication" (116), giving the governor an upper-hand on the islanders and thereby assists him with the political maneuvering that he wishes to conduct.

The confidence men up to this point in Melville's writings have sought to dupe their victims out of information, land, and as is more typically the case, money or something of monetary value. Yet there are con artists in Melville's writings who are far more ruthless in their desires and who wish to obtain something of far more significance or value than information, money, or vast areas of land. In *Israel Potter* and "The Encantadas," Melville presents confidence men who use their skills in conning and their knowledge of alcohol and its effects on inebriated individuals in order to obtain human beings. These con artists use alcohol to assist them in their goal of kidnapping the drinkers themselves.

In his 1969 study *Melville's "Israel Potter": A Pilgrimage and Progress*, still one of the few if not only book-length studies devoted exclusively to Melville's eighth novel,[13] Arnold Rampersad writes that the second section of *Israel Potter*,[14] which includes the parts of the novel about to be discussed herein that follow Potter "from the meeting with Dr. Franklin through the return to Squire Woodcock's," are largely moments of "comic relief."[15] Although there are comical parts in the section to which Rampersad refers, such as "Israel's flight from the Woodcock home dressed in the Squires' clothes and terrifying the household before he is himself petrified by what turns out to be a scarecrow" (Rampersad 51), there are also moments of the utmost seriousness, episodes in which Melville provides his commentary on the extreme and potentially life-threatening dangers of alcohol. On numerous occasions in *Israel Potter* the titular character himself acts as a con man who uses liquor in order to save himself from imprisonment and is also taken advantage of by con artists and alcohol by possible confidence men who seek to imprison him. In each case, alcohol has the potential to be used as a tool or weapon for the purpose of incapacitating and subduing the victims.

Episodes of the con artist are (seemingly) on display in *Israel Potter*'s sixth chapter. At this point of the novel Israel continues to seek shelter and protection on a farm when he is approached by the farmer, who is carrying a message for him:

> Late one night while hiding in a farmer's granary, Israel saw a man with a lantern approaching. He was about to flee, when the man hailed him in a well-known voice, bidding him to have no fear. It was the farmer himself. He carried a message to Israel from a gentleman of Brentford, to the effect, that the refugee was earnestly requested to repair on the following evening to that gentleman's mansion [33].

After being dressed by the farmer in clothes intended to disguise him, Potter sets off the next day and encounters the man who had requested his presence. Despite telling Israel that "no foul play was intended" for this meeting, the man is nonetheless a possible threat and confidence man. Squire Woodcock along with two other men, his possible shills the Rev. Horne Took and the pro–American British citizen James Bridges, have apparently, as Israel is told by Woodcock, formed a conspiracy in Britain to aid in the American Revolution:

> "I am John Woodcock," said the host, "and these gentlemen are Horne Tooke and James Bridges. All three of us are friends to America. We have heard of you for some weeks past, and inferring from your conduct, that you must be a Yankee of the true blue stamp, we have resolved to employ you in a way which you cannot but gladly approve; for, surely, though in exile, you are still willing to serve your country; if not as a sailor or soldier, yet as a traveller?" [34].

Subsequent to arriving at Woodcock's home, Potter is given a meal of cold beef and a glass of perry, an alcoholic beverage made from fermented pears. Three times during their conversation Potter is urged by Woodcock to drink more, but he is cautious about imbibing too much. He is suspicious of the men and he therefore refuses to drink more than two glasses of liquor. Based on his own ploy in Chapter 3 of the novel in which he successfully tempts the guards to imbibe heavily and who later passed out and enable Potter to escape,[16] he is cognizant that alcohol could be used as a weapon against those who are not vigilant, especially around those one may not know or trust:

> But after his second glass, Israel declined to drink more, mild as the beverage was. For he noticed that not only did the three gentlemen listen with the utmost interest to his story, but likewise interrupted him with questions and cross-questions in the most pertinacious manner. So this led him to be on his guard, not being absolutely certain yet, as to who they might really be, or what their real design [34–35].

Potter's vigilance should be commended in this instance, but it was not necessary; the men ultimately pose no danger to him whatsoever: "But as it turned out, Squire Woodcock and his friends only sought to satisfy themselves thoroughly, before making their final disclosures, that the exile was one in whom implicit confidence might be placed" (35). As discussed in Chapter 1 of this study on Melville's temperance fiction, Woodcock's interest in Potter is for him to carry sensitive documents to Benjamin Franklin in Paris in order to assist with the conspiratorial plot. Israel has escaped in this episode from being

• 5. Alcohol, Deception and Melville's Confidence Men •

taken advantage of by the false yet nonetheless potential confidence man and alcohol. He has escaped, that is, for now.

The previous episode illustrates that Israel Potter is fully aware of how excessive drinking could cause him to be placed in a situation with dire consequences. He cautiously avoids imbibing too much in Chapter 6 of the novel in order to protect himself from any possible danger that may arise from intoxication. Although he was able to resist the temptation to drink in Chapter 6 despite there being no true danger to him, he is not able to do so seven chapters later and, thereby, he is subjected to potential danger. Unlike the previous episode with Squire Woodcock, however, his excessive drinking in this instance places him in a truly ominous situation. Even those who are aware of and partake in "the game," as Israel does in Chapter 3 and as discussed in note 16 to this chapter, are susceptible to becoming victims of it.

In Chapter 12 of the novel Israel is sent back to England by Franklin and for his continued protection he is secluded in a secret compartment behind Woodcock's chimney. After many days in hiding, Potter emerges only to find that Squire Woodcock has died and that Tooke and Bridges are nowhere to be found. In the following chapter, Potter is again on the run and later approached, in a similar way to the Woodcock episode discussed earlier, by a seemingly affable stranger who lures Potter into drinking. As Israel will soon discover, this person is a true confidence man who gets from Potter exactly what is desired:

> While standing wrapped in afflictive reflections on the shore, gazing towards the unattainable coast of France, a pleasant-looking cousinly stranger, in seaman's dress, accosted him, and, after some pleasant conversation, very civilly invited him up a lane into a house of rather secret entertainment. Pleased to be befriended in this his strait, Israel yet looked inquisitively upon the man, not completely satisfied with his good intentions. But the other, with good-humoured violence, hurried him up the lane into the inn, when, calling for some spirits, he and Israel very affectionately drank to each other's better health and prosperity [83].

As was the case with Woodcock, Potter is continually urged to continue drinking, only this time he heeds the requests. He is unable, or at least unwilling, to refuse the invitation to continue drinking as he, much like Pierre, Turkey, "Cock-A-Doodle-Doo!"'s unnamed narrator, and the sailors on board the *Neversink* in *White-Jacket*, is in need of an

73

escape from the hardships and stresses from which he has been experiencing. This time and unlike Chapter 6 of the novel, for whatever reason, Potter does not have any reservations about imbibing in the company of these strange men and is coaxed easily into drinking excessively. He should have remembered his prior strength to resist imbibing with Woodcock and recalled Franklin's advice concerning temperance as discussed earlier in this study's opening chapter because, this time, he truly is in danger. Alcohol is being used against him by the confidence man in order to make him easier to subdue.

As the con artist kindly says to Potter as related by the narrator, "'Take another glass,' said the stranger affably. Israel, to drown his heavy-heartedness, complied. The liquor began to take effect" (83–84). It is only once Potter is drunk that the supposedly friendly strangers' plot becomes obvious. The confidence man and his shills are employed to round up runaway sailors, and since Potter is so intoxicated he admits to what they want to hear and his inebriation makes him easier to control. After admitting that he had been a whaler, Potter is kidnapped:

> "Ah!" said the other, "happy to hear that, I assure you. Jim! Bill!" And beckoning very quietly two brawny fellows, in a trice Israel found himself kidnapped into the naval service of the magnanimous old gentleman of Kew Gardens—his Royal Majesty, George III. "Hands off!" said Israel, fiercely as the two men pinioned him. "Regular game-cock," said the cousinly-looking man. "I must get three guineas for cribbing him. Pleasant voyage to ye, my friend," and, leaving Israel a prisoner, the crimp, buttoning his coat, sauntered leisurely out of the inn [84].

Within a week, and only because he failed to resist the alcohol that had been offered to him by the confidence man, Israel is put in a perilous position at sea:

> To be short, in less than a week Israel found himself at Portsmouth, and, ere long, a fore-topman in his majesty's ships of the line "Unprincipled," scudding before the wind down channel, in company with the "Undaunted," and the "Unconquerable"; all three haughty Dons bound to the East Indian waters as reinforcements to the fleet of Sir Edward Hughes [84].

The confidence man, with the assistance of alcohol, has successfully lured Potter into the position in which the con man sought Israel to be. Potter eventually escapes from his dire situation, yet there are others who meet their demise due to the actions of far more nefarious con men.

5. Alcohol, Deception and Melville's Confidence Men

As John Bryant has insightfully observed, the hermit Oberlus from the ninth sketch of "The Encantadas" ("Hood's Isle and the Hermit Oberlus"), Melville's series of ten sketches set in the Galápagos Islands that he himself visited or sailed near at various times from 1841 to 1843,[17] is a confidence man.[18] Unlike Bryant, however, I do not regard Oberlus as merely an "incompetent villain" ("Comic" 263). Rather and without question, Oberlus is a cunning and successful con man who uses sailors' thirst for and addiction to alcohol against them. He uses liquor as a weapon to bait successfully his victims and to lure some of them into incarceration and slavery and others to death.

At the beginning of the sketch we learn that Oberlus has been living in seclusion from civilization for half a century on Hood's Isle. Over the period of this isolation, he has developed a misanthropic view that instills in him "a vast idea of his own importance, together with a pure animal sort of scorn for all the rest of the universe" (141). This self-serving and individualistic attitude causes Oberlus to attempt to kidnap or destroy those who come on to his island. His appearance, as the narrator relates, is as equally vile as his actions that we will see later: "His appearance, from all accounts, was that of the victim of some malignant sorceress; he seemed to have drunk of Circe's cup; beast-like rags insufficient to hide his nakedness; his befreckled skin blistered by continual exposure to the sun; nose flat; countenance contorted, heavy, earthy; hair and beard unshorn, profuse, and of fiery red" (139).

The main part of the sketch's narrative begins with Oberlus seeing a sailor going into the thickets for wood. He becomes enraged that his island is being used for resources without him receiving some sort of compensation.[19] It is his island, he believes—"This island's mine by Sycorax my other," he says (140)—and nobody but him is entitled to its resources. As a result, Oberlus attempts to kidnap the sailor using a musket as a weapon. Although the gun misfires during the course of the attempted abduction, the sailor is nonetheless frightened and eventually subdued by Oberlus:

> Oberlus runs off a little space to a bush, and fetching his blunderbuss, savagely commands the negro to desist work and follow him. He refuses. Whereupon, presenting his piece, Oberlus snaps at him. Luckily the blunderbuss misses fire; but by this time, frightened out of his wits, the negro, upon a second intrepid summons, drops his billets, surrenders at discretion, and follows on [142].

The sailor, it appears, has been captured by Oberlus and his violent plan.

While leading his prisoner up the mountain, Oberlus's vigilance slackens and the sailor, who is a "powerful fellow," "suddenly grasps him in his arms, throws him down, wrests his musketoon from him, ties his hands with the monster's own cord, shoulders him, and returns with him down to the boat" (142). After being taken on board the sailor's ship, where Oberlus is whipped severely, handcuffed, and then taken back to his island to make known to his captors his home and possessions, the sailors destroy his hut and garden. While the sailors are thus occupied and distracted, however, Oberlus escapes into the mountains.

Despite fleeing to safety, Oberlus's failure to capture and detain the initial sailor creates in him a further hatred and a more diabolical desire to seek "revenge upon humanity" (142). He begins thinking about what went awry with his prior kidnapping attempt and he "pursues a quite different plan" (142) to take hostage that he will subsequently turn into slaves. He will no longer use violence in order to subdue his victims; rather, he ultimately decides to become a confidence man and gain the sailors' trust and complement the friendly nature he will begin to present by offering alcohol, something with which he is very familiar.

Oberlus is fully aware of the power that alcohol can have on an individual as he himself is an alcoholic: "Except for his occasional visitors from the sea, for a long period, the only companions of Oberlus were the crawling tortoises; and he seemed more than degraded to their level, having no desires for a time beyond theirs, unless it were for the stupor brought on by drunkenness" (140). Armed with this knowledge, Oberlus begins to set his new plan into action. Once further sailors arrive on the island later in the sketch, Oberlus uses charisma to instill confidence in them and employs alcohol to take advantage of them: "When seamen come ashore, he makes them like a free-and-easy comrade, invites them to his hut, and with whatever affability his red-haired grimness may assume, entreats them to drink his liquor and be merry" (142–143). Due to their addiction to, or at least their penchant for, alcohol and paired with the calming effect of Oberlus's supposedly friendly nature, the sailors need little coaxing, or "little pressing" as the narrator says, to indulge in drinking. Little do they know and much to their detriment, however, Oberlus's convivial and good-natured attitude is all a ploy; he has used the alcohol and the men's addiction to it as his new weapon. In the process, he has placed them in a more inescapable

5. Alcohol, Deception and Melville's Confidence Men

situation than he could have ever hoped to achieve by using the muscle or force of a gun. Once the sailors are inebriated and "rendered insensible" from the alcohol, as the narrator describes them, Oberlus's true character surfaces. The sailors are

> tied hand and foot, and pitched among the clinkers, and there concealed till the ship departs, when finding themselves entirely dependent on Oberlus, alarmed at his changed demeanor, his savage threats, and above all, that shocking blunderbuss, they willing enlist under him, becoming his humble slaves, and Oberlus the most incredible of tyrants [143].

Oberlus's harsh treatment of his captive results in the death of some of the sailors and those who survive are eventually brainwashed. He "makes murderers out of them" (143) and they become his slaves and soldiers: Oberlus has "a noble army now" (144). In the process of their degradation and in contrast to Charles Darwin's theory of evolution that he began to develop during his own time in the Galápagos islands in 1835, the captives experience, as William B. Dillingham has said, a process of a "reverse evolution to a lower form of life."[20]

Oberlus ultimately meets his demise at the end of the sketch. While still on his island Oberlus destroys three boats that were sent ashore for vegetables that he promised sailors who were in need of provisions and he makes his way off his island in the fourth to Peru. The captains of the two ships anchored off his island, in fear of Oberlus, had allowed him to go free. While in Payta (Paita), a city in the Northwestern part of the county, he convinces a local beauty to return with him to his island but he is arrested prior to their departure and he is sent to prison in South America, where the jails consist of "but one room, without windows or yard, and but one door heavily grated with wooded bars" and that are "both within and without the grimmest aspect" (146); his cell is the total opposite to Oberlus's accustomed habitat of fresh air and clear sky on his island. Despite Oberlus's capture and subsequent incarceration at the end of the sketch, the knowledge of and unquestionable success in the con game—pairing charisma with alcohol—that he demonstrates with the sailors in the earlier part of the sketch not only makes him one of the most "naturally tyrannical and cruel" characters in Melville's writings, as Paul McCarthy aptly describes him in *"The Twisted Mind"* (99), but also and in contrast to Bryant's earlier-mentioned assessment gives him the distinction of being Melville's most cunning, ruthless, and successful confidence man of all.

As Melville illustrates through the works considered throughout this chapter, the power that alcohol has and the extent to which it can be used as a powerful tool or weapon against others is profound. Even those who are fully cognizant of the perils in which one could be placed due to excessive imbibing, as is the case with Israel Potter, are not always able to refrain from imbibing. Then there are those, like the sailors in "The Encantadas," who drink while they are already in perilous positions, thereby making their situations far worse, deadly for some. In any case, Melville's warning to his readers in these works is clear: there are varying yet nonetheless detrimental consequences for drinkers who are unable to resist the offer of liquor from those who are essentially strangers. Even when being vigilant the urge to overindulge still exists and accompanying such excessive drinking are the risks associated with it. It is better to abstain from alcohol entirely, Melville suggests, in order to avoid the dangers that may exist from those who offer it.

CHAPTER 6

Loss of Rank, Loss of Reputation

Herman's father, Allan Melvill,[1] was a relatively successful importer of luxury goods until he suffered a fate similar to Jimmy Rose and was financially ruined during the economic depression of the early 1830s. In December of 1831, Allan traveled to New York City in an attempt to solicit new customers for his company; he was unsuccessful. On his return trip in January of 1832, Allan was forced to walk the final leg of his journey home to Albany across the frozen Hudson River after the ship *Constellation* on which he was travelling was forced to pull ashore in Poughkeepsie due to heavy ice. Subsequent to his return home, Allan continued to try and find a way out of his financial crisis yet in the process he failed to allow himself adequate recuperation time, and he later became delirious with fever. He eventually died in bankruptcy on the 28th of January, apparently in the throes of wild delirium.[2]

Since Melville had been withdrawn from school the October prior to his father's death he was now forced to find employment at the age of twelve in order to assist with the financial support of his mother and siblings. After holding a variety of menial positions and then advancing his education over the many years that followed, he eventually accepted a teaching position at the Sikes District School, southwest of Pittsfield. From the outset he despised teaching and for good reasons. For one, some of his class's "bigger boys" had threatened a rebellion against Melville in which they wanted to physically assault him (Parker, *Melville*

79

1: 118). Clearly dissatisfied with being a teacher, Melville then sought work on the Erie Canal Project. Despite being a certified surveyor and engineer in the late 1830s, however, he was unable to find employment. Ultimately and with no other option, Melville signed on as a cabin boy on board the merchant ship *St. Lawrence* bound for Liverpool, England, in June of 1839. This four-month voyage and the time that he would spend in Liverpool served a decade later as the inspiration for his 1849 novel *Redburn*.[3]

After returning home from his voyage he found his mother and sisters again in near poverty. Desperate for extra income he once again took a job as a school teacher, this time at the Greenbush & Shodack Academy in Lansingburgh, New York. A few months after accepting the teaching position, however, the school declared bankruptcy and Melville was never paid. Despite his indifference to teaching, Melville may have remained a teacher had Greenbush & Shodack offered him a "living wage" (Parker, *Melville* 1: 167). This, obviously, did not happen. In a further attempt to find employment Melville and his friend Eli Fly went as far west as Illinois. Again, there was nothing to be found. At the end of 1840 and with no other option for work, Melville signed on board the whaling vessel *Acushnet* and set sail for the whaling hunting grounds of the Pacific Ocean on 3 January 1841. When he finally returned home to America in 1844 with unbelievable tales of adventure, he devoted his time to what he hoped would become his new and financially-rewarding profession: authorship. Sadly, however, such success did not materialize. Although his first two novels *Typee* and *Omoo* netted him profits, his further writings did not fare nearly as well, to say the least.[4] This left Melville (after his marriage) and his family in a dire financial situation until he finally was offered—and finally accepted under no doubt a sense of inevitable defeat—full-time employment as an inspector of customs at the port of New York City in 1866,[5] more than two decades after returning from his voyages and adventures at sea.

Melville was clearly well aware that there were few job opportunities available for men in the first half of the nineteenth century other than joining the crew of various sea vessels.[6] Perhaps stemming from his knowledge of how rare gainful employment was for men in the United States during this era, Melville suggests to his readers in works including *Typee*, *Omoo*, and *White-Jacket* to take advantage of the only option available to them: as he and Ishmael did, take to the ship.[7] However,

6. Loss of Rank, Loss of Reputation

he also advises them to stay sober or run the risk of losing their professional rank and reputation—lose their jobs and livelihood essentially—and not to join such ships with the illusion, as certain sailors in *White-Jacket* do, that excessive drinking will be tolerated.[8]

The alcoholic first-mate of the *Julia* John Jermin from *Omoo* runs the risk of losing his reputation on board the whaling ship *Julia* due to his excessive and chronic drinking. In the novel's fifth chapter, Jermin begins his watch at midnight, bringing with him "a flask of spirits" (17). He later gets drunk and passes out, thereby allowing other sailors to highjack a whaling boat and escape from the ship. Although the runaways are captured the next day and Jermin suffers no consequences for his actions, or more specifically his lack thereof, this episode calls attention to the need for sailors on duty to remain vigilant and abstain from drinking. In other parts of *Omoo* and in many of his other works, however, Melville shows what can happen to those who are caught drinking while on duty or who are found to be in any form of alcohol-related dereliction of duty.

The first clear example from Melville's writing of a sailor who has truly lost his professional rank and reputation as a direct result of his drinking occurs in the second chapter of *Typee*, Melville's first novel—and first significant publication[9]—that fictionalizes the time that he spent on the island of Nukuheva after abandoning the whaling vessel *Acushnet* with Richard Tobias Greene in 1842.[10] The character in question is the English harbor pilot. As the whaling vessel *Dolly* approaches the bay of Nukuheva in Chapter 2, the narrator Tommo is stunned by the island's beauty. Unfortunately for him, and more specifically the islanders, he is immediately enraged by the presence of the French colonizers and missionaries:

> Towards noon we drew abreast the entrance to the harbor, and at last we slowly swept by the intervening promontory, and entered the bay of Nukuheva. No description can do justice to its beauty; but that beauty was lost to me then, and I saw nothing but the tri-colored flag of France trailing over the stern of six vessels, whose black hulls and bristling broadsides proclaimed their warlike character. There they were, floating in that lovely bay, the green eminences of the shore looking down so tranquilly upon them, as if rebuking the sternness of their aspect. To my eye nothing could be more out of keeping than the presence of these vessels; but we soon learned what brought them there.

The whole group of islands had just been taken possession of by Rear Admiral Du Petit Thouars, in the name of the invincible French nation [12].

After Tommo's diatribe about the French's presence on the island, and more generally about colonialism itself, the *Dolly* is approached by a whale boat steered by a "genuine South-sea vagabond" (12): the English harbor pilot.

Once the boat is aside the *Dolly* the harbor pilot is assisted on board by the sailors, who find him to be in an "interesting stage of intoxication" that has rendered him "helpless" (12). Despite his inebriation—"he was utterly unable to stand erect or to navigate his body across the deck" (12–13)—he wishes to assist the *Dolly*'s Captain Vangs in navigating the ship securely into the harbor. Although Captain Vangs wisely declines the pilot's services, the drunken vagabond cannot be silenced:

> [B]ut our gentleman was determined to play his part, for by dint of much scrambling he succeeded in getting into the weather-quarter boat, where he steadied himself by holding on to a shroud, and then commenced issuing his commands with amazing volubility and very peculiar gestures. Of course no one obeyed his orders; but as it was impossible to quiet him, we swept by the ships of the squadron with this strange fellow performing his antics in full view of all the French officers [13].

This is not the first time that the English harbor pilot has been drunk while on duty, nor is it the first time that his inebriation has been witnessed by his superior officers.

We subsequently learn that the harbor pilot had been a lieutenant in the English Navy, but lost his rank and "disgraced his flag" by some criminal and alcohol-induced behavior (13). After losing his position as lieutenant he deserted his ship, roamed among the islands of Nukuheva, and was present when the French took control. He had then been appointed pilot of the harbor by the "newly constituted authorities" (13): the French. The English harbor pilot's habitual drunkenness not only cost him his high-ranking position with the English Navy that he once held, but more importantly also forced him to switch political and national allegiances. For Melville, who was clearly an "ardent nationalist"[11] who asserted and sought for America's cultural and literary independence in his 1850 review essay "Hawthorne and his

Mosses" "with an astonishingly imperious, provocative arrogance,"[12] there would be very little as shameful or severe a consequence as having to abandon one's country, an outcome for the English harbor pilot that is caused solely by his alcoholism.[13]

"It is hardly to be doubted," the narrator say in Chapter 14 of *White-Jacket*, "that the controlling inducement which keeps many men in the American Navy, is the unbounded confidence they have in the ability of the United States government to supply them, regularly and unfailingly, with their daily allowance of [alcohol]" (53). Considering the number of apparent alcoholics on board the *Neversink*, it should be no surprise, then, that *White-Jacket* contains more detailed and frequent accounts than *Typee* of sailors whose careers are adversely affected by their alcoholism. One such character is Lieutenant Mad Jack. Despite being loved by all of the sailors around him, Mad Jack has one "fearful failing," as the titular narrator calls it: he drinks (34).[14] Just like the English harbor pilot, Mad Jack is an alcoholic whose addiction has gotten him into "very serious scrapes" (34). On more than one occasion his drinking had cost him his authority as an officer and caused him nearly to suffer the brutality of a flogging: "Twice he was put off duty by the Commodore; and once he came near being broken for his frolics." (34).[15] White-Jacket, like the rest of the crew, admires Mad Jack so much that, in an aside, he offers temperance advice to him, expressing his hope that Mad Jack would quit drinking:

> So far as his efficiency as a sea-officer was concerned, on shore at least, Jack might *bouse away* as much as he pleased; but afloat it will not do at all. Now, if he only followed the wise example set by those ships of the desert, the camels; and while in port, drink for the thirst past, the thirst present, and the thirst to come—so that he might cross the ocean sober; Mad Jack would get along pretty well. Still better, if he would but eschew brandy altogether; and only drink of the limpid white wine of the rills and the brooks [34].

By doing so, Melville, through White-Jacket, is also providing the advice to the novel's readers.

In Chapter 58 of *White-Jacket* Melville introduces and clearly chronicles the tribulations of arguably the *Neversink*'s most notorious alcoholic: Mandeville. Like the English harbor pilot in *Typee* and *White-Jacket*'s Mad Jack, Mandeville is without question an alcoholic who, despite the hardships that he has experienced as a result of his addiction to alcohol prior to the narrative, is simply unable to free himself from his dependency on drink and to prevent himself from repeating his alcohol-related mistakes. He cannot refrain from imbibing, despite knowing full well what horrific consequences—physical and professional—await him.

While in port at Rio de Janero, the man-of-war *Neversink* is in need of extra crew members. It is here that Mandeville enters the narrative. After boarding the ship in Rio and as if expecting some type of favoritism or preferential treatment, Mandeville introduces himself to one of the *Neversink*'s officers, Lieutenant Bridewell:

> "Mandeville, sir," said the man courteously touching his cap. "You must remember me, sir," he added, in a low, confidential tone, strangely dashed with servility; "we sailed together once in the old *Macedonian*, sir. I wore an epaulet then; we had the same state-room, you know, sir. I'm your old chum, Mandeville, sir." And he again touched his cap [242].[16]

Mandeville is not greeted by Bridewell with the civilities that he was clearly hoping for from his former fellow sailor and bunk-mate. Bridewell responds to Mandeville harshly, reminding him that there are certain rules on board a man-of-war that must be obeyed. Although he does not mention it explicitly, Lieutenant Bridewell is clearly referring to Mandeville's prior drinking habits and of the loss of professional rank and reputation that his alcoholism has cost him: "'I remember an *officer* by that name,' said the first lieutenant, emphatically, 'and I know *you*, fellow. But I know you henceforth for a common sailor. I can show no favoritism here. If you ever violate the ship's rules, you shall be flogged like any other seaman. I place you in the foretop; go forward to your duty'" (242). White-Jacket then explains precisely and with more specificity than Bridewell what transpired previously with Mandeville in order for him to be received so negatively upon boarding the *Neversink*.

Mandeville joined the United States Navy when he was "very young" and eventually rose to the rank of lieutenant (242). Yet his addiction to alcohol, brandy more specifically, caused him to lose everything. The first drunken incident that results in Mandeville's loss of rank and reputation occurs while he is on duty as commanding officer on deck in the Mediterranean Sea. Despite being on watch, he becomes intoxicated and later passes out due to his drunkenness, thereby leaving the ship without a commanding officer on deck. It is

6. Loss of Rank, Loss of Reputation

later and quite obviously suggested that he is subsequently flogged and stripped of his rank. After this disgrace, Mandeville has no other option but to join the merchant service, yet he is still unable to overcome his addiction to alcohol and his reputation as a sailor suffers further damage as he is berated and embarrassed by his captain: "Having no fortune, and no other profession than the sea, upon his disgrace he entered the merchant-service as a chief mate; but his love of strong drink still pursuing him, he was again cashiered at sea, and degraded before the mast by the captain" (242). Unfortunately for Mandeville, this will not be the last time that he suffers the consequences of his addiction.

Despite the professional degradation and physical punishment that he experiences in these past two episodes, Mandeville is still unable to free himself from his addiction to alcohol, or his "sin" as it is described (242), once he joins the *Neversink*'s crew. After being on board the man-of-war for only a week and failing to heed Lieutenant Bridewell's warning, Mandeville "was found intoxicated with smuggled spirits" (242) and would again be flogged. Mandeville disappears from this point on in the novel, yet he presumably continues to imbibe his smuggled spirits and to suffer whatever consequences await him for his ongoing drunken actions.

High-ranking officers (former and otherwise) like the English harbor pilot, Mad Jack, and Mandeville are not the only ones whose professional reputations and positions on board a ship suffer negatively as a result of intoxication and alcoholism. *Omoo*'s Dr. Long Ghost is not a member of the *Julia*'s actual whaling crew—he has "nothing but his professional duties [as surgeon] to attend to" (8)—yet he is nonetheless subjected to having his reputation and professional position destroyed by his bibulousness. Dr. Long Ghost's drunken behavior directly contributes to the loss of his reputation and of his position as surgeon on board the *Julia*.

Nineteenth-century American law dictated that whaling vessels were obligated to carry on board a physician, a doctor who typically lived in the captain's cabin. In the outset of the novel this is the case, yet accommodations are not all that Dr. Long Ghost and the *Julia*'s Captain Guy share. Alcohol is also a significant part of their relationship: "In the early part of the voyage," Typee says, "the doctor and the captain lived together as pleasantly as could be. To say nothing of many a can they drank over the cabin transom, both of them had read books, and one of them had travelled; so their stories never flagged" (8). Yet this amiable relationship that is based on fantastic tales and copious amounts of liquor does not last. Alcohol causes a rift between the two and ultimately results in the loss of Dr. Long Ghost's reputation and professional position.

During one of their evenings of heavy drinking together, Captain Guy and Dr. Long Ghost enter into a discussion on politics. As is typically the case when alcohol is mixed with conversations concerning sensitive issues like politics or religion, a disagreement arises and a dispute erupts between them. It is here that we see the violent nature that Long Ghost assumes when he is intoxicated: "But once on a time they got into a dispute about politics, and the doctor, moreover, getting into a rage, drove home an argument with his fist, and left the captain on the floor literally silenced" (8). Subsequent to assaulting the captain and knocking him out cold, Long Ghost suffers various consequences including solitary confinement and food rationing and he ultimately makes the decision to relegate himself to the more cluttered and far less comfortable quarters of the seamen's bunks:

> This was carrying it with a high hand; so he was shut up in his stateroom for ten days, and left to meditate on bread and water, and the impropriety of flying into a passion. Smarting under his disgrace, he undertook, a short time after his liberation, to leave the vessel clandestinely at one of the islands, but was brought back ignominiously, and again shut up. Being set at large for the second time, he vowed he would not live any longer with the captain, and went forward with his chests among the sailors, where he was received with open arms as a good fellow and an injured man [8].

Not long afterwards, Dr. Long Ghost resigns from his position as the *Julia*'s surgeon (10) and continues to live as a mere passenger *en route*, once again, for Sydney. Although Long Ghost on his own accord makes the decision to consign himself to the sleeping quarters of the common sailors and to relinquish his position as surgeon, he ultimately had no other choice. His alcohol addiction and the behavior he demonstrates while intoxicated left him with no other option.

Not only does Melville clearly illustrate in various works that drinking and drunkenness can have serious ramifications on one's professional rank and reputation, but in his final work *Billy Budd, Sailor* he illustrates the professional benefits of staying sober. As the narrator

6. Loss of Rank, Loss of Reputation

relates in the novella's eighth chapter, John Claggart—the master-at-arms on the *Bellipotent* by the time the narrative begins—joined the English Navy later in life. Since he entered the navy "as a novice" in the service, he was therefore "assigned to the least honorable section of a man-of-war's crew." However, "he did not long remain there" and was promoted quickly (67). One of the primary reasons for his quick ascension through the ranks to a position of power and authority, as the narrator makes clear, is his "constitutional sobriety" (67); Claggart does not drink. Unlike characters including the English harbor pilot in *Typee* and *White-Jacket*'s Mandeville, Claggart consistently refrained from drinking upon joining the navy and, as a result, he was quickly rewarded professionally for his avoidance of liquor. Drunkenness, Melville suggests, can destroy one's career whereas sobriety can lead to success and promotion.

Based on his own experiences, Melville was cognizant of how few employment opportunities existed for American men in the middle of the nineteenth century and of how difficult it is to live in near poverty. Keeping whatever work one could find, therefore, was essential. As Melville relates to his readers in *Typee*, *White-Jacket*, and *Omoo*, alcohol must be avoided while "on the job." There are harsh consequences for those who drink while on board their respective vessels—one of the few places where jobs during the nineteenth century were virtually guaranteed. From commanding officers to those who are employed to attend to the ship's ill sailors, professional rank and reputation can be negatively affected, in certain cases forever destroyed, by alcohol. Once the damage has been done, as is the case most specifically with Mandeville, rank and reputation are impossible to be restored. It is a warning that Melville provides to those who may be embarking on a voyage on board a man-of-war or a whaler: avoid alcohol or else suffer the professional ramifications of loss of reputation and the physical pains of a flogging.

Chapter 7

Alcohol, Ill Health and Penury

As the renowned historian Orville Vernon Burton discusses early in his insightful book *The Age of Lincoln*, it seemed "perfectly obvious" to temperance reformers in both the North and the South in the years leading up to the Civil War that American men had become "slaves to drink" and that their addiction to alcohol was both "ruining their health" and "wasting their fortunes" (34). It appears that Melville was well ahead of such temperance reformers in recognizing this. In many of his antebellum American works, some of which precede the Civil War by more than a decade, Melville himself calls attention to and relates to his audience the detrimental effects that alcohol will have on people's physical well-being and on their financial security. Excessive imbibing, Melville cautions his readers, will take from the drinkers the health that they can ill-afford to lose and will cost them the money that they do not have to spend. For the sake of one's health and finances, Melville illustrates in the works examined throughout this chapter that abstinence from alcohol is essential.

We currently know that chronic drinking will ultimately have varying yet nonetheless serious effects on one's health. Continual imbibing can cause alterations to skin pigmentation and therefore affect one's appearance, can contribute to cardiovascular disease, and can lead to liver cancer and cirrhosis.[1] Yet we were not always so enlightened about the dangers of frequent drinking. For much of early American history, in fact, "fermented alcoholic beverages such as beer and wine were regarded as healthful beverages, essential for life,"[2] and "alcohol was popularly believed to have medicinal qualities."[3] It "stimulated and supported the system," the proponents believed, and it "prevented fevers and infectious diseases, and furnished the stamina necessary for physical labor" (Blocker, Fahay, and Tyrrell 407). Beginning in the early decades of the nineteenth century, however, such beliefs slowly began to change.[4] Although doctors and other medical practitioners in the early years of alcohol research were not always correct or as accurate in identifying the causal relationship between alcohol and health as they are today, they nonetheless astutely made connections between alcohol consumption and physical and mental health. In 1822, for instance, Dr. James Jackson of Boston stated his belief that alcohol weakened mental function,[5] while the temperance supporter Senator Henry William Blair of New Hampshire, some sixty years later in *The Temperance Movement; or, The Conflict Between Man and Alcohol*, somewhat hyperbolically stated that drinking would ultimately result in the collapse of the body's vital organs and cause the body to decay: "Alcohol attacks the blood and consequently the integrity of every tissue and living atom of the body. It follows that its use produces disease of every organ and part of the frame" (84). Toward the end of the nineteenth century people had not only become increasingly aware that excessive and persistent drinking had no health benefits, but that it would rather and undoubtedly lead to serious health problems, something that was medically proven during the latter half of the nineteenth century: "When scientific knowledge about alcohol toxicity and its effects on the nervous system and bodily organs advanced during the second half of the nineteenth century, experts agreed that alcohol did not just overtax the nervous system; it also quite directly poisoned it."[6]

The health-related effects of excessive drinking and alcoholism, both the purportedly positive and the actually negative, were not lost on Melville. In "Benito Cereno" and to a greater degree in *Redburn* and *The Confidence-Man* Melville dismisses any notion that alcohol has any significant or worthwhile health benefits, while in *Omoo* and *Mardi* he demonstrates to his readers the harmful effects that drinking will ultimately have on one's health. Drinking for medicinal purposes will only create new or exacerbate existing conditions.

"Benito Cereno" is the novella in which Melville writes about the sealer *Bachelor's Delight* and its captain Amasa Delano. At the beginning of the story Captain Delano spots the distressed cargo ship *San*

Dominick, which is carrying Senegalese slaves among other "cargo." Delano boards the ship to see if he can be of any assistance, at which time he is introduced to Captain Don Benito Cereno. By the end of the novella Captain Cereno attempts to escape with Delano and it is only then that Delano finally realizes that the slaves have revolted during a time prior to the narrative and have taken control of the *San Dominick* and murdered most of its crew. Although Melville's primary commentary in the novella clearly surrounds the Peculiar Institution,[7] there is also a small discussion of alcohol and its supposed medicinal qualities.

When Don Benito finally begins to tell Captain Delano about the situation on board the *San Dominick*—a false story since the slave leader Babo is dangerously close—he speaks with a "husky whisper" and then becomes afflicted with a harsh cough and weakness: "Here there was a sudden fainting attack of his cough, brought on, no doubt, by his mental distress. His servant sustained him, and drawing a cordial from his pocket placed it to his lips" (248).[8] The liquor, however, does not cure Don Benito's mental state or cough. Although he was "a little revived" after taking the drink, shortly thereafter his condition worsens: "His cough returned and with increased violence; this subsiding, with reddened lips and closed eyes he fell heavily against his supporter" (249). The alcohol in this episode has done nothing to cure Benito Cereno's health. Given what he has and is truly experiencing on the *San Dominick*, however, perhaps I should play Devil's advocate and suggest that no amount of anything would be able to cure his cough or mental distress. As we see in further examples from other works, however, alcohol is never medicinally beneficial for those characters who are experiencing various health issues.

Melville appears to be heralding the medicinal qualities of alcohol in Chapter 8 of *Redburn*, yet by paying close attention to the narrator Wellingborough Redburn's words in this episode—the only words that should truly count since he is the one who is afflicted with an illness and experiencing the pain and discomfort—it is clear that this is not the case. At this early point in the novel Redburn has out of financial necessity, just like Melville himself had done in 1839 by signing on as a cabin boy on board the *St. Lawrence*, joined the crew of the merchant ship *Highlander* and is experiencing his first ocean crossing *en route* to Liverpool. As is typically the case for landlubbers who are on their maiden voyage across a turbulent body of water, he is stricken with sea sickness. In order to alleviate his illness, the Greenlander gives Redburn rum.[9] Although critics have maintained that the alcohol does indeed improve the ailing sailor's health—Carl Rollyson and Lisa Paddock state that the alcohol "proves beneficial" for Redburn's illness (173) while Robert Gale believes that the Greenlander "helps Redburn's initial seasickness by giving the youth a dose of rum"[10]—such views are not entirely true. It is simply the drink itself and not actually the alcohol that is contained in it that settles Redburn's stomach. As Redburn himself admits, having any other beverage would have been just as if not more beneficial to his health: "But to tell the truth," as Redburn tells us, "I found, in spite of its sharp taste, the spirits I drank was just the thing I needed; *but I suppose, if I could have had a cup of nice hot coffee, it would have done quite as well, and perhaps, much better*" (43, emphasis added). Contrary to what the Greenlander and critics alike maintain, therefore, the liquor has no further benefit in curing Redburn's sea sickness than would coffee or perhaps any other warm beverage, thereby rendering the alcohol in the rum as essentially a placebo and discrediting any legitimate medicinal qualities that the alcohol was thought to have.

In his next novel, *White-Jacket*, Melville continues to demonstrate that alcohol does not prevent or cure sailors' ill health. White-Jacket, like most of the sailors, knows that they will be stricken with sea sickness when they are on duty on the main-top. In order to prevent such illness many sailors go to the ship's apothecary, Pills, for a preventative cure. In a tin cup White-Jacket and other sailors would be given a partial alcoholic beverage, sherry-cobbler, to drink. After climbing to his post he would then consume the beverage and try to keep down its "unspeakable flavor" (327). As is the case in *Redburn*, the liquor-based drink does nothing to assist with the impending illness; in fact, it perhaps exacerbates it: "I do not know whether it was the wide roll of the ship, as felt in that giddy perch, that occasioned it, but I always got sea-sick after taking medicine and going aloft with it. Seldom or never did it do me any lasting good" (327). Further examples of alcohol's false curing qualities continue to be shown in *The Confidence-Man*.

It again appears that Melville is illustrating the healing qualities of alcohol in Chapter 24 of *The Confidence-Man*. Just as is the case in *Redburn* and *White-Jacket*, though, Melville is actually and unequivocally dismissing whatever positive health benefits the consumption of alcohol purportedly has. In fact, Melville goes a step further in *The Confidence-Man* and illustrates that the medicinal use of alcohol is actually detrimental to the drinker as it will result in further health problems; in this case, alcoholism. This episode in *The Confidence-Man* is therefore Melville's nineteenth-century cautionary equivalent to those who in the early twenty-first century use painkillers including Percocet and OxyContin only later to become addicted to them. In Chapter 24, the confidence man relates to another character on board the *Fidèle*, the bachelor, the story of the old lady of Goshen, a woman who shares distinct affinities with the female protagonist from Isaac Shepard's 1842 work *Confessions of a Female Inebriate*.[11] The similarities are so profound, in fact, that they suggest both a source of influence on Melville and offer more insight into the fate that awaits the lady of Goshen in *The Confidence-Man*.

Confessions of a Female Inebriate concerns a temperate woman who takes ill and is prescribed alcohol by her physician. After using alcohol medicinally, she becomes an alcoholic and her husband threatens to leave her if she is unable to give up her addiction. Shortly thereafter, the couple's daughter dies, throwing the wife into a deep depression. As time passes, her husband suggests that they host a small dinner party in order to assist them in dealing with their loss. The wife agrees but in the moments leading up to and during the party she, like the prodromal phase alcoholics from works including "Cock-A-Doodle-Doo!" and "Bartleby," drinks to deal with the various stresses that she is experiencing. This is clear in her discussion of her preparation for the dinner party that she and her husband are hosting:

> On the morning of the appointed day, one of my servants was taken severely ill; and in the afternoon I was disappointed in the attendance of another head-servant, hired for the occasion. I was at a loss what to do, as it was getting late. I was fatigued with some preparations I had been making; what did I do to remedy a temporary inconvenience? *I drank again.* Yes, I write it for a warning; and from that moment I felt like a lost spirit! I was distracted by the apprehension that Mr. L. [her husband] might suspect it, and to quiet this fearful foreboding *I drank again*. ... I finished my preparations; my guests began to arrive. I trembled so excessively from mere agitation that I could not stand. It was absolutely necessary that I should descend without delay. *I drank again*, to brace my nerves to the scene, and descended [77, emphasis added].

7. Alcohol, Ill Health and Penury

Before the party ends and no longer caring if her husband sees her drinking, she downs an entire glass of wine, causing her to pass out shortly thereafter. Staying true to his earlier threat, her husband leaves her the next day. For the next eight months she waits for him to come home, a hope that she ultimately abandons when she reads in the newspaper that he has died in London.

Like Shepard's female inebriate, the lady of Goshen is a temperate woman who becomes gravely ill. In response, her husband, the deacon, summons the doctor to assist her. The doctor prescribes alcohol, yet in order to feel its beneficial effects she must drink, as she is instructed by her physician, "as much as she can get down" (179). At first it appears that the doctor's remedy restores the hesitant woman's health: "Much against the grain, the sober deacon got the unsober medicine, and, equally, against her conscience, the poor old woman took it; but, by doing, ere long recovered health and spirits, famous appetite, and glad again to see her friends" (179). Although it seems that alcohol has alleviated the lady of Goshen's pain and has fully restored her condition, as Robert Gale maintains,[12] this is all merely an illusion. The effects of her drunkenness simply mask her pain. The alcohol is not, as nineteenth-century medicinal drinking proponents believed, a cure to her ailment. In fact, it has just made her situation worse. Once she begins drinking, we are told, she is unable to stop. The lady of Goshen, again like the female inebriate in Shepard's story who toward the end of the tale drinks to calm every small nerve, becomes an alcoholic: "[A]nd having by this experience broken the ice of arid abstinence, never afterward kept herself a cup too low" (179). As a result of her alcoholism, she will face a variety of alcohol-related health and social issues, thereby making her physical well-being ultimately worse than it had been in the first place.

Melville dismisses in "Benito Cereno," *Redburn*, *White-Jacket*, and *The Confidence-Man* the pervasive late-eighteenth and early-nineteenth-century beliefs that the excessive drinking of alcohol had certain health benefits and could cure certain ailments. In *White-Jacket*, *Omoo*, and *Mardi*, he illustrates some of the more common health problems that can be caused by imbibing to excess and in indulging too frequently. In doing so, Melville is suggesting to his readers that not only is there nothing positive about drinking alcohol, but that it is all, in fact, negative and harmful to one's health.

It was shown in the previous chapter that Mandeville from *White-

Jacket is an alcoholic who has had his rank as a sailor and his overall professional reputation affected by his alcoholism. Yet this is not all that is destroyed by his persistent drinking. Like many other characters from Melville's writings, Mandeville's physical appearance is also harshly marked by his liquor consumption; his appearance is clearly indicative of the physical effects of drinking: "[F]rom his haggard cheek and sunken eye, he seemed to have been in the sad habit, all his life, of sitting up rather late at night; and though all sailors do certainly keep late hours enough standing watches at midnight—yet there is no small difference between keeping late hours at sea and keeping late hours ashore" (241). Outward appearances, as Melville continues to relate elsewhere, are not the only physical or health-related problems that alcoholism and excessive drinking can cause.

In Chapter 72 of *Omoo* Melville illustrates with great clarity, accuracy, and even a bit of comedy the pain that will always be the result of imbibing too much alcohol: the hangover. Although it is not terminal like liver cancer or as constantly painful as the physical ailment that Melville will document in *Mardi* later in this chapter, the hangover is nevertheless an ever-present and at times a day's-long debilitating side-effect of excessive drinking. In this part of the novel, Typee, or Paul as he is sometimes referred to as, and Dr. Long Ghost are on the tenth day of their hegira, or flight from Tamai. They have just left Loohooloo and are nearing their destination of Taloo when they discover the shanty of the hermit Varvy, who appears to be deaf and mute. Although Varvy has little to offer them in the way of food, he urges Typee and Dr. Long Ghost with various types of gestures to drink with him his home-made liquor. Typee refrains from drinking, yet the alcoholic Long Ghost is ultimately unable to resist Varvy's coaxing and eventually he and his host are, to put it bluntly, sloshed:

> Fancy Varvy and the doctor, then, lovingly tippling, and brimming over with a desire to become better acquainted; the doctor politely bent upon carrying on the conversation in the language of his host, and the old hermit persisting in trying to talk English. The result was that, between the two, they made such a fricassee of vowels and consonants that it was enough to turn one's brain [258].

When Long Ghost awakes the following morning he has not only forgotten where he placed his boots, which attests to his highly-intoxicated or blacked-out state of the night before, but he is suffering in great

• *7. Alcohol, Ill Health and Penury* •

pain from his overindulgence in what is likely the most potent drink that he has ever had. As Typee describes once Long Ghost finally wakes up, "The next morning, on waking, I heard a voice from the tombs. It was the doctor solemnly pronouncing himself a dead man. He was sitting up, with both hands clasped over his forehead, and his pale face a thousand times paler than ever" (258). Dr. Long Ghost then himself explains his condition: "'That infernal stuff has murdered me!' he cried. 'Heavens! my head's all wheels and springs, like the automaton chess player! What's to be done, Paul? I'm poisoned'" (258–259). Excessive imbibing, as Dr. Long Ghost is now—and was likely already cognizant of based on his prior drinking experiences—well aware, has its physical consequences. If Melville's readers had not been prior to this episode in *Omoo*, now so are they.

Melville's discussion of Long Ghost's hangover is comical yet is nonetheless illustrative of the severe headache and other after-effects associated with drunkenness. In a more serious episode in *Mardi*, Melville provides a significant illustration of the physical pain and health problems that can be caused or exacerbated by alcohol consumption. He presents a character whose physical health and well-being is seriously affected—and will be forever so—by imbibing alcohol. During a huge feast in Chapter 95 of *Mardi*, Borabolla, the King of Mondoldo, issues a toast in which he glorifies the purity of his wine: "Brimming with a ram's horn, the mellowest of bugles, Borabolla bowed to his silent guest, and thus spoke:—'In this wine, which yet smells of the grape, I pledge you, my reverend old toper, my lord Capricornus; you alone have enough; and here the full skins to the rest!'" (291). Shortly thereafter, Borabolla is subjected to a twinge of discomfort that becomes progressively worse. The pain eventually becomes so intense for the King of Mondoldo that it causes him to collapse and drop his cup of wine. After Borabolla falls down and screams in agony, in the process revealing the cause of his pain, he vows never to drink alcohol again: "The goblet fell from his hand; the purples flew from his wine to his face; and Borabolla fell back into the arms of his servitors. 'That gout! that gout!' he groaned. 'Lord! lord! no more cursed wine will I drink!'" (292). This discomfort, however, does not last for long. As is usually the case for tipplers, neither does his vow to abstain from drinking.

In the previous episode Melville demonstrates for his readers the negative consequences of drinking. As the scene continues, he emphasizes for them Borabolla's recklessness with his health. Once Borabolla's pain subsides, he, like a typical drinker who no longer feels the negative effects caused by alcohol, rescinds his promise to give up his wine. He gives no thought whatsoever to the return of his gout, which is inevitable with further alcohol consumption,[13] but rather implores everyone to continue—and in his case resume—drinking: "'Come! let us be merry again,' he cried, 'what shall we eat? and what shall we drink? that infernal gout is gone; come, what will your worships have?'" (292). Even after experiencing the excruciating pain of gout, which is undoubtedly exacerbated by drinking (Terkeltaub 138), Borabolla refuses to quit consuming his wine, even after promising to do so. His health, clearly, will continue to deteriorate.

Melville is quite clear in *Redburn*, *The Confidence-Man*, *Omoo*, and *Mardi* about the supposed yet non-existent health benefits and of the unquestionable health risks associated with alcohol. Yet as Orville Burton notes, health was not the only aspect of men's lives that was being affected by their drinking. The second area of people's lives that was being destroyed by alcohol and intoxication, as late antebellum temperance advocates accurately noted, was their financial security. This fact was not lost on Melville either. Many of Melville's characters indebt or destroy themselves financially for the sake of drunkenness. Alcohol is the most important part of their lives, and their expenditure on liquor clearly attests to their addiction. In *White-Jacket* Melville generally refers to the "abject poverty" in which alcoholism can cause people to be placed (54); in "Cock-A-Doodle-Doo!," *Redburn*, and *Omoo* he demonstrates clearly and more specifically how this can occur.

It was shown in Chapter 2 that "Cock-A-Doodle-Doo!"'s narrator is a prodromal phase alcoholic who lives a depressing existence for a variety of reasons including debt and defaulted payments that result in him being hounded by his creditor. Very early in the story he calls attention to the financial difficulties that he is experiencing and of what he perceives as the impossibility of him being able to pay off his debts: "I can't pay this horrid man; and yet they say money was never so plentiful—a drug in the market; but blame me if I can get any of the drug, though there never was a sick man more in need of that particular sort of medicine. It's a lie; money ain't plentiful—feel my pocket" (77). Although the narrator is aware of his undoubtedly insurmountable debt and is frustrated and overwhelmed by it, he appears to be oblivious to the cause of one of the largest single contributing factors to his penury. Melville, however, does his best to ensure that readers are fully aware that the source of the narrator's poverty is his unrelenting alcoholism.

Despite recognizing and lamenting his dire financial situation, the narrator continues to spend large amounts of money on alcohol, thereby putting himself in a further financial crisis and making his overall situation worse. As opposed to saving any money that he may otherwise spend on alcohol for the purpose of paying off his creditor, the narrator simply continues to drink and waste his money. He has what seems to be a more than adequate supply of liquor at his home (80–81),[14] as Melville did at Arrowhead, yet he still goes out drinking and spends further money at his local pub (86), and even after going even further in debt he continues to spend whatever money he has on alcohol. As he says in his most notable example of this, "I saw another mortgage piled on my plantation; but only bought another dozen of stout, and a dozen dozen of Philadelphia porter" (95). Alcohol and inebriation clearly take precedence over financial security for the narrator, and as noted in Chapter 2, his alcoholism ultimately wins. That being said, there are more severe examples of people living in poverty who continue to spend money on alcohol.

"For people living in extreme poverty," it has been stated, "spending money on alcohol rather than on food and other necessities is an issue of tremendous concern."[15] Unfortunately, Melville clearly illustrates this point in *Redburn*. In Chapter 28 of the novel, the *Highlander* docks in Liverpool and Redburn and the sailors go for their supper. Once they arrive at the tavern Redburn is informed that it is too late for a cup of tea so he, despite having taken an oath of temperance (42) and thereby showing the lure that alcohol has, accepts the offer of a glass of swipes. After drinking it, Redburn describes the beverage as "a bastard kind of beer; or the washings and rinsing of old beer-barrels" (134). Redburn relates further that the poor people of Liverpool continue to spend their money on this rank, low-quality beer in order to feed their addictions, despite the fact that they are already destitute: "As for the taste of it, I can only describe it as answering to the name itself; which is certainly significant of something vile. But it is drunk in large quantities by the poor people about Liverpool, which, perhaps, in some degree, accounts for their poverty" (134–135). In this passage, Melville, through Redburn, illustrates how it is a never-ending cycle for alcoholics. They drink to forget their hardships and in doing so they spend money they do not have on alcohol, thereby creating further financial stresses and difficulties. There is always money, somehow, for alcohol, which simply leads to further penury.

Alcohol-related financial ruin does not simply affect those who, like Liverpool's destitute in *Redburn*, are already experiencing financial difficulties. Even those who were at some point affluent are not immune to losing their fortunes to the bottle. This is precisely what happens to *Omoo*'s Dr. Long Ghost. By having a wealthy character lose his riches to alcohol, Melville lucidly and emphatically demonstrates that anyone, regardless of caste, can be ruined financially by a severe drinking problem. Alcohol, Melville suggests through Long Ghost, does not discriminate.

At one time prior to the novel Dr. Long Ghost was a rich man. He had a "patrimonial estate [and] a nabob uncle" (8) that afforded him a position as a man of wealth. Yet this is no longer the case; he has fallen from his literal and figurative high estate. Typee informs readers that prior to joining the *Julia*'s crew Long Ghost had been a surgeon on board an emigrant ship bound for Australia. Subsequent to disembarking, he "went back into the country, and after a few months' wanderings, returned to Sydney penniless" (8). Although the cause of Long Ghost's fall from affluence to near penury is not explicitly mentioned in the text, Melville provides enough information to suggest clearly enough that Long Ghost is an alcoholic and that his financial ruin was caused by his love for and addiction to liquor.

There are various reasons to believe that Dr. Long Ghost is an alcoholic and that his loss of fortune can be attributed to it. First, his complexion. Like that of Mandeville, Long Ghost's appearance is indicative of an alcohol-related health condition. He is a "tower of bones," which could be a result of the malnutrition among alcoholics, "with a complexion absolutely colourless" (9), which is a further characteristic of those suffering from alcoholism as excessive drinking affects muscle and nerve tissue and can therefore affect the body's ability to look healthy.[16] Also, we know that prior to joining the *Julia* he had a history of drinking frequently with other men of wealth; he "had certainly at some time or other spent money, drunk Burgundy, and associated with gentlemen" (9). Most importantly, once he joins and subsequently leaves the *Julia* he continues to drink heavily. He gets drunk frequently with Captain Guy and his inability to control his inebriated behavior, as shown elsewhere in this study, results in his assaulting the captain and, as discussed earlier in this chapter, he continues to imbibe excessively—even after his professionally-traumatic experience—on the island with Varvy. All of these factors suggest a clear pattern of excessive inebriation and alcoholism. It is likely, therefore, that while wandering in Australia he associated with various drinkers and spent his fortune on imbibing excessively. This activity set the chain of events in motion that caused him to lose his fortune, join the *Julia*'s crew, assault Captain Guy in a drunken rage, be relegated to the sailors' quarters, relinquish his position as the ship's doctor, and be imprisoned with Typee in the Calabooza Beretanee in Papeetee, where his life was momentarily yet nonetheless ultimately at stake. His downfall, financial and otherwise, was initiated and then accelerated by alcohol.

Arguably the most significant example of how alcohol addiction could lead to financial difficulties occurs in *Redburn*. It is the most significant, I would argue, as the character's drinking in this case affects not only his own financial security, but that of others as well. In the novel's penultimate chapter Harry Bolton and Redburn seek their remuneration for their services from Captain Riga once the ship has arrived back in New York City. Yet Riga offers Bolton only a pittance and is unwilling to pay Redburn anything at all. Captain Riga, in fact, believes that Redburn actually owes him money due to his absence from the *Highlander* in Liverpool, for the money that had been advanced to him, and for tools that had been lost:

> "Hum, hum!—yes here it is: Wellingborough Redburn, at three dollars a month. Say four months, that's twelve dollars; less three dollars advanced in Liverpool—that makes it nine dollars; less three hammers and two scrapers lost overboard—that brings it to four dollars and a quarter. I owe you four dollars and a quarter, I believe, young gentlemen?" [306–307].

As Redburn listens in disbelief, Riga continues with his lesson in mathematics:

> "And now let me see what you own me, and then we'll be able to square the yards, Monsieur Redburn.... By running away from the ship in Liverpool, you forfeited your wages, which amount to twelve dollars and as there has been advanced to you, in money, hammers, and scrapers, seven dollars and seventy-five cents, you are therefore

indebted to me in precisely that sum. Now, you gentleman, I'll thank you for the money" [307].

Redburn is understandably infuriated or, to use his words, he is "thunderstruck" (307) with Captain Riga's outlandish claims. Redburn quickly realizes, however, why Riga is unwilling—unable, in fact—to pay him.

The reality behind Riga being unable to pay Redburn his earned wages, as Redburn ultimately realizes, has nothing to do with the sailor's absence from the ship or money loaned to him or for lost tools. Captain Riga simply does not have the money to pay Redburn because he himself is experiencing financial difficulties stemming from his frequent drinking. His "expensive habits," to which his excessive imbibing of alcohol is referred, has caused him to accumulate "large wine bills at the City Hotel." As a result, Riga "could not afford to be munificent" (307) with Redburn. Riga, being the alcoholic that he is, "cares little for anyone but himself" (McCarthy 36), thereby reinforcing the selfish nature of alcoholics that was discussed in this study's third chapter. His alcoholism and the large debt that it has caused essentially leave his sailors, at least on this voyage, without pay and out of luck. As is typically the case for those who surround alcoholics, Redburn is affected—in this case financially—by someone else's drinking.

Melville is quite clear in episodes from various works that alcohol not only lacks health benefits, as was long believed, but that it will ultimately exacerbate or cause serious health problems. Excessive drinking will also compromise the drinkers' finances, leaving them unable to settle debts or even provide the necessities of life for themselves or their families. Alcohol, as Melville lucidly illustrates, will only cause degraded health and poverty, harsh conditions Melville hopes that will persuade the drinkers to choose their physical well-being and financial security over alcohol and the health and financial hardships that it inevitably brings.

Chapter 8

Of Grog and Monsters: Melville's Addiction Narratives

It was shown in the first chapter of this study on Melville's temperance fiction that the narrator's wife in "The Apple-Tree Table," much like many wives in the mid-nineteenth century who supported the temperance movement, wants her narrator-husband to abstain from imbibing his alcoholic punch. She believes that his drinking "gets the better" of him and that it causes him to have various forms of hallucinations (368). In her mind and in using the supposed spirits that he believes to be trapped in the table as evidence against him, his punch drinking changes him into an over-exaggerating and drunken annoyance. While the wife may be justified in detesting her husband's drinking from a social or personal standpoint and in preaching temperance to him—who, after all, would enjoy being awoken from a refreshing sleep late every Saturday night or early each Sunday morning for such frivolous concerns as the narrator's—his resulting behavior is, in reality and in relation to some of Melville's other drinkers, nothing more than an aggravating and frustrating inconvenience for her. He does not become violent toward her, which is in contrast to the behavior of many other husbands in works of nineteenth-century American temperance fiction,[1] or have his true demeanor change significantly or barbarically as a result of his Saturday night ritual. He is, one could say, simply an irritating drunk.

Although "The Apple-Tree Table"'s narrator undergoes only minor changes in character and behavior once he becomes intoxicated, there are many other drinkers in Melville's works who experience significant alterations due to their inebriation. Alcohol can have a profound transformative effect on people, a fact that even some of Melville's characters recognize. In Chapter 84 of *Mardi*, for instance, King Donjalolo, also referred to as Fonoo based on his feminine appearance,[2] poetically describes during a glorious feast that is attended by the narrator Taji and twenty-five other kings how alcohol, in this case wine, can affect and transform one's judgment and behavior: "Who with wine in him fears? who thinks of his cares? / Who sighs to be wise, when wine in him flares?" (258).[3] A further and without question more graphic example of how alcohol can alter one's actions comes in Chapter 3 of *Moby-Dick*. "Better sleep with a sober cannibal," the narrator Ishmael says once he finally meets his bed-mate and soon-to-be fellow whaler Queequeg at the Spouter Inn, "than a drunken Christian" (36). Apart from the novel's opening line—"Call me Ishmael" (18)—this sentence is one of the most recognized from the entire novel. Yet what, exactly, does it mean as it pertains to alcohol? A sober cannibal like Queequeg could eat you, so what could alcohol cause a good, God-fearing Christian to do? One could imagine little else as horrific than being the victim of cannibalism, yet there are apparently worse fates than being eaten, possibly alive, by another human being: alcohol could cause this undisclosed yet incomprehensibly evil act to be committed by otherwise righteous people. In this statement, therefore, Melville is pointing to the fact that alcohol is something that will exert total control over the drinkers and their actions, destroying any notion that their sober selves may have of right and wrong, good and evil. Taking direction from King Donjalolo's speech and Ishmael's contemplation on alcohol, the focus in this chapter is on Melville's works where the characters are transformed by their addiction to alcohol and resulting intoxication. The writings under consideration in this chapter are Melville's addiction narratives.

Examples of addiction narratives can be found in, among other collections, Rebecca Shannonhouse's 2003 anthology *Under the Influence: The Literature of Addiction*, which contains excerpts from Thomas De Quincey's famous *Confessions of an English Opium Eater* (1821), Virgil Easton's "How the Opium Habit Is Acquired" (1888), and Leo Tolstoy's "The Ethics of Wine-Drinking and Tobacco Smoking" (1891).[4] The works contained therein not only illustrate just how pervasive a topic addiction in literature is, but document how powerful the dependency on intoxicants is for the characters who are affected by it. That being said, the works that Shannonhouse includes in *Under the Influence* illustrate only one kind of addiction narrative: the documentary-type story that simply traces the overwhelming control that drugs or alcohol have on the characters and their lives. Notably absent from her compilation are works that demonstrate the drastic and violent changes that addicts can experience while under the influence of alcohol or other intoxicants.

As opposed to works that merely chronicle individuals' addiction and the difficulties that they experience in overcoming it, as is the case in the aforementioned works from Shannonhouse's anthology, this chapter is interested in the more Gothic-related strain of addiction narratives, the more horrifying alterations that various intoxicants can cause. As Carol Margaret Davison succinctly outlines in her introductory essay to a special issue of the journal *Gothic Studies* that is devoted exclusively to drug and alcohol dependency in Gothic literature, the Gothic and addiction go "virtually hand-in-glove."[5] As a result, it should come as no surprise that many works of Gothic fiction, as the essays in Davison's issue of *Gothic Studies* clearly illustrate, are also graphic examples of addiction narratives.

In Gothic addiction narratives, or Gothic pharmographies as Davison coins them in a separate yet equally enlightening essay of hers,[6] people who are typically caring and well-meaning individuals when they are sober can experience a terrifying and horrific transformation when they are lured to overindulge. When characters from works including E. T. A. Hoffman's *The Devil's Elixirs* (1815), Edgar Allan Poe's "The Black Cat" (1843), Robert Louis Stevenson's *The Strange Case of Dr. Jekyll and Mr. Hyde* (1886), and Bram Stoker's *Dracula* (1897) are under the influence of alcohol or other narcotics,[7] whether literal or figurative, the ruthless *other* or *Doppelgänger*, the "twin, shadow double, demon double, and split personality"[8] that is a "frequently noted feature of Gothic fiction,"[9] surfaces and leads the somewhat possessed individual into conducting or participating in various forms of heinous and illicit activities.[10] This is precisely what we see in Melville's addiction narratives.

With the possible exceptions of *Pierre* and "Bartleby, the Scrivener," both of which contain Gothic elements and have been examined as Gothic productions, by no means would I suggest that Melville's works that will be discussed in this chapter are examples of Gothic literature.[11] They do, however, share more distinct affinities with the type of addiction-related transformations that we see in the Gothic pharmographies of Hoffman, Poe, and Stevenson, among others, than they do with the generic autobiographical-type works that we find in Shannonhouse's anthology. As is the case with the addicts in the aforementioned Gothic works, some of Melville's characters are also typically rational and well-meaning individuals when they are sober. Once they are under the influence, however, their *Doppelgänger* surfaces, marking the drinkers' transformation into entirely different people. The resulting *others*, like the altered inebriated husbands from the nineteenth century who became abusive toward their wives when intoxicated (Mattingly, Introduction 10; Renker 125), are heartless, crude, violent, and at times even murderous individuals who demonstrate no similarities whatsoever to their sober counterparts.[12] The *others* are the result of excessive imbibing and, in this regard, Melville's addiction narratives serve as yet another type of warning that he uses to convince his readers to abstain from drinking. Avoid alcohol, Melville is urgently suggesting to his audience, and in turn avoid the monster.

A brief episode of how alcohol can turn people into callous individuals occurs in Book 6, Part 3, of *Pierre*. At the beginning of this scene Isabel is relating to Pierre what blank or vague memories of her childhood she can remember. She "never knew a mortal mother" and "cannot recall one single feature of such a face" (114), yet she is able to recollect being raised by two elderly foster parents. Although the old couple showed her "no affection" and avoided physical contact with her, as Wendy Flory remarks,[13] Isabel herself—the one who is subjected to their treatment—admits that they were "not entirely unkind" to her (115). In one incident that Isabel shares, however, alcohol causes a change in the elderly couple's behavior that results in her being nearly abused and starved for the night. In this moment, a hungry Isabel approaches the old couple's table for bread. They are both seemingly intoxicated on "a bottle of some thin sort of reddish wine," however, and, due to their drunkenness, they deny Isabel her meal when she attempts to eat with them at their table: "But instantly," as Isabel relates to Pierre, "the old man made a motion as if to strike me, but did not, and the woman, glaring at me, snatched the loaf and threw it into the fire before them" (116). While on the surface such an action may not be as monstrous as the murderous episodes in *Jekyll and Hyde* or "The Black Cat," consider what this elderly couple has done while in their drunken stupor: they have deprived a young child of her meal.

A further example of a character who is turned into a harsh and menacing monster as result of his drinking occurs in Melville's 1876 epic poem *Clarel*. Throughout its 18, 000 lines—longer than Virgil's *Aeneid*, Chaucer's *Canterbury Tales*, and Milton's *Paradise Lost*—that are divided into four parts and one-hundred and fifty cantos, *Clarel* tells the story of the young titular theology student whose faith has started to waver, so he travels to Jerusalem in an attempt to restore it. Yet hidden deeply within the 18, 000 lines of religious contemplation of *Clarel* is also commentary on the transformative effects of alcohol.

Clarel's third part, Mar Saba, and eleventh canto, "The Beaker," involves a festive gathering with free-flowing and copious amounts of wine. The Lesbian, a cheerful supply merchant, is serving wine to the Anglican priest Derwent and the others at the gathering and he complements the wine-drinking and sociality with singing. The celebratory atmosphere of the party, though, is quickly changed when the Arnaut, a massive Albanian warrior who is described as the biblical giant Og, wishes to be served more wine and at a faster pace. He is not impressed with the singing and other harmonious events during the feast because they delay how frequently his wine glass is filled. He then offers, demands in fact in what Walter Bezanson describes as the Arnaut's intimidating and "deep bass voice,"[14] to pour the wine himself. Shortly thereafter, the Arnaut becomes an intoxicated, barbarous host:

> When all were served with wine and rhyme
> "Ho, comrade," cried armed Og sublime,
> "Your singing makes the filling scant;
> The flask to me, let *me* decant."
> With that, the host he played—brimmed up
> And off-hand pushed the frequent cup;
> Flung out his thigh, and quaffed apace,
> Barbaric in his hardy grace [III xi 191–199].

Barbarism, as we shall see, is exacerbated by liquor for many of Melville's other characters as well.

Many of Melville's characters become excessively violent once they are intoxicated, which is in contrast to their genial sober demeanor. Consider, for instance, the narrator of "Cock-A-Doodle-Doo!" As noted in earlier parts of this study, the narrator of this short story is an alcoholic who refuses to refrain from drinking even though it is ruining his financial security. As is the case with all prodromal phase alcoholics, however, his drinking does not calm his nerves and allow him to evade his various difficulties including his dire financial situation. Rather, his drinking turns him into an aggressive bully. After offering to show the dun his collection of Barclay and Perkins, the intoxicated narrator physically removes the bill collector from his home: "Without more ado, I seized that insolent dun by the slack of his coat—(and being a lean shad-bellied wretch, there was plenty of slack to it)—I seized him that way, tied him with a sailor-knot, and, thrusting his bill between his teeth, introduced him to the open country lying round about my place of abode" (81). Subsequent to throwing the dun out of his house, the narrator in a further fit of rage orders his servant boy Jake to assault the bill collector, who the narrator falsely says is a beggar, in even more juvenile ways: "'Jake,' said I, 'you'll find a sack of blue-nosed potatoes lying under the shed. Drag it here, and pelt this pauper away: he's been begging pence of me, and I know he can work, but he's lazy. Pelt him away, Jake!'" (81). If one peruses the story closely, they will notice that the only time the narrator exhibits such violent behavior is when he is drunk,[15] thereby illustrating the changes that alcohol can cause in one's actions and demeanor.

Like "Cock-A-Doodle-Doo!"'s narrator and as was again discussed earlier in this study, the aging law copyist Turkey from "Bartleby, the Scrivener" is an alcoholic. Also like "Cock-A-Doodle-Doo!"'s narrator, he also demonstrates the negative and violent alterations that drunkenness causes. Despite his advanced age, his demeanor and behavior change for the worse once he becomes intoxicated. Alcohol transforms him from a reserved and calm scrivener into a rude and violent one. When Turkey is sober, which is only the case prior to his lunch breaks, he is the "civilest, nay, the blandest and most reverential of men" (42). Yet in the afternoons and once inebriated, Turkey's impertinent *other* appears. When he is drunk he becomes "slightly rash with his tongue—in fact, insolent" (42) toward his boss. He also has a propensity toward violence as he threatens to assault Bartleby and "black his eyes" for his passive aggressiveness (51). Turkey's post-drinking behavior is certainly not that of a civil man; it is the alcohol that turns Turkey from a calm and passive person into an impudent and violent individual.

• 8. Of Grog and Monsters •

Yet another example of a character who is transformed into an aggressive person by his intoxication occurs in *Omoo*. The *Julia*'s surgeon Dr. Long Ghost in *Omoo* is a respectful and hard-working individual when he is sober. As a result, he is well-liked and enjoys amiable relationships with Captain Guy and the *Julia*'s crew. During the time that he shared living quarters with Captain Guy they "lived together as pleasantly as could be" (8) and for the sailors he is, to use Typee's words, "as entertaining a companion as one could wish" (9). As soon as he becomes intoxicated, however, this all changes. Once he is under the influence of alcohol he becomes to a greater degree than Turkey a violent brute who is unable to control his *Doppelgänger*.

When he is drinking with Captain Guy one evening and as discussed in an earlier chapter, Dr. Long Ghost becomes infuriated during a discussion concerning politics. Instead of controlling his anger, Long Ghost's *other* presents itself and beats the captain senseless and ultimately unconscious: "But once on a time they got into a dispute about politics, and the doctor, moreover, getting into a rage, drove home an argument with his fist, and left the captain on the floor literally silenced" (8). Despite being an agreeable person when he is sober, Dr. Long Ghost becomes an enraged and unruly drunk once he is under the influence of liquor. His *other* takes over and causes Long Ghost to suffer the consequences of his *Doppelgänger*'s actions. In this case, the *other*'s violence results in Long Ghost's incarceration and subsequent relinquishment of his position as surgeon on board the *Julia*.[16]

The transformative effects of alcohol continue to be on display in the poem "Bridegroom Dick." In this part of the poem the titular speaker and retired sailor continues to relate his various experiences at sea to his wife Bonny Blue. In this tale, Dick tells Blue about Captain Turret. As Dick says to her, Turret was a kind and forgiving leader when he was sober and whose humanity is on display in one specific episode when Turret would have been justified in flogging one of his sailors, the Finn, according to the Articles of War[17]:

> Now the culprit he liked, as a tall captain can
> A Titan subordinate and true *sailor-man*;
> And frequent he'd shown it—no worded advance,
> But flattering the Finn with a well-timed glance.
> But what of that now? In the martinet-mien
> Read the *Articles of War*, heed the naval routine;

107

> While, cut to the heart of a dishonor there to win,
> Restored to his senses, stood the Anak Finn;
> In racked self-control the squeezed tears peeping,
> Scalding the eye with repressed inkeeping.
> Discipline must be; the scourge is deemed due [301–311].

In the end and disregarding the law, however, Turret displays his kindness by refusing to have the Finn flogged. As Turret instructs his officers,

> "Untie him:—So!
> Submission is enough.—Man, you may go."
> Then, promenading aft, brushing fat Purser Smart,
> "Flog? Never meant it—hadn't any heart.
> Degrade that tall fellow?" [325–329].

This clearly illustrates the kindness and sympathy that Captain Turret possess while he is sober.

Although Turret is a leader with good judgment, a genial demeanor, and a sympathetic spirit while he is not under the influence of liquor, he is transformed by his excessive imbibing into a harsh superior officer. He, more specifically his *Doppelgänger*, is a man who demonstrates no affinities whatsoever to the individual who showed mercy toward the Finn in the earlier near-flogging episode. As Dick relates to his wife and as just illustrated, Turret was the "Manliest of men in his own natural senses," but was

> driven stark mad by the devil's drugged stuff,
> Storming all aboard from his run-ashore late,
> Challenging to battle, vouchsafing no pretenses
> A reeling King Ogg, delirious in power,
> The quarter-deck carronades he seemed to make cower [257–263].

The transformative effects that liquor has on Turret are undeniable. When sober, he is a respected and forgiving individual. Once intoxicated, he becomes a violent, power-hungry, antagonizing captain who will maintain order in any way he wants and challenge to battle any ship he desires, regardless of what consequences it may have for him or his crew.

Dr. Long Ghost and Captain Turret are not the only sea-faring individuals who are transformed grotesquely due to an addiction to alcohol and who have their *other* surface and control their actions. As noted earlier in this study, the first mate of the *Julia* in *Omoo*, John Jermin, is an alcoholic. When he is sober, which is a rarity as Jermin is at

• 8. Of Grog and Monsters •

all times "more or less under the influence" of alcohol (7), Jermin is precisely like Dr. Long Ghost and Captain Turret when they are off the bottle: he is a caring and affable man with "a heart as big as a bullock's" (7). When he becomes intoxicated, however, he experiences a metamorphosis, again like Long Ghost and Turret, that turns him into a drunken brute whose alcohol-induced rages "are uncontrollable," as Paul McCarthy rightfully observes (24); he becomes an authoritarian renegade with no regard for his crew: "[A] more obstreperous fellow than Jermin in his cups," Typee says, "you seldom came across" (7). He "was always for having a fight" (7) while under the influence and his attempts to uphold order on board the *Julia* are marked by intimidation and violence. To use Typee's words, "the bluff, drunken energies of Jermin were just the thing to hold them in some sort of noisy subjection. Upon an emergency, he flew in among them, showering his kicks and cuffs right and left, and 'creating a great sensation' in every direction" (11). Dr. Long Ghost, Captain Turret, and John Jermin should be avoided by their respective crews when they are under the influence of alcohol. There are, however, more horrifying examples of just how transformative Melville believes alcohol to be and far more disastrous consequences for those who encounter people whose drinking causes them to be thrust into an uncontrollable rage.

Melville illustrates another profoundly negative change due to alcohol in Chapter 32 of *Omoo*, yet this time the effects of drunkenness are murderous. In this chapter, Typee relates the violent history between the French colonizers and the native islanders in Tahiti.[18] As it stands in the novel, the hatred between the natives and the French remains and their animosity has resulted in hostilities and bloodshed. Although such is to be expected in battles or war—the soldiers are doing what they have been trained and commanded to do and the islanders are merely defending what has been theirs for centuries—the French take it to a further extreme. In doing so, they become similar to the monstrous murderers that we see in many Gothic addiction narratives, or Gothic pharmographies. As a result of their drinking, the French become vicious killing machines, an enraged and uncontrollable army of *Doppelgänger*s whose actions would be classified today as near war crimes. In discussing a specific battle between the French and the native islanders at Mahanar on the peninsula of Taraiboo, Typee describes just how savage the supposedly civilized French become once they are drunk: "In this affair, the islanders fought desperately, killing about fifty of the enemy, and losing ninety of their own number. The French sailors and marines, who, at the time, were reported to be infuriated with liquor, gave no quarter; and the survivors only saved themselves by fleeing into the mountains" (115). While blood would have been shed regardless in this battle, it could have been significantly worse. Due to their intoxication, the French would have massacred them all—an attempted near genocide—had it not been for the islanders' retreat. This slaughter was caused and then seriously intensified strictly by the French soldiers' excessive inebriation.

Excessive drinking, according to Melville, can result in callous, dark, horrific, and Gothic transformations for otherwise rational individuals. Drinkers are turned into a variety of violent, heartless, irate, and even murderous monsters. The rational individual is momentarily killed by the *other* or *Doppelgänger* that surfaces during the moments of intoxication. Melville is detailed and graphic in these episodes in order to ensure that his audience fully recognizes the evil they can become when drinking. Basically, Melville wishes to prevent drinking among his readers by scaring the alcohol out of their hands. If this technique fails, then Melville has one last warning to his readers about what awaits them if they do not give up the bottle and their addiction to the contents therein. The final warning that he presents and as will be shown in the final chapter is one of no return; he discusses the fate that awaits those drinkers who continue to imbibe: a horrific and early death or unimaginable personal destruction.

CHAPTER 9

Melville's Dark Temperance

Over the last eight chapters it has been shown how prevalent alcohol consumption was in the United States up to and including the mid-nineteenth century and, more specifically, how in a variety of ways Herman Melville urges his readers to disassociate themselves from drinking, drinkers, and alcohol. He uses various techniques in his writings in order to convince his audience to avoid alcohol and thereby the perils of associating with it in any way: he preaches temperance to his readers, shows how they can become reliant on alcohol for their mere day-to-day functioning, chronicles how they can be taken advantage of with or betrayed strictly for the sake of liquor, gives warnings about the dangerous situations in which excessive drinking can cause them to be placed, demonstrates how their careers, professional reputations, financial security, and health can be seriously affected if not destroyed by drinking, and demonstrates to them how alcohol and intoxication can utterly control and alter their behavior and character. There is nothing good, Melville consistently illustrates in his novels, short fiction, and poetry examined up to this point, about alcohol or its consumption. He is, however, not finished outlining for his readers just how dangerous and life-altering alcohol and addiction to it can be. Despite being fairly blunt and direct about the consequences of chronic and excessive drinking in the episodes from the works considered thus far, his harshest, most graphic, and ultimate commentary about the horrific end that awaits those who are unable to refrain from excessively imbibing alcohol have yet to be examined. We have yet to see Melville's works of dark temperance.

• ALCOHOL IN THE WRITINGS OF HERMAN MELVILLE •

The alcoholic sailors on board the *Neversink* in *White-Jacket* admit that they will continue to drink excessively no matter what harsh or even deadly consequences they may face. As White-Jacket relates, "Tell him that the delirium tremens and the mani-a-potu lie in ambush for drunkards, he will say to you, 'Let them bear down upon me, then before the wind; anything that smacks of life is better than to feel Davy Jones's chest-lid on your nose'"(176).[1] Such statements are clearly the case of the proverbial *be careful what you wish for*. It is a challenge that the sailors offer alcohol—*give us your worst*, essentially—and it is a challenge that Melville accepts on liquor's behalf. In the episodes from *Redburn* and *Moby-Dick* that are considered in this final chapter, Melville illustrates to his readers what the drinkers' inevitable fate will be.

As outlined in Chapter 1, temperance literature shows the benefits of abstaining from liquor by featuring "straightforward, didactic expositions or exempla against drinking, with emphasis on the benign rewards of the virtue rather than the brutal results of the vice" (Reynolds, "Black" 22); it illustrates the positives that arise from staying sober. Works of dark temperance do the opposite. As opposed to focusing on the benefits of abstaining from alcohol like traditional temperance literature does, dark temperance works focus on and graphically illustrate the negative consequences that await the drinkers if they continue to imbibe. They outline how characters are, in a variety of ways, "suck[ed] to [their] doom by [their] affection for liquor" (Reynolds, *Beneath* 71).[2] Although Melville provides hope to his readers for overcoming alcohol addiction in his temperance fiction, his dark temperance shows that eventually all hope for sobriety and recovery for drinkers will be lost. Quit drinking, Melville urges his readers in the episodes from these final works, or you will share the same fate that these characters experience: a horrifying early death or, perhaps, something even worse.

The beginning of *Redburn's* tenth chapter contains Melville's most traditional example of dark temperance.[3] In this episode, Redburn and some of the other sailors are standing on deck during their Atlantic crossing and are suddenly frightened by a mysterious noise that they hear coming from below. They then witness a sailor running up on deck and screaming in unimaginable terror. This causes Redburn to believe that someone down below has been or is in the process of being murdered. As he relates, "While the scene last described was going on, we were all startled by a horrid groaning noise down in the forecastle; and all at once some one came rushing up the scuttle in his shirt, clutching something in his hand, and trembling and shrieking in the most frightful manner, so that I thought one of the sailors must be murdered below" (50). While trying to ascertain precisely what he and the other sailors have heard and seen, Redburn recounts the rest of the episode: "But it all passed in a moment; and while we stood aghast at the sight, and almost before we knew what it was, the shrieking man jumped over the bows into the sea, and we saw him no more" (50).[4] Despite launching a rescue boat in an attempt to find him, the sailor drowns. Redburn tells us that the man's death is a direct result of his drunkenness. His inebriated state caused him to develop delirium tremens, which are "an almost obligatory feature of dark-temperance novels" (Reynolds, "Black" 28),[5] and to jump overboard and put an end to his life. Again, this illustrates just how powerful and demonic alcohol's controlling influence can be:

> It seemed that he was one of the sailors who had been brought aboard dead drunk, and tumbled into his bunk by his landlord; and there he had lain till now. He must have suddenly waked up, I suppose, raging mad with the delirium tremens, as the chief mate called it, and finding himself in a strange silent place, and knowing not how he had got there, he had rushed on deck, and so, in a fit of frenzy, put an end to himself [50].

Put an end to himself, or did the alcohol do it for him? I, in agreement with Paul McCarthy, suggest the latter. For this sailor, "a physical state of intoxication [has created] a mental state which leads in this instance to self-destruction" (McCarthy 38). The physical state of intoxication has for this seaman, and by extension for all of those men who would continue to drink, caused an avoidably-early death.[6]

A brief yet profoundly powerful illustration of the early and horrific death that awaits excessive drinkers occurs in Chapter 36 of *Redburn*. In this episode, Redburn is visiting what the town's people call the Church of St. Nicholas, which he believes to be "the best piece of antiquity in all of Liverpool" (177). As he observes in the graveyard adjoining the church, there are frequent examples of both drunkenness and of the ultimate price that those who are unable to overcome their addiction to alcohol must pay:

> At noon, when the lumpers employed in loading and unloading the shipping, retire for an hour to snatch a dinner, many of them resort to

the grave-yard; and seating themselves upon a tomb-stone use the adjoining one for a table. Often I saw men stretched out in a drunken sleep upon these slabs; and once, removing a fellow's arm, read the following inscription, which, in a manner, was true to the life, if not to the death:—

HERE LYETH YE BODY OF
TOBIAS DRINKER. (178)

Drinker, as his name clearly suggests, has been doomed by alcoholism, as will be the drunkard who is passed-out on his grave stone. As he sleeps off his drunkenness on the tomb, it is as if we wait for the hand of the deceased, representing alcoholism, to reach out and breach the surface of the grave *à la* conclusion to Brian De Palma's 1976 film version of Stephen King's novel *Carrie* (1974), and pull the passed-out alcoholic into the grave as well. Although readers will not witness it, the hand will metaphorically surface eventually and drag the drunkard into the grave that, Melville is saying, will be the final yet earlier-occurring resting place that inevitably awaits us all.

Melville's most graphic example of a death caused by intoxication, delving into the supernatural, also occurs in *Redburn*. In the novel Melville links an American Gothic convention with excessive drinking: spontaneous combustion. Like the paternal Wieland from Charles Brockden Brown's Ur-American Gothic novel *Wieland; or, The Transformation* (1798), who was "reduced to ashes" after "a very bright spark was seen to light up his clothes,"[7] and also the alcoholic Krook from Charles Dickens's 1853 Victorian novel *Bleak House*, Miguel Saveda in *Redburn* is literally, albeit supernaturally, transformed into a monster and dies.[8] Just as Dickens uses spontaneous combustion as a way of demonstrating the "evils of addiction" in *Bleak House* (Snodgrass 81–82), Melville shows in *Redburn* the horrors of alcoholism by killing Saveda in such a horrific and excruciatingly painful manner.

In Chapter 48 of *Redburn* the *Highlander* is ready for its "departure from the English strand" when Saveda and two other sailors board the *Highlander* heavily intoxicated (243). For two of them, the effects of their drunkenness wane after a number of hours: "Of the three newly shipped men, who in a state of intoxication had been brought on board the dock gates, two were able to be engaged at their duties, in four or five hours after quitting the pier" (243). For Saveda, however, there is no recovering. A few hours after he and his drinking companions arrive on the *Highlander* and after he is placed out of sight in his bunk because of his intoxication, the crew notices an "intolerable smell" (244) coming from the sailors' quarters. Given the rodent problem on board the ship the odor is first "attributed to the presence of some dead rat among the hollow spaces in the side planks." Upon further examination, the sailors finally realize that the smell is coming from Saveda, who the sailors believe to be dead:

> "Blast that rat!" cried the Greenlander. "He's blasted already," said Jackson, who in his drawers had crossed over to the bunk of Miguel. "It's a water-rat, shipmates, that's dead; and here he is"—and with that, he dragged for the sailor's arm, exclaiming, "Dead as timber-head!" Upon this the men rushed toward the bunk, Max with the light, which he held to the man's face [244].

After examining the body, which reveals that Saveda is in fact still alive, something occurs that frightens the crew beyond belief. Saveda is transformed into a drunk, flaming monster:

> But hardly had the words escaped, when, to the silent horror of all, two threads of greenish fire, like a forked tongue, darted out between the lips; and in a moment, the cadaverous face was crawled over by a swarm of worm-like flames. The lamp dropped from the hand of Max, and went out; while covered all over with spires and sparkles of flame, that faintly crackled in the silence, the uncovered parts of the body burned before us, precisely like a phosphorescent shark in a midnight sea. The eyes were open and fixed; the mouth was curled like a scroll, and every lean feature firm as in life; while the whole face, now wound curls of soft blue flame, wore an aspect of grim defiance, and eternal death. Prometheus, blasted by fire on the rock [244].

Saveda is quickly thrown overboard by the sailors in order to rid the *Highlander* of the horror.

The sight that the sailors have witnessed and their resulting action of throwing Saveda overboard has a lasting effect on them: "After the event no one sailor but Jackson would stay alone on the forecastle, by night or by noon; and no more would they laugh or sing, or in any way make merry there, but kept all their pleasantries for the watches on deck" (245–246). The experience has an even more profound effect on the titular character Wellingborough Redburn. As he says about the flaming Saveda, "He froze my blood, and made my soul stand still" (246).

Only a horrifying monster could have this hold on Redburn, and only alcohol, Melville suggests, could cause such a monstrous death.

As is the case in *Redburn*, *Moby-Dick* contains instances where alcohol ultimately leads to an early and grisly death. In Chapter 36, "The Quarter-Deck," Captain Ahab is finally admitting to his crew what his true intention for the whaling mission is. Instead of simply hunting whales for economic reasons, which is the chief-mate Starbuck's sole interest for any whaling voyage, Ahab is using the *Pequod* and its crew to help him exact revenge on the whale that had in an episode prior to the narrative bitten off his leg: Moby Dick. Without question realizing that persuasion would be required in order for his crew to assist him in his quest and for him to avoid a revolt—which could have happened had the sole objector to Ahab's plan Starbuck had any say[9]—Ahab becomes a type of confidence man. He gets the sailors on board with his mission by both supplying them with alcohol while at the same time giving his dark yet nonetheless rousing speech that is intended to inspire the crew and prompt them to focus their attention on satisfying his vengeance by finding and killing Moby Dick:

> "Drink and pass!" he cried, handing the heavy charged flagon to the nearest seaman. "The Crew alone now drink. Round with it, round! Short draughts—long swallows, men; 'tis hot as Satan's hoof. So, so; it goes round excellently. It spiralizes in ye; forks out at the serpent-snapping eye. Well done; almost drained. That way it went, this way it comes. Hand it me—here's a hollow! Men, ye seem the years; so brimming life is gulped and gone. Steward, refill!" [141].

After the sailors have agreed to Ahab's plot somewhat under the influence of the rum, the captain reaffirms the *Pequod*'s mission: "Death to Moby Dick! God hunt us all, if we do not hunt Moby Dick to his death!" (142). In order to gain the crew's confidence further, Ahab offers them more alcohol and then he retires to his cabin. In the end and stemming from the rum that was used to coerce the sailors to agree with the pact, all save Ishmael are in one way or another—eaten or drowned—killed by the White Whale at the novel's end. Had it not been for the alcohol that they consumed during Ahab's speech, it could have been possible that Starbuck would have attempted to and succeeded in persuading the crew otherwise; minus the alcohol, the sailors could have possibly been saved. In the end, however, God did hunt them all except for the wanderer Ishmael, who was merely another orphan found by the devious-cruising *Rachel*.

A drinker who experiences a fate worse than death, if such a thing is possible, in *Moby-Dick* due to his alcoholism is Perth. He is the "begrimed, blistered old blacksmith" from the novel (368) who forges Captain Ahab's special harpoon that is intended to kill Moby Dick and that Ahab satanically baptizes with the blood of the whalers Tashtego, Queequeg, and Dagoo: "*Ego non baptizo te in nomine patris, sed in nomine diaboli!*" (372).[10] Like "Cock-A-Doodle-Doo!"'s Merrymusk and "The Apple-Tree Table"'s narrator, Perth is a recovered alcoholic. Unlike them, however, his adoption of sobriety occurs only after his life is irreversibly destroyed by his drinking. He will be forever forced to endure the hell that he and his alcoholism have created.

Prior to joining the *Pequod*'s crew, Perth lived what was essentially the American Dream. He had been "an artisan of famed excellence, and with plenty to do; owned a house and garden; embraced a youthful daughter-like, loving wife, and three blithe, ruddy children; every Sunday went to a cheerful-looking church, planted in a grove" (368–369). When Perth nears the age of sixty, however, his life is forever changed, destroyed in fact, by a cunning intruder. As Ishmael relates, "But one night, under the cover of darkness, and further concealed in a most cunning disguisement, a desperate burglar slid into his happy home, and robbed them of everything" (369). The thief that enters Perth's home is not a person who is literally intent on stealing the blacksmith's material possessions. Rather, the so-called intruder is alcohol.

Melville is not sympathetic with Perth, and by extension is not so with other continual drinkers who face similar issues of addiction. He places the blame, and rightfully so, on the old blacksmith himself for the damage that his alcoholism causes: "And darker yet to tell, the blacksmith himself did ignorantly conduct this burglar into his family's heart. It was the Bottle Conjuror! Upon the opening of that fatal cork, forth flew the fiend, and shrivelled up his home" (369).[11] After Perth starts drinking and his addiction becomes more severe, the amount of work that he conducts in his basement shop becomes less and less because his time is spent drinking more and more. As Ishmael relates, "The blows of the basement hammer every day grew more and more between; and each blow every day grew fainter than the last'" (369).

With no money coming into the household due to his lack of work, his wife and children are left to starve and later die, and Perth becomes homeless after his house was sold. For so long and like the old lady of Goshen from *The Confidence-Man*, Perth had avoided liquor for most of his life. Yet even at his advanced age, Melville clearly points out, alcohol still has the power to affect one's existence and to inflict harm and devastation.

The grief of what Perth has caused through his alcoholism is more than he can bear and he begins to hear voices, perhaps either alcohol-induced or those withdrawal hallucinations that are common among both heavy and habitual drinkers who have given up alcohol,[12] that prompt him to go to sea:

> "Come hither, broken-hearted; here is another life without the guilt of intermediate death; here are wonders supernatural without dying for them. Come hither! bury thyself in a life which, to your now equally abhorred and abhorring, landed world, is more oblivious than death. Come hither! put up *thy* grave-stone, too, within the churchyard, and come hither, till we marry thee!" [369].

As opposed to committing suicide, which is not explicitly suggested in the narrative but an action that Captain Ahab vaguely alludes to in surprisingly-sympathetic recognition of Perth's past trauma,[13] Perth heeds the advice of the voices and attempts to escape the devastation that his alcoholism has caused him by joining the *Pequod*'s crew and thereby surrounding himself by work. Such attempts to escape, as Paul McCarthy accurately states, are inevitably futile: "Such memories cannot be forgotten" (60), and he will be forever haunted by the damages that he and his alcoholism have caused. Perth's alcoholism may have been temporary, but the effects of the destruction that it has caused will live forever—and it will live forever for Melville's readers who continue to imbibe relentlessly.

Melville's dark temperance illustrates the ruinous effects that alcohol will ultimately have on those who fail to abstain from drinking heavily. It is the ultimate and horrific end that will face the drinkers should they continue to imbibe to such excessive extents. In the end, alcohol will take away everything that has ever meant anything to the drinker, whether that be their own lives or those of whom they love. For Melville, alcohol truly was something that would ultimately destroy

• 9. *Melville's Dark Temperance* •

the lives of those—and of those around them—who were unable to eventually resist and refrain from imbibing. He has in the works from this chapter provided his final warning, offered his last call of advice, urging his audience to abstain from drinking and, in doing so, the horrors associated with it.

Conclusion

In the Introduction I presented two central questions that were sought to be answered throughout the course of this study: why did Melville write so frequently and with such clarity in his works about alcohol and imbibing, and what was he trying to relate to his mid-nineteenth-century audience about drinking and intoxication? These questions, I believe, have been answered: Melville wrote about alcohol and inebriation so frequently because they were such an enormous part of his life and of his society at large that it would only make sense that he would write about them so consistently, and in his writings he continually urges his readers to avoid alcohol and inebriation by promoting temperance and by illustrating alcohol's various evils. In the process of arriving at these answers, however, another query has presented itself: why did Melville write so harshly about alcohol and intoxication when he himself, as is crystal clear from some of his journals and in many correspondences written by or about him that will be considered in detail in the Afterword, was the most ardent lover of liquor? Why would he lambaste the pastime that he seemingly loved so much? As is typically the case with Melville, the answer may very well have to do with Melville's own experiences with alcohol. He implores his readers to avoid alcohol because he was intimately acquainted with the variously negative—in some cases horrific—consequences that drinking and intoxication would inevitably cause. To varying degrees and depending on which legends in Melville scholarship one believes, he is so knowledgeable about alcohol's detrimental effects because he either experienced or witnessed such alcohol-related hardships firsthand. In turn, he passes this knowledge onto his readers with the hope that they will avoid similar fates that Melville or those around him experienced.

The works that were examined in Chapter 1 were classified as, or at least contain elements of, temperance fiction. There are many reasons to suggest why Melville would have written in this genre. First, the temperance movement itself was in such full-swing during the period in which Melville was writing his works that contain temperance features that it would have been impossible that he was unaware of the movement itself.[1] Secondly and considering that works of temperance literature were so pervasive in mid-nineteenth-century America and that Melville was such an avid reader, it would have been virtually impossible for him not to have been familiar with them or their conventions.[2] Finally, there were many women in Melville's extended family who urged men to avoid alcohol.[3] Melville's aunt Priscilla Melvill, for instance, believed that Judge Shaw was an alcoholic and she insisted that Melville not drink around or offer Shaw any alcohol, thinking that it "might undermine his father-in-law's resolves by offering him just a little wine" (Parker, *Melville* 2: 401). Moreover, if Melville's family truly did have concerns about his own drinking, as some critics have claimed,[4] then surely he would have been cognizant of such objections. In mid-nineteenth-century works including *Israel Potter*, "Cock-A-Doodle-Doo!" and "The Apple-Tree Table," then, Melville is reflecting the push for temperance that was occurring in his society at the time and, in the two short stories, illustrating the female presence of at least one—perhaps more—woman in his extended family who was urging men including Shaw and possibly himself to temper their drinking.

As was shown in Chapter 2, many characters in Melville's writings including "Bartleby"'s Turkey and "Cock-A-Doodle-Doo!"'s narrator use alcohol as a means of escape and for dealing with the hardships that they experience. There is reliable information to suggest that Melville to a certain degree did the same. Not only did Melville's granddaughter Eleanor Melville Metcalf maintain consistently throughout her adult years that Herman sought "the solace of brandy" (215) in order to cope with life's various challenges, but in his personal documents Melville himself clearly admits that he indeed used alcohol as a way of escaping his own stresses. In 1851 and while experiencing the frustration of com-

• Conclusion •

pleting *Moby-Dick*, for instance, Melville writes to Hawthorne that he would like to drown his various frustrations in alcohol:

> In a week or so, I go to New York, to bury myself in a third-story room, and work and slave on my "Whale" while it is driving through the press. *That* is the only way I can finish it now,—I am so pulled hither and thither by circumstances. The calm, the coolness, the silent grass-growing mood in which a man *ought* always to compose,—that, I fear, can seldom be mine.... What I feel most moved to write, that is banned,—it will not pay. Yet, altogether, write the *other* way I cannot. So the product is a final hash, and all my books are botches.... I feel cheerfully disposed, and therefore I write a little bluely. *Would the Gin were here!* [*Correspondence* 191, emphasis added].

Melville suggests further albeit inversely in a journal entry from his time in Egypt in 1857 that alcohol could be useful in alleviating stressful situations:

> Upon entering Cairo, saw the crescent & star—arms of Sultan in the sky. Large extent of square. Canal about it. Lower level than walks around. Avenues of acacas & other trees. Shrubs. Seems country. No fences. The booths & cafes. Leapers, tumblers, jugglers, smokers, dancers, horses, swings, (with bells) sherbert, &c. Lovely at evening. In morning, golden sun through foliage. Soft luxurious splendor of mornings. Dewy. Paradise melted & poured into the air. Soft intoxication; no wonder these people never drink wine [76–77].

In this passage Melville basically states that alcohol is not needed in this beautiful and peaceful environment where paradise is melted and poured into the air because there is nothing depressing about it; there is no need for "these people" to drink wine because there is nothing from which they need to escape. This inherently suggests that alcohol *would* be required and perhaps useful in order to cope or deal with a more stressful and disordered setting and experience, which is how his fictional prodromal phase alcoholics deal with their various ordeals.

There are at least two events from Melville's life—one perhaps more likely than the other—that may explain why he in works including "The Paradise of Bachelors" and "Jimmy Rose" expresses his belief that drinkers are untrustworthy and selfish individuals. The first involves his fellow American author Nathaniel Hawthorne. On 5 August 1850 while attending a social gathering in Stockbridge, Massachusetts, hosted by David Dudley Field and that included other notable men of

• Conclusion •

American letters including editors Evert A. Duyckinck and James. T. Fields, and writers Cornelius Matthews and Oliver Wendell Holmes, Melville met Hawthorne, who had by this time just published *The Scarlet Letter*. Shortly following this meeting Melville purchased the farmhouse he would name Arrowhead on the outskirts of Pittsfield, Massachusetts, which was within roughly six miles of Hawthorne's home in Lenox. Over the next year-and-a-half Melville and Hawthorne spent much time together drinking and discussing "ontological heroics" with each other (Melville, *Correspondence* 196), in the process forging one of the most intense and important friendships in American literary history.[5]

At some point during the second week of November, 1851, after roughly fifteen months of socializing, imbibing, and philosophizing, Melville traveled from Arrowhead in Pittsfield to visit Hawthorne in Lenox where the two dined together on a wintry afternoon at the Curtis Hotel, or the Little Red Inn. While enjoying liquor and cigars, Melville presented Hawthorne, his only invited guest, with a copy of the recently-published *Moby-Dick*. When Hawthorne opened the cover he saw the book's dedication:

IN TOKEN
OF MY ADMIRATION FOR HIS GENIUS,
THIS BOOK IS INSCRIBED
TO
NATHANIEL HAWTHORNE

"Take it all in all," Hershel Parker writes, "this was the happiest day of Melville's life" (*Melville* 883). It would quickly be followed, however, by perhaps one of his saddest.

Shortly after their private afternoon together at the Curtis Hotel and much to Melville's shock, Hawthorne and his family would leave Lenox for West Newton without, apparently, saying any good-byes, leaving Melville without his most revered of drinking partners. Melville was left alone in the harsh New England winter. There are no records of how Melville felt about Hawthorne's decision to leave, yet it is safe to say, as others have, that "his friend's departure left an enormous void" in Melville's life (Robertson-Lorant, "Mr. Omoo" 43). While I agree with Erik Hage when he states that "there is no evidence that any drama presaged the rift between the two writers" (1), is it at least *possible* that

• CONCLUSION •

Melville was so affected, felt so betrayed by Hawthorne's decision to leave that he viewed him as selfish in making what Melville would have thought to be such a quick and rash decision? Considering the other speculative unsubstantiated views that others have presented concerning the essential end of their friendship as Melville knew it, then *yes* it certainly is possible.[6]

The other individual by whom Melville unquestionably felt betrayed is Evert A. Duyckinck. Melville met Duyckinck in New York City in late 1847 when Melville became involved in the literary scene. Over the next four years they forged a close bond and during this time Melville would (in part, again, for financial reasons) write for Duyckinck's *Literary World*—where "Hawthorne and his Mosses" appeared in two installment in August 1850[7]—and drink at times excessively with him and others. Despite the close relationship that they developed over this period, Duyckinck set aside friendship and liquor when he reviewed *Moby-Dick* in the *Literary World*, an act that would result in the two becoming estranged for a number of years thereafter. In his two-part review of the novel in the *Literary World* (on 15 and 22 November 1851) Duyckinck panned *Moby-Dick* largely on religious grounds. Taking one excerpt of the review that deals with the novel's defamation of "sacred" things, Duyckink writes:

> This piratical running down of creeds and opinions, the conceited indifferentism of Emerson, or the run-a-muck style of Carlyle is, we will not say dangerous in such cases, for there are various forces at work to meet more powerful onslaught, but is out of place and uncomfortable. We do not like to see what, under my view, must be to the world the most sacred associations of life violated and defaced [Leyda, *Log* 1: 437].

Such a review by a friend who undoubtedly knew Melville's artistic temperament would have certainly cut deep wounds.[8] And it did. In complete and utter disgust with Duyckinck's review, Melville nearly immediately thereafter cancelled two subscriptions of the *Literary World*: his own and that of his friend Eli Fly (Rollyson and Paddock 58). The two would remain at odds (Melville at least) for years.

As Robertson-Lorant writes, "Melville must have felt as though both Hawthorne and Duyckink had thrown him to the cannibals" (*Melville* 293) in their respective actions. He possibly felt this way toward Hawthorne for leaving and at Duyckinck for his damning review, leading Melville to arrive at an awareness that those who drink with others may simply be selfish individuals. Perhaps he initially felt that they simply tolerated him for the alcohol that he had to offer them at Arrowhead. Given Melville's moody and depressive nature, this surely must have at least crossed his mind.

Although there seems to be no specific mention or direct moments in Melville's life that clearly point to his distrust of those who offer alcohol only to be taken advantage of by them, he suggests in his letter about his ocean crossing in 1856 to his brother Allan that he was, indeed, wary of possible confidence men. Did he avoid the passengers on board the *Glasgow* who he described as "not all of a desirable sort" (301) for fear that these drinkers who gambled and drank the entire time during the voyage over the Atlantic would use liquor to try and take advantage of others who may be enticed into gambling? It is certainly plausible.

Melville was intimately acquainted for two reasons with the consequences that existed for those who drank to excess or smuggled liquor on board vessels: he was aware as it had happened to some of his family members and he had witnessed it first-hand while at sea. As for the first reason, when Melville was about twelve years old his cousin Thomas Wilson Melvill's professional reputation suffered a serious set-back stemming from an alcohol-related incident that could have cost him his career. While on board the naval ship *Vincennes* in late 1831, Melvill, who was "no doubt under the influence of alcohol" (Robertson-Lorant, *Melville* 90), was involved in a verbal altercation with and later assaulted a drunken sailor who had accused him of (like Chips and Bungs from *Omoo*) stealing liquor from the ship's hold. As Wilson Heflin relates the incident,

> One day while climbing the fore ladder of the craft, he passed near Thomas Spence, an ordinary seaman who was confined in double irons for drunkenness and was guarded by a sentry. Spence swore at Midshipman Melvill, clenched his fists, and accused him of going frequently into the spirits room and robbing it.[9]

Melvill, who was indeed a heavy drinker at this point in his life but who later "altered his ways" and gave up the habit (Heflin 9), reacted to this accusation immediately by jumping with both feet on Spence's torso. Although he was punished—he was relieved of duty for seven months—

the sentence that he was given was for the assault on Spence and not for the theft of the liquor. In fact, the truth surrounding Spence's allegation was never discussed during Melvill's court martial as the legal system by which he was tried did not permit anyone to ask if the "grossly provocative accusation was true" (Parker, *Melville* 1: 75). Nonetheless, alcohol was the central issue in the incident.

Melville's cousin Thomas was not the only relative of his whose professional reputation was affected due to alcohol-related events. On more than one occasion alcohol directly contributed to the professional downfall of another of Melville's cousins, Guert Gansevoort. Gansevoort was a decorated sailor whose naval career began in 1823 and who, nearly twenty years later, was a lieutenant on board the *Somers*: the scene of the only American ship to undergo a mutiny, attempted or otherwise, that resulted in executions. In November of 1842 there were rumors on board the *Somers* that there was an impending mutiny, and there was a court inquiry of the allegations. The court initially found insufficient evidence to convict the three men who were suspected of organizing the mutiny; however, under pressure from the captain, the court was forced to reconvene and, this second time around, it returned with guilty verdicts (Delbanco 298). On 1 December 1842, the *Somers'* officers, including Gansevoort, sentenced Philip Spencer, Elisha Small, and Samuel Cromwell on the charges of conspiracy to commit mutiny. In a similar manner as Melville relates in his works "Bridegroom Dick" and *Billy Budd, Sailor*, all three were executed and buried at sea. The *Somers'* case and having played such a significant role in the execution of fellow American sailors haunted Gansevoort for much of his life and perhaps exacerbated his tendency to drink, an addiction that would negatively affect the remainder of his career.

Like many of Melville's fictional sailors, his cousin Gansevoort drank heavily while he was on duty and his alcoholism while "on the job" reached a breaking point for his commander Captain David Glasgow Farragut. On 18 September 1856 Captain Farragut had Gansevoort suspended from the United States Navy's *Decatur* for being frequently drunk on duty, in this particular instance at eleven in the morning (Parker, *Melville* 2: 429). This scare would do little to deter Gansevoort from continued intoxication on duty, though. Six years later he would be given more responsibility on board another navy vessel, yet again his alcoholism would cost him his revered position.

• Conclusion •

In the fall of 1861, Guert was hoping to be named commander of the sloop-of-war *Adirondack*, a position for which there was intense competition. One of his primary competitors was John I. Almy, who was well aware of Gansevoort's past alcohol-related difficulties while on board the *Decatur*. In writing Henry A. Wise on 21 of March 1862, Almy stated that "he has had his Commander's command—that is the Sloop-of-War 'Decatur' in the Pacific until he had the command of her taken away from him on account of habitual Drunkenness, and his habits are not over and above steady and correct now" (Garner 146). Despite Almy's concerns, legitimate ones as it would again turn out, Gansevoort was awarded command of the *Adirondack* in March of 1862.

Gansevoort's family was filled with pride, as he was himself, on the appointment. In July and just prior to the ship's setting sail, Melville's brother, Allan, took his family to see Guert and they were given a tour of the ship. Yet only five weeks after he was awarded command of the *Adirondack*, his alcoholism again possibly cost him and what was dearest to him, aside from alcohol perhaps: command. While sailing in the Caribbean Guert Gansevoort ran his vessel aground while he was possibly intoxicated and was again court-martialed for his dereliction of duty. The court-martial began on 15 October. Allan Melville described the situation and Guert's mindset in a letter to Catherine Gansevoort, Herman's cousin, on 7 November: "It was a mortification to his pride for full forty long years he had waited for the command of a vessel & when he had rec'd it, everything so complete—he was happy, but its loss has completely broken him" (Parker, *Melville* 2: 519). In the end, Gansevoort would be found not guilty of the charge and almost unbelievably he was granted command of another ship, the *Roanoke*, in 1863.

Even if his family had not experienced their misfortunes with alcohol at sea, Melville was conscious of the ramifications for excessive drinking while on duty due to his own time as a sailor when he was a member of the man-of-war *United States*. He witnessed first-hand how sailors on board the ship were "caught and lashed" when the ship was in port and, as was typically the case, had liquor smuggled on board (Parker, *Melville* 1: 284). Hershel Parker describes how severe the consequences were for sailors who were perpetually intoxicated:

> Smuggling liquor on board [the *United States*] went on throughout the stay in Callo, and punishment for drunkenness and for quarrelling became almost a daily scene. On 8 January a man took twelve lashes

• CONCLUSION •

> with the "cats" for smuggling liquor. In the succeeding days men were lashed for drunkenness (the most common offence), for gambling, for disobedience, for desertion, for drunkenness and mutinous language, for drunkenness and disorderly conduct; for fighting, for assaulting the master-at-arms, for "abuse to sentinel," for "neglect of duty on pass": and for insolence. Each of these floggings followed quarters and prayers. Melville witnessed them all, and had the more time to brood upon them because so little work had to be done all day long [1: 282].

He would witness these lashings about 150 times while on board the *United States* (Meltzer, *Melville* 70).

Drinking while on the job and neglecting one's duty would cost sailors their rank and reputation, not to mention a flogging, and Melville passes on such episodes as warnings to his audience. The ocean is certainly no the place to imbibe and expect to maintain one's position and reputation. As is the case in Melville's familial and personal experiences, there are many sailors from Melville's works—*Typee*, *Omoo*, and *White-Jacket*—who suffer a loss of professional reputation and rank as a result of their addiction to alcohol.

Like various characters from his works including Mandeville and Dr. Long Ghost, Melville himself at times demonstrated the physically-altering affects of drinking. As two college students Titus Munson Coan and John Thomas Gulick on their visit to Arrowhead in 1859 noticed, and as will be discussed in more detail in the Afterword, Melville's appearance to them on this visit seemed to be "slightly flushed with whiskey drinking" (Parker 2: 397). Naturally, this observation could have been simply from this day on which Melville was drinking and not be a clear indication of long-term or permanent facial distortion from chronic alcoholism. Also like many of his characters, it is clear and in more direct relation to his works that Melville also suffered painfully from a variety of health issues including sciatica and arthritis that required some type of alleviation. If critics including Laurie Robertson-Lorant and Raychel Haugrud Reiff are to be believed, then Melville also used alcohol medicinally; he used it "for relief of his physical pain and emotional distress" (Robertson-Lorant, *Melville* 370) and to get "relief from his tightened muscles" (Reiff 24). Yet like his characters including the lady of Goshen from *The Confidence-Man*, Melville's medicinal drinking only made his condition worse. He apparently developed a growing dependency on alcohol, which exacerbated the "highs and lows to which he was subject," and as a result "his moods became more unpredictable and dangerous" than they had been previously (Robertson-Lorant, *Melville* 371; Metcalf *Melville* 215). Like that of some of his characters, then, Melville's use of alcohol for such medicinal purposes either made his various conditions worse or created new ones with which he was forced to deal, thereby possibly causing him to continue drinking in search of further yet unattainable relief.

In addition to illustrating in his writings how alcohol is actually detrimental to one's health, Melville also shows in works including "Cock-A-Doodle-Doo!" and *Redburn* how it can ruin one's financial security. Without question, finances were a constant concern in the Melville household. As Melville writes to Hawthorne in his famous letter concerning the composition and publication of *Moby-Dick*, "Dollars damn me" (*Correspondence* 191). Yet Melville's financial situation was so poor even before *Moby-Dick*, in fact, that his eventual father-in-law Judge Lemuel Shaw was initially opposed to his daughter's intention to marry a writer who would likely be unable to support her financially. He eventually offered his blessing and the two were married on 1 August 1847. His concern, however, was certainly legitimate as Shaw provided significant financial support to Melville right from the couple's wedding and up until his death in 1861. For instance, he financed the purchase of Herman and Elizabeth's first home in New York City in 1847 and in 1850 advanced them money, strictly on Melville's request, so that Herman could buy the farmhouse on the outskirts of Pittsfield, Massachusetts, that Melville would name Arrowhead. In 1856 Shaw would give Melville an additional $5,000 in order to provide for his family, clearly an incredible sum of money at the time.[10] Shaw also frequently offered what could be classified as non-essential financial support as he funded many of Melville's trips, including one to Nantucket in 1852 and his more costly one to Europe and the Holy Land—his health respite—in 1856–1857.

Despite his own financial hardships—his writings after all never offered him a living wage[11]—and constant reliance on his father-in-law for money, Melville always, somehow, had a more-than-adequate supply of alcohol at Arrowhead during the 1850s and early 1860s. Roughly five months after their meeting, for instance, Melville in a letter to Hawthorne invites his friend to Arrowhead to indulge in an all-day drinking marathon, which suggests a more-than-ample supply of liquor: "Hark—There is some excellent Montado Sherry awaiting you & some most potent Port. We will have mulled wine with wisdom, & buttered toast with story-telling & crack jokes & bottles from morning till night" (*Correspondence* 176). Hawthorne himself later calls attention to Melville's plentiful supply of quality alcohol in a letter that he wrote to G. W. Curtis, who was at this time an editor for *Harper's New Monthly Magazine*.[12] As Hawthorne writes, "Herman Melville (whom you praise in your book) lives about six miles off, and is an admirable fellow, and has some excellent old port and sherry wine" (Leyda, *Log* 1: 410). Other notable instances of Melville's supply of liquor and drinking habits at Arrowhead include the aforementioned 1859 visit to the farm by Williams College students Titus Munson Coan and John Thomas Gulick, who were on what Coan described as a "literary pilgrimage" (Parker 2:397), during which Gulick states that Melville's "countenance is slightly flushed with whiskey drinking" (Parker 2: 397), when Melville three months later invites Daniel Shepherd to come over for what Andrew Delbanco describes as a "binge" (Delbanco 266),[13] and when he implores Evert Duyckinck, with whom he had by this time reconciled (May 1862), to join him for some "whiskey punch" (Melville, *Correspondence* 373). One must wonder how much of Melville's alcohol supply came as a result of his father-in-law's financial contributions and how much were, somehow, purchased from Melville's own earnest earnings. In this regard, Melville has much in common with the narrator from "Cock-A-Doodle-Doo!," the man who despite lacking money and piling up further and further debt always had the coin to continue enjoying his stout.

In many of his works and as outlined in Chapter 8, Melville urges his readers not to drink by demonstrating how typically rational and well-meaning individuals can be transformed into their demonic *other* or *Doppelgänger* once they are under the influence of alcohol. "Cock-A-Doodle-Doo!"'s narrator, "Bartleby"'s Turkey, "Bridegroom Dick"'s Captain Turret, and *Omoo*'s two most notorious drinkers Dr. Long Ghost and John Jermin, among others, are all clear illustrations. How does this relate to Melville's life, however? It is certainly likely that he had witnessed such alterations in others during his time at sea on board vessels where drinking and drunkenness were commonplace, yet is it possible that Melville himself during one of his many drunken escapades that will be discussed more thoroughly in the Afterward experienced a similar alteration in his own behavior? If—and I stress *if*—one believes certain unverifiable yet nonetheless intriguing and certainly disturbing legends in Melville scholarship, then the answer is undoubtedly *yes*.

Melville's depiction of women in his works has been for generations lambasted by many critics for being misogynistic and for being generally "womanless."[14] Taking the allegations of supposed women hatred a step further and according to one story that dates back to the early years of the Melville revival that was introduced by critics including Henry Murray and Charles Olson and that was propagated most significantly in the latter years of the twentieth century by Elizabeth Renker in her 1994 essay "Herman Melville, Wife Beating, and the Written Page," Melville was frequently emotionally and physically abusive toward his wife, Elizabeth (Olson 92; Renker 123–150; Hardwick 52).[15] Melville's drinking got so bad and he was such an uncontrollable alcoholic on at least one occasion, the legend goes, that he came home "drunk one night" and in such a monstrous state similar to some of his characters that it caused him to beat on Elizabeth and to then violently throw her down the back stairs of their house (P. Metcalf 15). Although there is no concrete evidence to support such allegations, and while some renowned Melville scholars dismiss—or at least distance themselves from—such claims,[16] what is certain is that Elizabeth "was seen to be living a nightmare" because of Melville's behavior toward her (Hardwick 154) and that she, with the urging and support of her family and the Rev. Henry Whitney Bellows (minister at the All Souls Unitarian Church in New York City, where Herman and Elizabeth were both part of his congregation), was presented with an opportunity to leave Herman in the mid–1860s.[17] For her safety, Bellows proposed a staged kidnapping of Elizabeth that would take her from New York to Boston. Is it possible that Melville's supposed ongoing alcoholism and the accompanying violent changes in his behavior that it purportedly caused, leading to the related spousal abuse theory, is the reason for both its prominence in Melville's writings and for Elizabeth's decision to contemplate such a difficult decision for a nineteenth-century wife?[18] Naturally, it is impossible to say. All that is certain is that Melville either altered his (drinking) habits and behavior or simply Elizabeth's heart changed; she ultimately chose to stay with Herman until his death in 1891, writing to the Rev. Bellows on 20 May 1867 that she would submit herself to "whatever further trials may be before" her (Melville,

• CONCLUSION •

Correspondence 860). What precisely did she mean? We can never know as she took whatever secrets she may have had about this dark period in her marriage to Herman to the grave with her when she died in 1906. Little did she know at the time of her writing to Bellows, however, there would certainly be darker times and further trials to come for both her and Herman in less than four months.

In his works of dark temperance Melville illustrates the horrific and inevitable end that awaits those who continue to imbibe relentlessly: death and destruction to the drinker or to those around them. Melville was well-aware of how alcohol could destroy the lives of those who drank continually; he saw this clearly during his time on board the *United States*, among other vessels. Yet there is perhaps one episode from Melville's life—the most horrific of all that happened for him more than a decade after *Redburn* and *Moby-Dick* were published—in which Melville is possibly eerily prophetic. It involves the death of his oldest son, Malcolm, and is somewhat related to the aforementioned yet unsubstantiated spousal abuse theory.

By the summer of 1867 and once talk about the kidnapping plot had seemingly subsided, the Melvilles' oldest child, Malcolm, had taken a job as a clerk at an insurance company and had joined the New York State National Guard and was issued a pistol that would prove to be fatal. Since he was now making his own money he could afford to spend nights out on the town, so to speak, with his friends. Melville, however, was concerned that his late nights would "expose him to the manifold dangers and temptations that lay in wait for unwary youths in the taverns and back alleys of New York" (Robertson-Lorant, *Melville* 513). Melville detested his son's late nights to such an extreme and was so infuriated that Malcolm continued to break his 11 o'clock curfew that he took away his key to the house in an attempt to ensure that Malcolm would come back home on time (Leyda, *Log* 2: 687). On the night of 10 September 1867, Malcolm again broke his curfew and his father, shortly before going to bed himself, ordered the house locked. Elizabeth, however, waited up for her son to come home, which did not happen until 3 a.m. on the morning of 11 September. Upon Malcolm's return home and according to Catherine Gansevoort, Melville's cousin, Elizabeth did not severely scold him for his four-hour tardiness, but reminded him that it was inconsiderate. As Gansevoort wrote to her brother Henry on the 16th of September, "Cousin Herman is I think a very

• Conclusion •

strict parent & Cousin Lizzie thoroughly good but inefficient. She feels so thankful that she did not scold him or remonstrate as she intended" (Leyda, *Log* 2: 691).

When Herman arrived home from work on the evening of the 11th of September, unusually late by some accounts,[19] Malcolm was still in bed. After speaking with Elizabeth, the reason for her being thankful that she had not scolded Malcolm harshly became evident.[20] After his conversation with his wife, Herman finally went to his son's room and "forced the door and found Malcolm on the bed in his night clothes, his pistol in his right hand and a hole in his right temple. He had been dead for several hours" (E. H. Miller 317). On 12 September the coroner's office deduced that Malcolm's death was a suicide. Curiously and without explanation, however, four days later the *Evening Post* published the following retraction from the coroner's office: "We, the undersigned jurors in the inquest of the death of Malcolm Melville, on the 11th inst., desire to correct any erroneous impression drawn from the verdict of 'suicide.' We believe that his death was caused by his own hand, but not that the act was by premeditation or consciously done" (Leyda, *Log* 2: 690).

There is no doubt that Malcolm shot himself, but was his death a true suicide or a horrific accident? If one believes the coroner's office's aforementioned retraction of the initial verdict and the views of Malcolm's descendents, then it was clearly the latter.[21] Yet if it was an unequivocal and factual suicide, as nearly all modern critics seem to say,[22] then what prompted it? Could alcohol have played a role? Although Malcolm had become more rebellious toward his parents (as all teenagers become) in the time before his death, relatives in retrospect claimed that "he had *no* vices" and that he was not "debauched by alcohol" (Parker, *Melville* 2: 642). Further supporting such claims, when he returned home in the early hours of 11 September 1867 his mother, Elizabeth, apparently did not notice any trace of liquor on his breath. Is her account entirely reliable, though? Could Elizabeth's reluctance to tell Herman in the morning about Malcolm possibly having been imbibing be to avoid any inevitable anger that it would have instilled in Herman? He was, after all and according to his cousin Catherine, a "very strict parent" (Leyda, *Log* 2: 691). Given the legends concerning Melville's drinking habits and his moodiness during this time in his life, such a concern on Elizabeth's part would have certainly been under-

• CONCLUSION •

standable and plausible. Further speculation about Malcolm's possible drinking is fueled by the fact that he on the night of 10 September was "at an entertainment at Yorkville" (Leyda, *Log* 2: 687) that saw him and his friends "probably" go to Niblo's Gardens, "a popular night club ... which featured musical comedies with girls who 'wore no clothes to speak of'" (Robertson-Lorant, *Melville* 513; Cohen and Yannella 192, 197n38). Going to such an establishment of ill-repute could certainly increase the likelihood that Malcolm could have been drinking. Could such a possible intoxicated state, paired with the "fact" that Malcolm slept with his pistol under his pillow (Robertson-Lorant, *Melville* 514), have contributed in some way to his death, accidental or otherwise? Of course, it is *possible*.

Even if Malcolm himself was not a drinker or at least not drinking that night, is it possible that alcohol somehow still played a role in his death? Malcolm's death occurred during the years when his father apparently was drinking heavily (according to which critic you believe) and when his supposed abuse toward his wife was at its height. If the abuse allegations are indeed true, then Malcolm would have undoubtedly been aware either by seeing or hearing such episodes as he was still living with his parents. In further support of this possibility, some have argued that the pistol Malcolm shot himself with, inadvertently or otherwise, was on-hand and ready "if his father, whether in an intoxicated or crazy state, ever again physically abused his mother."[23] Such arguments are simply speculative as there is no concrete evidence to support them (Robertson-Lorant, "Melville" 36–37n42), yet is it feasible to believe that Malcolm's action was a manner in which to get away from the household atmosphere that his father's, like Perth's, drinking had caused? Certain other scholars speculate that this, indeed, is yet another possible scenario: Malcolm committed suicide to escape "his father's cruelty toward him" (Rollyson and Paddock 119) and that the suicide was Malcolm's "act of hostility toward his father for a lack of attention and affection (Renker 129). In reality, this is all conjecture and we will never know for certain, but such speculation should not be necessarily dismissed for, as is always the case, "so much about Melville is *seems to be, may have been,* and *perhaps*" (Hardwick 141).

Regardless of how much Melville himself appeared to enjoy imbibing during his life, particularly during the late 1840s to the early 1860s based on the available factual documents, his writings for decades show

· *Conclusion* ·

unequivocally that he wished that others would abstain from alcohol and its consumption. Various episodes from all of his novels, much of his short fiction, and some of his poetry serve as warnings to his readers, showing them what the harsh consequences for involvement or association with alcohol in any way will be. He wanted his audience to avoid the dark realities of drunkenness and alcohol in general and he did so stemming from first-hand experiences that he likely either went through or witnessed. Despite not wanting a "Temperance Heaven," as he writes in his famous letter to Nathaniel Hawthorne in 1851 (*Correspondence* 191),[24] Melville's writings clearly, consistently, and without question illustrate that he wished for a sober world.

Afterword: Melville and the Bottle

While the critics and scholars referenced in the early part of the Introduction who speculate as to the nature of Melville's drinking have seemingly either over- or under-interpreted Melville's imbibing habits for their own design, Stanton Garner has apparently done the opposite. He states in his thorough book *The Civil War World of Herman Melville* that Melville, particularly during the 1850s, drank to an "unknown" extent (41).[1] In making such a claim, Garner has curiously overlooked various documents from the late 1840s to the early 1860s that give us substantial factual information about Melville's drinking. That being said and as I stated in both the Introduction and Conclusion, I was not nor am I here seeking to even contemplate what I have coined as the Melville Question, or to set out and to discuss in any way whether or not Melville was an alcoholic. Given the length of time that has passed since his death and that of those who could provide first-hand insight into the debate, paired with the absence of documents that specifically refer to his drinking as problematic in even some small yet direct way, finding an unequivocal answer to this question is, quite simply, impossible. Considering that I use Melville's own drinking as one of the reasons for the recurrence of alcohol throughout many of his works,[2] however, I would be remiss if I failed to offer commentary on how frequently Melville drank.

My hope, in a sense, for this Afterword is the same as eminent

• Afterword •

Melville scholar Jay Leyda's desire for his invaluable work *The Melville Log: A Documentary Life of Herman Melville, 1819–1891*. As Leyda writes in the introduction to his study, "In the making of this book I have tried to hold to one main aim: to give each reader the opportunity to be his own biographer of Herman Melville, by providing him with the largest possible quantity of materials to build his own approach to this complex figure" (1: xi). I here reiterate that I am not interested in finding an answer to the Melville Question, but perhaps this information will assist others in their quest, no matter how futile such an endeavor may ultimately be.

Like Thomas Gradgrind from Charles Dickens's novel *Hard Times* (1854), I am simply interested in presenting the facts as we know them about Melville and the bottle.[3] I will here relate the factually-known instances of both Herman's history of imbibing and his association with alcohol as presented in such personal writings as journal entries and letters written by or about him that are found in the Northwestern-Newberry edition of Melville's letters (*Correspondence*) and journals (*Journals*) and from similar writings by other individuals including Nathaniel Hawthorne that are found in either these same publications or that are included in Jay Leyda's *The Melville Log*. Chronicling these factual episodes of Melville's relationship with liquor that appear in such personal documents will make it absolutely clear as to why alcohol and its consumption are such insistent themes in his works.

Naturally, it is impossible to determine the exact day that Melville began drinking, frequently or otherwise, but it is certain that during the early 1840s he drank heavily and had a fairly high tolerance for alcohol.[4] We know this from a 4 January 1861 letter that Melville received from Richard Tobias Greene, with whom Melville sailed on board the whaler *Acushnet* from 3 January of 1841 until the two abandoned the ship and together took refuge on the of Marquesan island of Nukuheva on 9 July 1842. In this letter Greene, whom Melville had not seen in nearly twenty years, writes that he hopes to visit Melville at some point and that Herman would still be able to hold his liquor as good as he did nearly two decades earlier: "Hope you enjoy good health, and can yet stow away your 'five shares of duff!' I would be delighted to see you and 'freshen the nip' while you would be spinning a yarn as long as the Main top bowline. I shall most certainly avail myself of your kind invitation if I ever travel that way, which may not be far distant" (*Correspondence* 679).[5]

• AFTERWORD •

The first known series of references that Melville himself makes about his own drinking—and there are many of them—are found in a number of journal entries from the fall and early winter of 1849. At this point in his life Melville was on board the steamer *Southampton* and was *en route* from New York to his final destination of London for what was primarily a business trip to negotiate the details of a contract for the publication of *White-Jacket*. In addition to completing his business dealings, Melville also went to the Continent and visited, among other countries, France, Germany, and Belgium. He returned to America at the end of January 1850. Likely knowing or anticipating that he would consume a large amount of alcohol during this trip, Melville actually started off the journey by keeping a checklist in his journal of what he had to drink while on board.[6] It is probably wise that he kept this list for only the first day or two of the trip. If he had kept his running-record going, as the examination of the journal in this Afterword will attest, then he would have certainly needed more paper.

Melville did not spend his days alone wasting away with a bottle for the duration of the Atlantic crossing. He spent much of his time and many late nights with two highly educated individuals who provided Melville with the type of philosophical contemplation and discussion that he had began to incorporate into his writings in his relatively recently-published novel *Mardi* (published in March of 1849). One was George Adler, a German philosophy and literature professor at New York University and whom Melville had previously met through Evert Duyckinck. The other was Dr. Frank Taylor, the *Southampton's* surgeon, whom Melville met on the ship for the first time. For the duration of the voyage, Melville, Adler, and Taylor spent significant time together philosophizing and drinking. The three men also shared a frequent glass of various types of alcohol with Theodore McCurdy, the son of the rich merchant Robert McCurdy, and on at least one occasion with the *Southampton's* captain, Robert Griswold. We can say with certainty, then, that Melville was not a solitary drinker; he had plenty of company during his drinking stints on board the ship.

Melville first references his drinking on the *Southampton* on the 15th of October when he admits to having "a small bottle of London Stout" for dinner (7). Five days later he "for the first time went into the Ladies' Saloon, & heard Mrs. Gould the opera lady sing. There was quite a party" (8). The 21st appears to have been mundane; Melville's journal for the day is brief, running only three fragmented sentences: "Rainy—near the Banks. Can not remember what happened today. It came to an end somehow" (8). Considering that each of his previous entries are substantially longer and provide more detail concerning his activities for the day, this brevity is curious. Melville's journal entry for the 22nd, however, may give us some insight as to why:

> I forgot to mention, that *last night* about 9 ½ P.M. Adler & Taylor came into my room, & it was proposed to have whiskey punches, which we *did* have accordingly.... We had an extraordinary time & did not break up till after two in the morning. We talked metaphysics continually, & Hegel, Schlegel, Kant & c were discussed under the influence of the whiskey [8].

Was Melville's October 21 journal entry brief because the day was uneventful and written prior to 9:30 in the evening, or was it composed after Adler and Taylor departed and with Melville feeling the effects of the whiskey, hence his inability to remember what happened or how the day ended? Either way, Melville was unquestionably inebriated on board the *Southampton* on the 21st. It would certainly not, however, be his last night on the ship in such a state.

It appears that Melville refrained from drinking from the 22nd to the 24th inclusive. Considering how much he consumed on the 21st, taking a few days off was probably a good idea. On the 25th he drank champagne with Adler, Taylor, and McCurdy, and on the 27th had "some" mulled wine, again with the same three men. As was the case on the 21st, the drinking and discussion on the 27th kept Melville and his companions up extremely late; they separated "at about 3 in the morning" (9). Although it is impossible to say how much "some" mulled wine means, it seems likely that "some" is an understatement considering the late hour they departed each other's company. Melville, certainly tired and possibly feeling the effects of a hangover from the night before, was not too productive on the 28th. He "read a little, dozed a little & to bed early" (10). This, as it would turn out, would be much needed rest.

Melville drank to varying degrees on the final three days of October and on six of his final seven days on board the *Southampton*. The 29th appears to have been a day of little drinking, having only some stout with Taylor (10). He imbibed a little more heavily on the 30th, having a "superb dinner" with "a good deal of wine & porter on the table" (10).

• AFTERWORD •

The final day of October was another night Melville and McCurdy were up late, spending it drinking mulled sherry (10). Melville's drinking habits did not change along with the month.

On November 1, upon the suggestion of Taylor, Melville returned "McCurdy's civilities" (10). On this night they were also joined by the ship's Captain Griswold, who "ordered a pitcher of his own" (10). The 3rd of November, it would seem based on Melville's description, was the most riotous night of all. There was likely no discussion of metaphysics or other matters of philosophy; it was, quite simply, a raucous party: "In the evening all hands in high spirits—Played chess in the ladies' saloon—another party at cards; good deal of singing in the gentlemen's cabin & drinking—very hilarious and noisy" (11). As would be expected, the following day was much more subdued. There were "long faces at dinner—no porter bottles" (11). Despite the long faces resulting from excessive imbibing the night before and hence the absence of alcohol on the tables on the 4th of November, Melville "cracked some Champaign" with McCurdy on the 5th and retired around midnight (12).[7] He was woken up five hours later on the morning of the 5th by Captain Griswold, signaling Melville's final day on board the *Southampton* and his first day on land.

Spending nearly four weeks at sea in relatively cramped quarters with little else to occupy his time, one could say that frequent drinking is understandable if not expected. When Melville finally got his footing on shore, the sights that were there to be seen and the business that he went there to do might have certainly enabled him to occupy his time with more productive activities. This is not what we see, however. From the 5th of November to the 16th of December Melville notes that he drank with sobering frequency. He imbibed on twenty-two different occasions: November 5, 6, 11, 12, 15, 16, 18, 21, 23, 24, 26, 29, and December 2, 9, 10, 11, 12, 15, 16, 17, and 21. It was not just the frequency of Melville's drinking that increased. So did its intensity.

After departing from the *Southampton*, Melville writes that the change from ship to shore was "delightful." It was so delightful, in fact, that Melville, Taylor, and Adler complemented their first breakfasts on land, as some of Melville's characters do, with "ales & pipes" (12). Heading to the railway station on November 6th to catch the train to London, Melville swallowed a glass of ale (13). Once in London on the 11th he drank some more ale (16) and on the next day he had "a noble dinner

• *Afterword* •

of turtle soup, pheasant &c: with glorious wine" (17). Melville drank a bit again on the 15th of November, having a pint and a half of Scotch ale at the "Edinburgh Castle," the best, Melville says, he ever drank (18–19).

On 16 November Melville drank heavily again and calls attention to his drinking as something that should be expected. At the Mitre Tavern, Melville had "bread & cheese, & ale (of course)." He also had a glass of ale at the Dr. Johnson Tavern, and then it was on to the Cook Tavern for two more glasses of stout—enough to make him blush—and then refrained from drinking, it appears, until the 21st, when he had his fair share. He dined at the Queen's Hotel "on ox-tail soup—chops—ale—port wine." Later in the evening, "Porter passed around in tankards.... Afterwards, Gin, brandy, whiskey & cigars" (24).

November 22 appears to have been a dry day for Melville, but the following two days consisted of heavy drinking: "At dinner the stiffness, formality, & coldness of the party was wonderful. I felt like knocking all their heads together.... After the ladies withdrew, the three decanters—Port, Sherry, & Claret—were kept going the rounds with great regularity" (26). The following night—returning at midnight based on his entry—Melville, basically, tied one on. To use his words, "Just returned from East Sheen with an indefinite quantity of Champagne Sherry, Old Port, Hock, Madeira, & Claret in me" (26–27). On the 26th, Melville again dined at the Mitre Tavern and then to the Blue Posts Tavern with David Donaldson and "took some of their renowned punch" (30).

On the 29th Melville had a bottle Bordeaux; on the 2nd of December he had "chilly wine"; on the 8th on a train bound for Cologne, Germany, he encountered "a young Frenchman—a genuine blade, who carried a flask of Belgian Gin in his pocket with a glass" (31, 32, 35). On his first full day in Cologne on December 9, Melville took in the food and drink of the city: "A regular German dinner & a good one, 'I tell you.' Innumerable courses—& an apple-pudding was served between the courses of meat & poultry. I drank some yellow Rhenish wine which was capital, looking out on the storied Rhine as I dined" (36). Shortly thereafter, Melville "stopped at a beer shop—& took a glass of *black ale* in a comical flagon of glass" (36). At around 9:30 the night of the 10th Melville departed Cologne for Coblentz. Prior to his departure he took in a few last drinks in Cologne. When he returned to his hotel from his walk, he found "a large party assembled, filling up all the tables in the Dining Saloon. Every man his bottle of Rhenish, and his cigar" (36). Melville himself had a bottle of *Rudenshimer*" (37). At his first dinner in Coblentz Melville drank "nothing but Moselle wine" (37), and on the 11th of December he enjoyed more drinking. Between 3:00 and 6:30 in the afternoon till evening he drank some "Rhenish on the Rhine" and then drank a bottle of Steinberger (38). The following day—the 12th—Melville sauntered around, drank "a little beer here & ate a bit of cake there" (38–39).

After returning to England and successfully completing his business concerning *White-Jacket* on the 15th of December,[8] Melville had a glass of stout at the Cock near Temple Bar, then went home to read a few chapters of *Tristram Shandy* (41). On the 17th, after taking a letter to the post office and a pair of pants to the tailor, he drank a "pint of ale" (43), and following his supper on the 21st he drank some more mulled wine (45). This December 21st entry is the last explicit reference to Melville's drinking in his 1849–1850 journal. Unlike his outward-bound trip across the Atlantic to England, he did not keep a journal during his return to America. Therefore, it is impossible to determine if or to gauge how much he drank. Considering the amount of alcohol that he consumed on the outward-bound part of the voyage and the extent to which he drank while on land, it would seem likely that he imbibed—at times heavily—on the way home. Likely but not conclusive and therefore lending nothing of significance.

Eight months after arriving home from his travels in Europe, Melville and his wife, Elizabeth, who were married in 1847, were invited to attend a social gathering in Stockbridge, Massachusetts, hosted by David Dudley Field,[9] and that included other men of American letters including poet and physician Oliver Wendell Holmes, writer Cornelius Matthews, Boston publisher James. T. Fields, New York editor Evert A. Duyckinck, and the famous author of the recently-published novel *The Scarlet Letter*: Nathaniel Hawthorne. The meeting between Melville and Hawthorne on 5 August 1850 was marked with heavy amounts of champagne that all the men together drank during a supposed rain storm on Monument Mountain. This marks the beginning of a friendship between men who are currently regarded as two of nineteenth-century America's most famous authors, a relationship whose brevity is exceeded not only by its intensity but by the alcohol that was consumed by the two of them during each other's company. Three days

• *Afterword* •

after the monumental encounter on Monument Mountain, Hawthorne writes in his journal that he gave Melville, in addition to Duyckinck and Matthews, "a couple of bottles" of champagne (Leyda, *Log* 1: 385) and on 15 August, Duyckinck himself sent Melville twelve bottles of the same, a dozen "beautiful babies" as Melville describes them in a 16 August letter of *thanks* to Duyckinck (*Correspondence* 168). Unable or unwilling to wait, the first bottle was opened the following day.

Around the 29th of January, 1851, Melville wrote his first known—at least first existing—letter to Hawthorne. Right from their first correspondence, alcohol and the hope of sharing moments of drinking, from Melville's perspective at least, was a significant and frequent topic of discussion. In this initial letter, Melville invites Hawthorne to drink with him at Arrowhead. His desire for Hawthorne to imbibe with him at the farm is so intense in the letter that he even jokingly threatens Hawthorne with arrest if he does not accept the offer: "Hark—There is some excellent Montado Sherry awaiting you & some most potent Port. We will have mulled wine with wisdom, & buttered toast with story-telling & crack jokes & bottles from morning till night. Come—no nonsense. If you don't—I will send Constables after you" (176).

On the 12th of February, Melville again wrote Evert Duyckinck to tell him about a trip that he took to see Hawthorne in Lenox a few weeks earlier and in which he expresses his hope that Hawthorne would soon repay him the visit. Again, alcohol was to be a part of the meeting:

> After long procrastination, I drove down to see Mr. Hawthorne a couple of weeks ago. I found him, of course, buried in snow; & the delightful scenery about him, all wrapped up & tucked away under a napkin, as it were. He was to have made me a day's visit, & I had promised myself much pleasure in getting him up in my snug room here, & discussing the Universe with a bottle of brandy & cigars. But he has not been able to come, owing to sickness in his family.—or else, he's up to the lips in the *Universe* again [180].

Although we never see Hawthorne's response to Melville's letters as Herman destroyed nearly all of his received correspondences,[10] we can gain insight into Melville's drinking from documents that his friends and acquaintances wrote to each other about him. In an April, 1851, letter, for instance, Hawthorne wrote to G. W. Curtis that calls attention to the amount and quality of alcohol that Melville has at

• AFTERWORD •

Arrowhead: "Herman Melville (whom you praise in your book) lives about six miles off, and is an admirable fellow, and has some excellent old port and sherry wine" (Leyda, *Log* 1: 410). About a month later, Melville would write to Hawthorne and it is clear from the letter that he thought Hawthorne was far more than simply an "admirable fellow." For Melville, the relationship had exploded into a deep reverence and admiration. In this letter from May of 1851, Melville expresses his equal devotion to both Hawthorne and alcohol:

> If ever, my dear Hawthorne, in the eternal times that are to come, you and I shall sit down in Paradise, in some little shady corner by ourselves; and if we shall by any means be able to smuggle a basket of champagne there (I won't believe in a Temperance Heaven), and if we shall then cross our celestial legs in the celestial grass that is forever tropical, and strike our glasses and our heads together, till both musically ring in concert,—then, O my dear fellow mortal, how shall we pleasantly discourse of all the things manifold which now so distress us,—when all the earth shall be but a reminiscence, yea, its final dissolution an antiquity [191–192].[11]

On 29 June 1851, frustrated with the delays and difficulties of writing *Moby-Dick* and while the book was "half through the press" (*Correspondence* 195), Melville writes again to Hawthorne about going to Lenox to visit him and to sit down to deep philosophical discussion, accompanied of course by alcohol: "When I am myself quite free of my present engagements, I am going to treat myself to a ride and a visit to you. Have ready a bottle of brandy, because I always feel like drinking that heroic drink when we talk ontological heroics together" (196). This letter was written at the height of the men's friendship, yet unfortunately for Melville the intense relationship, like all good things in life, would ultimately have an end.

At some point during the second week of November, 1851, Melville traveled from Pittsfield to Lenox to visit Hawthorne and the two dined together at the Curtis Hotel, or the Little Red Inn. While enjoying liquor (again) and cigars, Melville presented Hawthorne with a copy of the recently-published *Moby-Dick*, which as noted in the Conclusion Melville inscribed thus:

IN TOKEN
OF MY ADMIRATION FOR HIS GENIUS,

• *Afterword* •

THIS BOOK IS INSCRIBED
TO
NATHANIEL HAWTHORNE

On 21 November, only a few days after being presented his copy of *Moby-Dick*, Hawthorne and his family boarded the train in Pittsfield and moved from Lenox to West Newton, leaving Melville to wonder why he left.

Although their friendship would never again reach the same level of intensity with the same degree of trust (on Melville's end anyway) that it had from August 1850 to November 1851, Melville and Hawthorne continued to communicate, albeit infrequently, with alcohol remaining a frequent topic of conversation. In a 17 July 1852 letter to Hawthorne, Herman discusses his time drinking wine in Massachusetts, where Melville had been with Lemuel Shaw on a tour of Nantucket from 6–14 June,[12] and overhearing a couple talk about Hawthorne's most recently-published (three days earlier) book *The Blithedale Romance* (230). Three months later, Melville would write Hawthorne again and lament the fact that the two had not seen each other since Hawthorne had moved from Lenox—a span of nearly a year. As Melville writes on 25 October 1852, "I don't know when I shall see you. I shall lay eyes on you one of these days however. Keep some Champagne and Gin for me" (240). Melville would, indeed, finally lay eyes on and visit Hawthorne again in December of 1852 in Concord after he had spent Thanksgiving with his in-laws in Boston. The specifics that we have about the meeting—what they did while together—are virtually non-existent, but Melville did write Hawthorne between the 3rd and 13th of December thanking him for the visit (242). After this letter the two men would meet only twice more; there would only be a few final drinks that the two men would share together. They would have to wait nearly four years.

Despite Herman's intense relationship with him from 1850–1851, Hawthorne was not the only individual with whom Melville imbibed with during this period. In August of 1851 and in between letters to Hawthorne, Melville wrote to Samuel Savage (Elizabeth Melville's stepmother's nephew)[13] alluding to past and future drinking: "My dear Sam—I thank you for your letter, which by its pleasant mood—its allusions to 'Jolly Gods' nectar' 'cigars' 'London Dock' and 'rambles' 'dis-

• AFTERWORD •

cussions' &c awaked in me hearty desires that you would come back to us for a few days & live over again those 'rambles' & tap anew the cask of 'London Dock'" (202). As noted in Chapter 37 of *White-Jacket*, London Dock is a type of liquor (152–154).

From 1853 to 1856 Melville was a highly productive even if not financially successful writer, completing more than a dozen works of shorter fiction including the masterpieces "Bartleby, the Scrivener" and "Benito Cereno," and at least two novels: *Israel Potter* and *The Confidence-Man*.[14] Such constant writing left him physically and mentally exhausted. In an attempt to improve his health, Melville would embark on a recuperative journey that would take him to Scotland, England, the Levant, and the Holy Land, a voyage that was funded by his father-in-law Lemuel Shaw. It would be on this trip that Melville and Hawthorne would meet for the final time and would raise together their last glass of booze.

Melville began keeping a journal of this voyage on 8 November 1856, two days prior to seeing Hawthorne again.[15] While this journal does not contain as intense or frequent descriptions of drunkenness as does his journal from 1849 to 1850, it nonetheless demonstrates further albeit tame drinking episodes between the two reunited yet certainly not entirely reconciled friends. The meeting between Melville and Hawthorne in 1856 would be their first since their brief encounter in Concord, Massachusetts, in 1852 as Hawthorne had moved to England in 1853 after being awarded by his friend Franklin Pierce, who was elected President of the United States the previous year, a political appointment as United States Consul in Liverpool. Melville recounts in his journal their meeting and while his description of it lacks the passion and enthusiasm that filled his letters six years earlier, there are some things that do not change: the two shared a day of drinking together. After meeting Hawthorne on the 10th at the Consulate and traveling by train together to Southport on the 11th, the two men had, according to Melville in his journal entry, "An agreeable day. Took a long walk by the sea. Sand & grass. Wild and desolate. A strong wind. Good talk. In the evening Stout & Fox & Geese" (51).[16] The phrasing of this sentence suggests that he and Hawthorne had some stout first and then went to the Fox and Goose, a Southport pub,[17] for further drinking.

Although Melville curiously makes no mention of it, Hawthorne relates in his own journal to another drinking experience that the two shared on the 15th of November. After visiting the cathedral in Chester, the two men "sat down in a small snuggery, behind the bar, and smoked cigars and drank some stout" (Leyda, *Log* 2: 530–531). This could have been the final drink that the two would share together as Melville would sail from Liverpool on the 18th on board the *Egyptian* to continue on his European and Near-Eastern vacation and there is no further mention of another drink in any surviving documents.[18] They would meet only once more: briefly in early May of 1857 when Melville was on his return journey to the United States. There is no discussion of alcohol or its consumption at all by either individual during this encounter either: Melville tersely states in his journal that he "Saw Hawthorne" (129), while Hawthorne fails to make note of this meeting in any of his own surviving documents (Horsford with Horth 529). Hawthorne died roughly seven years later, on 19 May 1864, with Melville not attending the funeral. "[U]ninvited or unwilling to attend," as David Laskin writes, "we do not know" (93). For the two men who had drank so heavily together in the early 1850s while intensely discussing their "ontological heroics," the well had finally run dry and their final moments in each other's company were marked, it appears, with indifference.

Melville's soul may have been refreshed after returning from his trip in 1857, but he, like Ishmael, returned with little or no money in his purse; he was still in dire need of money. With little other choice, he decided to do what other American literary figures including Ralph Waldo Emerson and Henry David Thoreau did: he joined the lecture circuit or lyceum. This was clearly a risky endeavor for Melville because it did not guarantee him any remuneration; the speakers needed to rely on people willing to pay to see them in order to earn any money. Not only would lecturing not guarantee him the income that he needed that prompted him to join the lyceum in the first place, it would also potentially diminish further whatever reputation Melville had left, which at this point in time was clearly not much if any. As Andrew Delbanco notes, public speaking in antebellum America "was indeed a form of beggary" (258). Dr. Oliver Wendell Holmes apparently classified it even more crassly to Melville's cousin Henry Gansevoort. As Gansevoort paraphrases Holmes in his diary, "a lecturer was a literary strumpet subject for a greater than whore's fee to prostitute himself" (Leyda, *Log* 2: 597). Melville was a member of the lecture circuit from 1857 to 1860, speaking on various subjects under the titles of "Statutes in Rome," "The South Seas," and "Travel" in cities including Baltimore, Boston, Chicago, Detroit, and New York. Melville's career as a lecturer was about as critically and financially successful as were books like *Mardi* and *Pierre*.

Many of Melville's reviewers were just as harsh on his lecturing as his critics had been on *Pierre* years earlier. One who attended a 28 February 1859 performance described lecturing as "not his forte," while a reviewer from a Charlestown lecture (10 February 1858) noted the displeasure of the audience: "Some nervous people, therefore, left the hall; some read books and newspapers; some sought refuge in sleep, and some, to their praise be it spoken, seemed determined to use it as an appropriate occasion for self-discipline in the blessed virtue of patience" (Leyda, *Log* 2: 603, 592). Despite such negative feedback, his story-telling talent was not lost on or criticized by all. After attending a lecture on "The South Seas" given for the New York Historical Society on 7 February 1859, for instance, Melville's cousin Henry Gansevoort praised Melville's oratory performance in such a way that it calls attention to Melville's drinking. He insinuates that he had witnessed Melville delivering private family talks and telling entertaining tales in a frequently inebriated state: "It was in Cousin Hermans true vein. He was emphatically himself, and the lecture was to me like a quantity tied together—of his vivid and colloquial sketches (always too short) told under the inspiration of Madeira after dinner or drawn forth by some proper association elsewhere. He should be invited to deliver it at Albany" (Leyda, *Log* 2: 600–601). By stating that Melville's "true vein" was to be under the "inspiration of Madeira," Gansevoort basically says that Melville frequently drank to excess during such family story-telling episodes.[19]

The year before quitting the lecture circuit, Melville was visited at Arrowhead by two students from Williams College. On 19 April 1859 Titus Munson Coan and John Thomas Gulick traveled to the Melville farm for what Coan described as a "literary pilgrimage" (Parker 2: 397). Subsequent to his visit to Arrowhead, Gulick provides information that, as Parker notes, "cannot be passed over" (2: 400) as it relates to Melville and alcohol. As Gulick describes, Melville had "a form of good proportions, is about 5 ft. 9 in. in height, stands erect and moves with firm, manly grace.... His head is of moderate size with black hair, dark eyes, a smooth pleasant forehead and rough heavy beard and

• Afterword •

moustache. His countenance is slightly flushed with whiskey drinking, but not without expression" (Parker 2: 397). Since Gulick had never met Melville prior to this encounter, it is significant that he would have noticed the imbibing (from either extended periods of drinking or merely from earlier that day) etched on Melville's face. Was Melville flushed from drinking that day, or was his appearance affected like characters including Mandeville from extended periods of drinking? The answer is uncertain, yet the observation nonetheless important to Melville's drinking.

Three months after the college students' visit, Melville was in need of another alcohol-filled visit from someone. This time the drinking companion he sought was the lawyer and Allan Melville's (Herman's brother) law partner, Daniel Shepherd, who Melville had already likely met in Lake George, New York, in August of 1856 (editorial note to *Correspondence* 337). In July of 1859, Melville urges Shepherd in a poetic letter to come visit and drink with him at Arrowhead:

> Come, Shepherd, come visit me:
> Come, we'll make it Arcady; ...
> —Of Bourbon that is rather new,
> I brag a fat black bottle or two [337–339].

It is uncertain whether or not Shepherd accepted Melville's invitation, or that Melville's letter was ever sent at all (editorial note to *Correspondence* 337), but it nonetheless demonstrates Melville's urge to drink heavily at Arrowhead as he had done previously with Hawthorne.

Beginning in the 1860s, references to or discussions of imbibing in factual documents become less frequent until they disappear altogether (from extant documents anyway) after a letter that he wrote to Evert Duyckinck in February of 1860: "If you have nothing better to do, come round tomorrow (Sunday) evening, and we will brew some whiskey punch and settle the affairs of the universe over it—which affairs sadly need it, some say" (373). This request sounds something like the discussion of "ontological heroics" that Melville shared with Hawthorne, and is the last direct reference that is made to drinking in Melville's life. This is not to say that he quit drinking from this point on; in fact, such a suggestion is in direct conflict with the arguments of those who claim that Melville either started or continued to drink heavily toward the end of the 1860s (Bryant, "Writer" xxxix; Delbanco

• AFTERWORD •

275–276) and that he under the influence of alcohol possibly became abusive toward Elizabeth during this period (Olson 92; Renker 123–150; Hardwick 52, 111; Delbanco 275–276). Since this letter to Duyckinck is the last direct and explicit reference to Melville's drinking that exists from known factual documents including letters or journal entries by or about Melville, however, it will be the final commentary provided in this Afterword.

Like many other American authors, male and female, Melville clearly liked—loved, in fact—to drink. Does this necessarily mean that he was an alcoholic? Does it prove that he was, indeed, physically abusive to his wife and children? Naturally, these questions are impossible to answer and, as I have stated throughout, they are not questions to which I seek answers. All that is certain, from my perspective, is that Melville like countless others throughout history drank frequently and that he infused his writings with the variously negative repercussions that can be associated with a love of drink.

Appendix: A Concordance of Melville's Characters and Alcohol

Over the course of this study it has been clearly and thoroughly illustrated that Herman Melville's novels, short stories, and poetry are rife with characters who are negatively affected by alcohol in various ways. Although there are for certain nearly 90 individuals from more than 20 of Melville's works who fit this description, if we include the large groups of drinkers such as the violently-inebriated French soldiers from *Omoo* and the innumerable drunken crew members on board the *Highlander* (*Redburn*) and *Neversink* (*White-Jacket*)—imbibers whose actual numbers are indeterminate—then the number of characters who are associated with or affected by alcohol would astoundingly extend into the hundreds.

I present here, therefore, a clear type of concordance to the most notable examples of Melville's characters who are in some way involved with or affected by alcohol or inebriation. This concordance is organized alphabetically by work title and then again by the character names therein (prioritized by given names in cases where surnames are also provided and by rank titles including *Captain* or *Lieutenant*).

"The Apple-Tree Table" (1856)

Narrator: Alcoholic narrator who frustrates his wife weekly with his drunken behavior and trivial concerns on Saturday nights. Based on his wife's urging, he eventually adopts sobriety near the middle of the story.

Narrator's wife: Temperate woman and seeming prohibitionist who successfully gets her husband to quit drinking after being subjected to his weekly and frustrating drunken behavior.

• APPENDIX •

"Bartleby, the Scrivener" (1853)

Narrator: Unnamed narrator of the story and master-in-chancery whose legal documents are shoddily transcribed in the afternoon by the alcoholic scrivener Turkey. Turkey's alcoholism and the poor quality of his work in the afternoons put the accuracy of the narrator's sensitive and important legal papers at great risk.

Turkey: Elderly alcoholic scrivener whose work ethic, transcribing accuracy, and calm demeanor are drastically and negatively affected by his excessive mid-day drinking. His alcoholism also puts the narrator's legal documents at great risk. He continues to be an alcoholic at the story's conclusion.

"Benito Cereno" (1855)

Captain Amasa Delano: Captain of the slave ship *San Dominick*. Despite the beliefs that alcohol could cure and prevent many ailments, Captain Delano's mental state and harsh cough are not cured by the liquor that is given to him.

Billy Budd, Sailor (An Inside Narrative) (1924; published posthumously)

Captain Graveling: Captain of the ship *Rights of Man* whose liquor and most valuable sailor (Billy Budd) are essentially stolen by the unscrupulous drinker Lieutenant Ratcliffe.

Lieutenant Ratcliffe: Thievish and unscrupulous lieutenant of the H. M. S. *Bellipotent* who barges onto the *Rights of Man* and subsequently into Captain Graveling's stateroom early in the novella and steals his liquor. He also takes with him Billy Budd, Captain Graveling's most valuable sailor.

"Bridegroom Dick" (1888)

Captain Turret: Alcoholic captain of a man-of-war who when sober is kind and forgiving. Once he is intoxicated, however, he is transformed into a harsh and unforgiving tyrant who shows none of the sober qualities that endear him to his crew.

Lieutenant Tom Tight: After the execution of a sailor who had been charged with mutiny, the alcoholic Lieutenant Tight is approached by other sailors who offer him liquor in the hopes that it will cause him to reveal privileged information concerning the condemned sailor's trial and subsequent execution. Despite drinking, he does not provide the sailors with any of the information that they sought.

Sailors who tempt Lieutenant Tom Tight: After the execution of a

• *Appendix* •

sailor on the charge of mutiny, many sailors approach Lieutenant Tom Tight and supply him with alcohol in the hopes that he will give them confidential information about the sailor's trial and death. Despite being inebriated he does not divulge any information.

Clarel (1876)

The Arnaut: Massive Albanian warrior who in the Mar Saba part of the poem (Part III) becomes enraged that his wine glass is taking so long to be filled. He then begins to fill it himself and in the process becomes intoxicated and barbaric.

The Cypriote's dame / lady: In Part III, Mar Saba, the Cypriote says that he has just delivered wine to his lady that she needed. *Need* is different than *want*, so perhaps this attests to some form of alcohol reliance on her part.

"Cock-A-Doodle-Doo!" (1853)

Bill collector / dun: The narrator's creditor. He is refused payment and physically abused by the alcoholic narrator.

Jake (narrator's servant boy): The servant boy Jake is lied to by the alcoholic narrator and prompted by him to assault the bill collector by throwing potatoes at him after the narrator has violently thrown the dun out of his house.

Merrymusk: The wood sawyer and former wild partier / alcoholic who ten years prior to the narrative gave up the bottle for the sake of his temperate and, at the time, soon-to-be bride.

Merrymusk's wife: The wood sawyer Merrymusk's wife. She is the reason behind Merrymusk's abandonment of alcohol ten years prior to the story's narrative.

Narrator: The unnamed narrator of the story who lives a life filled with various stresses. He uses alcohol as a way of coping with such difficulties yet his alcoholism only exacerbates his innumerable problems including his financial worries. His drunkenness also causes him to become excessively violent toward his bill collector. His drinking problem becomes progressively worse over the course of the story until he is entirely consumed by it at the end of the narrative.

The Confidence-Man (1857)

Charles Arnold Noble: The new friend of Francis Goodman, the confidence man. He drinks (although not as much) with Goodman and is ultimately asked for money. He refuses but later succumbs to the con man's request to drink further, thereby placing him at further risk of eventually being duped out of his money.

• APPENDIX •

Francis Goodman: The confidence man who tries to get money out of Charles Arnold Noble. He drinks continuously in order to gain Noble's trust. He is ultimately unsuccessful.

The old lady of Goshen: Elderly lady who becomes ill and who is then instructed by her doctor to take alcohol in order to cure her ailment. The liquor seems to cure her illness when in reality it is all just an illusion. She ultimately becomes an alcoholic, which will only contribute to further and more harsh medical conditions.

The old lady of Goshen's doctor: He prescribes alcohol for the old lady of Goshen's illness, but the "medicine" he instructs her to take only exacerbates her problems as she later becomes an alcoholic.

The old lady of Goshen's husband (the deacon): He seeks the advice of the doctor for his temperate wife's illness. The doctor then prescribes alcohol for her and she subsequently becomes an alcoholic.

"The Encantadas" ("Hood's Isle and the Hermit Oberlus") (1854)

Oberlus: Alcoholic hermit who had secluded himself on Hood's Isle fifty years prior to the narrative. He uses alcohol against various sailors who come onto what he perceives as his island. Once they are all intoxicated, Oberlus is able to subdue, imprison, and brainwash them. His actions result in the death of some of the sailors.

Sailors: Sailors who come on to Oberlus's Hood's Isle in search of supplies. They are taken advantage of by the hermit Oberlus with alcohol and they are subsequently and as a direct result of their drinking incarcerated, enslaved, and brainwashed. Some of them die.

Israel Potter (1855)

Benjamin Franklin: American ambassador to France who gives Israel Potter and others temperance advice and also his various reasons for abstaining from drinking.

Inn's landlord (Chapter 3): Landlord who stereotypes Israel Potter as a Yankee alcoholic who must therefore need liquor after his time on the run trying to elude capture.

Israel Potter: Israel Potter is offered temperance advice by Benjamin Franklin, uses alcohol to free himself from a nearly inescapable situation, and is then himself taken advantage of with liquor by confidence men when he gets drunk with them. They then kidnap Potter in his drunken state and send him to sea.

Israel Potter's kidnappers: Individuals who are confidence men. They get Israel Potter drunk and later kidnap him and send him to sea.

• *Appendix* •

"Jimmy Rose" (1855)

Jimmy Rose: Titular and formerly affluent character who is taken advantage of for his alcohol by his party-goers who appear to be genuinely fond of him. Once he is ruined financially, however, it becomes clear that his liquor is all that his party-goers truly appreciated.

Party-goers: People who go to Jimmy Rose's numerous parties and who consume excessive amounts of his liquor for free. These same people, however, abandon him once he is ruined financially by poor business handlings and a fierce storm that sinks ships carrying his merchandise.

Mardi (1849)

Borabolla (King of Mondoldo): After celebrating in a speech the purity of his wine, Borabolla is stricken with an onslaught of gout, no doubt caused and exacerbated by his drinking. During the pain that he experiences he vows never to drink alcohol again. Once the pain subsides and like a typical alcoholic, however, he rescinds his promise to abandon the bottle and quickly resumes his drinking.

Hautia: The queen of Flozella-a-Nina who likens wine and its consumption to sinning. Nevertheless, she encourages people to continue drinking.

Taji: *Mardi*'s narrator. As he relates in Chapter 33, he discovers the ill-fated captain of the *Parki*'s secret stash of liquor and decides for a variety of reasons to keep it known only to himself. He periodically returns to it to ensure that it remains undisturbed and, it is clearly implied, that he is the only one who consumes it.

Moby-Dick (1851)

Aunt Charity: Temperate woman who gives Dough-Boy ginger water to smuggle on board the *Pequod* to give to the sailors to drink instead of alcohol.

Captain Ahab: Monomaniacal captain of the *Pequod* who in Chapter 36 gets the sailors to agree with his vengeful plot to kill Moby Dick by giving a dark yet stirring speech while at the same time getting them intoxicated on rum.

***Grampus*'s crew:** Group of whalers who have arrived back in New Bedford after three years at sea. They come into the Spouter Inn where they will be taken advantage of by the bartender Jonah and the alcohol that he serves.

Dr. Jack Bunger: Surgeon on board the whaler *Samuel Enderby*. Although he claims to be a temperate man, the captain says otherwise; Dr. Bunger according to Captain Boomer frequently gets secretly drunk.

Jonah: Unethical bartender at the Spouter Inn. He serves to his cus-

• APPENDIX •

tomers alcohol in glasses that distort for his benefit how much liquor is actually being poured. The sailors are paying more for than what they are actually being served.

Jonah's Spouter Inn customers: All of those who go to the Spouter Inn, where they and their hard-earned money will be taken advantage of by Jonah.

Pequod's crew: At the novel's end, all crew members on board the *Pequod* but Ishmael are killed because they agreed to Captain Ahab's plot to get revenge on the White Whale. They were willing to assist Ahab because they were somewhat under the influence of alcohol at the time of his dark yet inspirational speech.

Perth: Recovered alcoholic blacksmith on board the *Pequod*. Like the old lady of Goshen from *The Confidence-Man* who around the age of sixty had become an alcoholic, Perth's late-life addiction led to the death of his wife and children. Despite giving up the bottle after their deaths and going to sea, the damage that his addiction has caused is irreparable.

Perth's wife and children: When their husband and father Perth becomes an alcoholic around the age of sixty, he fails to continue working and in the process is unable to make a living. As a result, his wife and children are left to starve to death.

Omoo (1847)

Armand-Joseph Bruat: French governor. He uses alcohol against the islanders and gets them heavily intoxicated, hoping that they will become more willing to give up control of the island.

Bungs: The *Julia*'s alcoholic cooper. He and Chips (the ship's carpenter) secretly steal alcohol by siphoning it off the ship's hold. Bungs also betrays his ship-mates in the episode concerning the Round Robin that the crew has signed in protest of the conditions on board the *Julia* and of Captain Guy's behavior. Bungs is an unscrupulous alcoholic who only looks after himself and his own best interests.

Captain Crash: Former British naval officer who lost a ship off New Zealand. Subsequently, he had been making a living by smuggling French alcohol. When the ship *Leviathan* anchors in the harbor he gets drunk with the sailors and causes such a ruckus that the islanders approach them and a riot ensues. Only Crash is brought before the court, however, as it is he who is deemed responsible for the brawl. The tribunal finds him guilty not only of inciting the riot but also for aiding and abetting a fourteen-year-old girl with her "naughtiness" and other crimes. As his punishment he is banned from the island.

Captain Guy: Despised alcoholic captain of the *Julia*. He is also affected by Dr. Long Ghost's excessive drinking when he is knocked unconscious by the doctor during a disagreement between the two concerning politics.

• *Appendix* •

Chips: The *Julia*'s carpenter. He along with the assistance of Bungs (the ship's cooper) secretly steals alcohol by siphoning it off the ship's hold. The two are frequently intoxicated together, leaving the rest of the crew to ponder jealously the source of their alcohol.

Dr. Long Ghost: Alcoholic surgeon on board the *Julia*. He is frequently drunk throughout the novel and his intoxication causes dramatic changes in his behavior, resulting in him assaulting Captain Guy and rendering him unconscious. This act causes him to relinquish his position as the ship's surgeon and to join the rest of the crew in the cramped sleeping quarters. His alcoholism has also cost him the financial security that he once had prior to the narrative.

Fourteen-year-old girl: Young girl who is accused of committing various crimes. Captain Crash, the tribunal believes, is the one responsible for her corruption, claiming that he either forced or assisted her into committing the crimes.

French soldiers: The French soldiers in the novel's thirty-second chapter become an enraged army of uncontrollable drunks who and as the result of their intoxication attempt genocide against the islanders

John Jermin: Alcoholic first-mate of the *Julia*. When he is sober he is a cordial and affable individual; once he becomes intoxicated, however, he is transformed into a harsh and violent brute.

Julia*'s crew:* Not only are many of the *Julia*'s crew members alcoholics (Dr. Long Ghost, John Jermin, Captain Guy), but others are subjected to the harsh treatment that they experience from those including John Jermin and Captain Guy.

Kitoti: The island chief who is taken advantage of by Armand-Joseph Bruat. Bruat uses alcohol against the islanders in order to get them intoxicated in order for them to be more willing to go along with his plan for taking over the island.

Old Mother Tot: Old lady whose alcohol-serving cantina is shut down by the acting British consul Wilson. She later sees and then criticizes the apparent-alcoholic Wilson for being extremely intoxicated himself.

Tahitian islanders: In Chapter 32, the islanders are engaged in a battle with the French soldiers. As the battle continues, the islanders are brutally hunted by the drunken French soldiers. Had it not been for their retreat into the forest, then the islanders would have been exterminated by the French. This excessive use of force by the French soldiers is caused and exacerbated strictly by their inebriation.

Varvy: Alcoholic hermit with whom Dr. Long Ghost gets intoxicated. He offers both Long Ghost and Typee his home-made alcohol; only Long Ghost indulges, resulting in the worst hangover that the doctor has ever had.

Wilson: Acting British consul. He hypocritically shuts down Old Mother Tot's cantina for serving liquor only to be later seen by her heavily intoxicated himself.

• APPENDIX •

"The Paradise of Bachelors" (1855)

The nine bachelors: The nine single men that the narrator and R. F. C. drink with at the Temple Cloisters. Although these nine men seemingly appreciate each others' company, they are truly only selfish and self-centered alcoholics who take advantage of each other and who wish for the party and its accompanying drinking to continue as long as possible.

Pierre (1852)

Isabel Banford: Pierre Glendinning's putative half-sister. As she relates to Pierre, Isabel is subjected to at times harsh treatment by her elderly foster parents while they are under the influence of wine.

Isabel Banford's elderly foster parents: Elderly couple who for a time take care of Isabel during her childhood. At times they are harsh to her, including one notable episode when they are seemingly intoxicated on wine and nearly physically abuse her and then deny her her meal by throwing her supper into the fire.

Mary Glendinning: Pierre Glendinning's mother. Once she begins to feel separation from her son she tells him that if he were ever to leave her that she would deal with her loss by seeking solace in her wine and eventually become an alcoholic wine bibber.

Pierre Glendinning: Titular character. He comes to rely on alcohol in order to cope with the various stresses that he is experiencing while writing his novel. He is eventually able to overcome his use of alcohol as a coping mechanism.

Redburn (1849)

Captain Riga: Alcoholic captain of the *Highlander*. His drinking problem has put him so deeply in debt that he upon returning to the United States is unable to pay Harry Bolton or Wellingborough Redburn what they are truly owed for their services on board the ship; Riga's alcoholism affects the financial security of others.

The Greenlander: Unscrupulous sailor on board the *Highlander* who extorts money for his alcohol addiction from the stuttering passenger.

***Highlander*'s crew:** There are numerous instances throughout the novel where the *Highlander* crew's alcoholism is on display both on and off the ship.

Liverpool's bartenders: Bartenders at the taverns in Liverpool who Redburn compares to various vile creatures who take advantage of their customers with the alcohol that they serve them.

Liverpool's destitute (swipe drinkers): Poor people of Liverpool who continue as Redburn relates to spend whatever money they have

Appendix

on the poor-quality beer called swipes. Their expenditure on swipes simply contributes further to their financial difficulties.

Miguel Saveda: Sailor who boards the *Highlander* heavily intoxicated. Many hours later he through the process of spontaneous combustion bursts into flames and is subsequently thrown overboard by the sailors on deck.

Passed out drinker on tomb: Alcoholic who has passed out on Tobias Drinker's tomb in the cemetery near the Church of St. Nicholas, foreshadowing the fate that will ultimately be his.

Shrieking suicidal drunken sailor: Unnamed sailor on board the *Highlander*. During a fit of the delirium tremens he runs on deck from below and jumps overboard into the ocean, thereby committing suicide.

Stuttering passenger: Passenger on board the *Highlander* who tends to his own business throughout the voyage but who is nevertheless taken advantage of by the Greenlander. The stuttering passenger must give the Greenlander money for alcohol before the Greenlander releases him from the "spread eagle."

Tobias Drinker: Deceased character who, as him name implies, has been doomed by alcohol. It is on Drinker's tomb that another passed-out alcoholic rests.

Wellingborough Redburn: Titular narrator who is denied his due pay at the novel's end by Captain Riga, who is unable to remunerate him due to the debt that he has incurred from his drinking problem.

"The Scout Toward Aldie" (1866)

The Colonel: Gives his prisoner Reb alcohol in the hopes that it will cause Reb to reveal important information concerning the location of Mosby's Raiders.

Reb: Confederate prisoner of the Colonel's men. He is tempted with drink by the Colonel to reveal vital and classified information about Mosby's Raiders. Reb accepts the offer but is not tricked into giving the Colonel any information.

"The Two Temples" (1924; published posthumously)

Narrator: Nameless narrator who is stereotyped by the young English bartender as being a typical world-renowned American drunkard.

Young English boy bartender: Stereotypes the narrator and all Americans in general as being alcoholics who would always be interested in drinking.

• APPENDIX •

Typee (1846)

English harbor pilot: Former British naval officer who prior to the narrative had his rank and reputation destroyed by his alcoholism and associated criminal activity. He has by the early part of the novel joined the French and been appointed pilot of the harbor. As is clear in the episodes related, he continues to be afflicted with alcoholism.

King Mehevi: Closet alcoholic. Despite being a member of the Hawaiian Temperance Society he continues to drink constantly.

"Under the Rose" (1924; published posthumously)

Greek translator: Alcoholic and one-armed Greek translator who is unable or unwilling to perform any duties unless he is intoxicated. He agrees to translate a poem for the Ambassador, but states that he is in need of wine in order to do so.

White-Jacket (1850)

Bland: Master-at-arms on board the *Neversink* who is instructed by Captain Claret to find out who has been smuggling liquor onto the ship. The smuggler is eventually identified as the despicable Scriggs, but Scriggs in an attempt to save himself reveals the truth behind his smuggling racket: the master-at-arms Bland is his accomplice. Bland nevertheless is let off easy compared to Scriggs by Captain Claret.

Captain Claret: Alcoholic captain of the *Neversink* who at times relies on Mad Jack to take control of the ship. He is also infuriated with the smuggling that occurs on board his vessel so he instructs the master-at-arms Bland to find out who is responsible. A seaman named Scriggs is ultimately identified as the smuggler, but then Scriggs in an attempt to save himself reveals that Bland is his accomplice. Captain Claret punishes Scriggs harshly yet does very little to reprimand the master-at-arms Bland.

Cockswain: Smuggler who assembles a team of men to smuggle alcohol on board the *Neversink*. One of his accomplices gets drunk on shore, however, and is then overheard by the old sheet-anchor-man talking about the smuggling racket. The Cockswain is then blackmailed by the sheet-anchor-man: hand over his liquor or be exposed as a smuggler. Not wanting to risk being flogged for his activity, the Cockswain begrudgingly complies.

Landless (Happy Jack): Alcoholic sailor on board the *Neversink* who freely admits to White-Jacket that rum and tobacco are truly all that he and the other sailors desire.

Mad Jack: A beloved lieutenant of the *Neversink* who suffers from an

• *Appendix* •

addiction to alcohol and who is indirectly offered temperance advice by White-Jacket. Despite being an alcoholic, he is able to refrain from drinking during times that require him to be alert, such as when Captain Claret is too intoxicated to guide the ship safely in areas that are renowned for, among other dangers, fierce storms.

Mandeville: Disgraced former naval officer who ultimately joins the *Neversink*'s crew as a lowly seaman and where he is reunited with his former fellow officer: the ship's first lieutenant, Lieutenant Bridewell. Despite Bridewell's warning to Mandeville about his alcoholism and the professional and physical destruction that his addiction to liquor has caused him in the past, Mandeville is unable to overcome his love of drink and within just a few days of joining the ship he is found yet again to be intoxicated on board and while on duty on smuggled spirits. Once again he is flogged for his actions.

Neversink's **crew:** Throughout the novel it seems that the entire crew of the *Neversink* is either an alcoholic, a smuggler of spirits, or both.

Old toper of a top-man: Alcoholic sailor on board the *Neversink* who tells White-Jacket that he will never give up his grog, despite knowing full-well that it is in a variety of ways destroying him.

Scriggs: A deplorable sailor on the *Neversink*. He is in cahoots with the master-at-arms Bland in smuggling liquor on board the ship. Once Scriggs is identified as the one who has been bringing the alcohol illegally on board, he turns on and outs Bland in an attempt to save himself. Scriggs is locked up in the brig for his illegal activity while Bland is let off relatively easy.

Sheet-anchor-man: Individual on board the *Neversink* who overhears one of the Cockswain's accomplices talking about the smuggled liquor that is about to be brought on board. The sheet-anchor-man approaches the Cockswain and tells him that if he fails to give over the alcohol then he will report the Cockswain as a smuggler, at which point he will be certainly flogged. The Cockswain has no choice but to comply.

Yarn: The *Neversink*'s boatswain who successfully smuggles liquor on board and stores it in his stateroom. He is witnessed doing so, however, and before he can secure his contraband it is stolen by the unscrupulous alcoholic sailor who had seen him putting it into his room.

Chapter Notes

Preface

1. Richard Worth, *Teetotallers and Saloon Smashers: The Temperance Movement and Prohibition* (New York: Enslow, 2009), p. 21.

2. Although most of Melville's works considered herein were written from 1846 (*Typee*) to 1856 ("The Apple-Tree Table"), others relevant works such as *Clarel*, "Bridegroom Dick," and *Billy Budd, Sailor* were written and / or published in the last quarter of the nineteenth century (*Billy Budd* was published posthumously; 1924).

3. As Ryan C. Cordell also notes, "much literary criticism" of the mid-nineteenth century "fails to account for—or even notice—temperance at all, though in reach, scope, and longevity it was the dominant reform movement of its day, especially in the middle classes ("'Enslaving You Body and Soul': The Uses of Temperance in *Uncle Tom's Cabin* and 'Anti-Tom' Fiction," *Studies in American Fiction* 36 [2008]: 3).

4. I borrow the phrase about book shelves groaning due to the weight of Melville criticism from Eugene McNamara's review of Richard Harter Fogle's critical study *Melville's Shorter Tales* (1960). When I was a graduate student at the University of Windsor (Ontario, Canada), where McNamara is a professor emeritus, I purchased a copy of Fogle's book in a quaint used book store in Windsor. In it was a cut-out copy of the newspaper review. Tragically, the snippet provided no indication for proper citation of the review.

5. Edwin Haviland Miller, *Melville* (New York: George Braziller, 1975); Laurie Robertson-Lorant, *Melville: A Biography* (New York: Clarkson Potter, 1996); Hershel Parker, *Herman Melville: A Biography*, 2 vols. (Baltimore: Johns Hopkins University Press, 1996–2002). Checking the respective indexes in Roberton-Lorant's and Parker's biographies under the search words and terms "Temperance movement" (Parker 1: 938), "Alcohol and alcoholism" (Parker 2: 969), and "Melville, Herman, and drinking" (Robertson-Lorant 699) will provide readers with the many references to drinking and drunkenness in both Melville's life and in his society. Melville's drinking was so frequent, or so many believe, that even in creative works about him he is represented to the point of exaggeration and farcically as an alcoholic. See, for instance, Jay Parini's novel *Passions of H. M.: A Novel of Herman Melville* (New York: Doubleday, 2010) and Rick Mitchell's play *The Composition of Herman Melville* (Bris-

tol: Intellect Books, 2002). Some of the discussion of Melville's drinking by Miller and Robertson-Lorant is based on more hypothetical rather than factual information and therefore at times creates controversies concerning the type of drinker Melville was. Parker's discussion of Melville's drinking is consistently supported with factual documentation.

6. See W. J. Rorabaugh's groundbreaking study *The Alcoholic Republic: An American Tradition* (Oxford: Oxford University Press, 1979) and Sharon Sallinger, *Taverns and Drinking in Early America* (Baltimore: Johns Hopkins University Press, 2002).

7. See, for instance, Corey Evan Thompson's "Herman Melville's 'The Apple-Tree Table' as Temperance Fiction," *The Explicator* 71 (2013): 135–139 and "The Prodromal Phase of Alcoholism in Herman Melville's 'Bartleby, the Scrivener' and 'Cock-A-Doodle-Doo!,'" *The Explicator* 71 (2013): 275–280 (both of which in somewhat different forms appear in this study). Also, see parts of David S. Reynolds' *Beneath the American Renaissance* (Oxford: Oxford University Press, 1988) and "Black Cats and Delirium Tremens: Temperance and the American Renaissance," *The Serpent in the Cup: Temperance in American Literature*, eds. Debra Rosenthal and David S. Reynolds (Amherst: University of Massachusetts Press, 1997), pp. 22–59, and page 38 in Paul McCarthy's *"The Twisted Mind": Madness in Herman Melville's Fiction* (Iowa City: University of Iowa Press, 1990).

8. Herman Melville, *White-Jacket*, eds. Harrison Hayford, Hershel Parker, and G. Thomas Tanselle (1850; Evanston: Northwestern University Press, 1970), p. 176.

9. For an excellent and user-friendly introduction to literary theory and criticism that clearly differentiates the various means of literary analysis, see, among others, Steven Lynn, *Texts and Contexts: Writing About Literature with Critical Theory*, 2d ed. (New York: Longman, 1998).

Introduction

1. Ralph Waldo Emerson, "The Poet," *Emerson's Essays: First and Second Series* (New York: Gramercy, 1995), p. 209. Emerson makes this claim believing that such indulgence gives poets and other literary types "extraordinary power to their normal powers" of artistic creativity (209). For an extended study that examines the link between artistic creativity and alcoholism, see Olivia Laing's book *The Trip to Echo Spring: Why Writers Drink* (Edinburgh: Canongate Books, 2013).

2. For discussion of such writers' various addictions see Milton Meltzer, *Edgar Allan Poe: A Biography* (Minneapolis: Lerner, 2003); Jeffery Meyers, *Hemingway: A Biography* (New York: Da Capo, 1986); Edward O'Reilly, *F. Scott Fitzgerald: A Biography* (Westport, CT: Greenwood, 2005); David Minter, *William Faulkner: His Life and Work* (Baltimore: Johns Hopkins University Press, 1997); Tom Clark, *Jack Kerouac: A Biography* (New York: Da Capo, 2001). Female writers, naturally, are not exempt from addiction. Elizabeth Bishop and Dorothy Parker, for instance, both struggled with alcohol abuse. See Brett C. Miller, *Elizabeth Bishop: Life and the Memory of It* (Berkeley: University of California Press, 1993); Marion Meade, *Dorothy Parker: What Fresh Hell is This?* (New York: Penguin, 1989).

3. Lewis Mumford, *Herman Melville* (New York: Harcourt, Brace, 1929), p. 156; David Laskin, *A Common Life: Four Generations of American Literary Friendship and Influence* (New York: Simon & Schuster, 1994), pp. 29–30, 64. Hennig Cohen also alludes to Melville's appreciation of the social aspect of drinking when he states that "For Melville, wine, Burgundy or Falemian, represented geniality, a quality in short supply in the rather withdrawn life that he led at the time" (Hennig Cohen, ed., *Selected Poems of Herman Melville* [New York: Fordham University Press, 1992], p. 258). Arrowhead is the name that Melville gave to the farmhouse on the outskirts

of Pittsfield, Massachusetts, that he purchased in 1850. It was his residence from 1850–1863 and he named it such due to the Native American artefacts including literal arrow heads that he found scattered throughout the 160 acre property.

4. Charles Olson, *Call Me Ishmael* (1947; Baltimore: Johns Hopkins University Press, 1997), p. 92; Elizabeth Hardwick, *Herman Melville* (New York: Viking, 2000), pp. 52, 111; Elizabeth Renker, "Herman Melville, Wife Beating, and the Written Page," *American Literature* 66 (1994): 123–150; Joseph Adamson, *Melville, Shame, and the Evil Eye* (Albany: State University of New York Press, 1997), p. 25. Carl Rollyson and Lisa Paddock, *Herman Melville A to Z: The Essential Reference to his Life and Work* (New York: Facts on File, 2001), p. 119. Paul Metcalf, Melville's great grandson, refers to such allegations in a letter that he wrote to Clare Sparke in February of 1988. He discusses the rumors "about Herman beating on Lizzie, about Herman coming home one night drunk and throwing her down the back stairs." Indirectly distancing himself from such allegations attributed to his great grandfather, Metcalf doubts how much of this story is true "or how much was embellished (or even invented)" (Paul Metcalf, ed., *Enter Isabel: The Herman Melville Correspondence of Clare Sparke and Paul Metcalf* [Albuquerque: University of New Mexico Press, 1991], pp. 14–15).

5. Raychel Haugrud Reiff, *Herman Melville: "Moby-Dick" and Other Works* (Tarrytown: Marshall Cavendish, 2008), p. 24. Laurie Robertson-Lorant has also asserted that Melville used alcohol as a type of medicinal painkiller for his various health issues: "In the mid–1850s, Melville suffered attacks of sciatica and rheumatism that drove him to summon his neighbour, Dr. Oliver Wendell Holmes, Jr., and to use alcohol as a painkiller in conjunction with the medicine Dr. Holmes prescribed" ("Melville and the Women in his Life," *Melville and Women*, eds. Elizabeth Schultz and Haskell Springer [Kent, OH: Kent State University Press, 2006], p. 29).

6. See also Bradley A. Johnson, *The Characteristic Theology of Herman Melville* (Eugene: Pickwick Publications, 2012), p. 95.

7. John J. Ross, "The Many Ailments of Herman Melville," *Journal of Medical Biography* 16 (2008): 21–29.

8. Lynn Michelsohn, Afterword, *In the Galapagos Islands with Herman Melville: "The Encantadas, or Enchanted Isles."* By Herman Melville (Roswell: Cleanan Press, 2011), p. 139.

9. John Bryant, "Herman Melville: A Writer in Process," *Herman Melville: Tales, Poems, and Other Writings*, ed. John Bryant (New York: Modern Library, 2002), p. xxxix; Andrew Delbanco, *Herman Melville: His World and Work* (New York: Knopf, 2005), pp. 275–276. Melville's granddaughter, Eleanor Melville Metcalf, believed that the "closing-in" of Melville's life during the 1870s "drove him at times to desperate irascibility and the solace of brandy" (*Herman Melville: Cycle and Epicycle* [Cambridge: Harvard University Press, 1953], p. 215).

10. Robert Milder, *Exiled Royalties: Melville and the Life We Imagine* (Oxford: Oxford University Press, 2006), p. 187.

11. Various references to and discussions of Melville's own drinking will occur throughout this study's nine chapters and Conclusion. For the most thorough (and although at times repetitive) illustration of Melville's own factual experiences with alcohol and intoxication, though, see the Afterword.

12. Reynolds' focus typically rests on *Redburn*, *White-Jacket*, and *Moby-Dick*. See his works *Beneath the American Renaissance* and "Black Cats and Delirium Tremens: Temperance and the American Renaissance" for his temperance / alcohol-related discussion of these works.

13. In terms of established literary conventions, "The Bell-Tower" has much more in common with traditional British Gothic literature than it does with the American Gothic. See Corey Evan Thompson's "The Locale of Melville's Gothicism" for further discussion of the differences between British

and American Gothic literary conventions and, more specifically, of how "The Bell-Tower" adheres more to the British than American Gothic literary mode (*Papers on Language and Literature* 43 [2007]: 190–193).

14. Herman Melville, "The Fiddler," *Great Short Works of Herman Melville*, ed. Warner Berthoff (New York: Perennial Classics, 2004), pp. 195, 197. All subsequent references to Melville's short fiction are from this edition and will be cited parenthetically in the text. Although alcohol plays no major role in "The Fiddler," the story nonetheless inversely enters into Melville's commentary on temperance. See note 27 to Chapter 2 for further discussion.

15. Alcohol also has a minor presence in the second half of the diptych "Poor Man's Pudding and Rich Man's Crumbs" (1854) when the narrator's guide discusses the amount of money spent on food and wine (174), and in canto four, "The Cypriote," Part III, Mar Saba, in *Clarel* when the Cypriote talks about bringing his lady her "holy wine" (Herman Melville, *Clarel*, ed. Walter E. Bezanson [1876; New York: Hendricks House, 1960] III, iv, line 75). Considering the Cypriote's words—he says that his dame is in "need" of her wine (75)—there is possibly more than a simple appreciation of alcohol on the dame's part. *Need* implies a necessity that goes beyond mere desire and could therefore suggest a dependency on or addiction to alcohol. The text is not clear enough in this regard to substantiate such a claim.

16. As far as we know, "The Two-Temples" is the only short story that Melville composed during the 1853–1856 short fiction stage of his literary career that was rejected for publication. *Putnam's Monthly Magazine* editor Charles F. Briggs describes in a 12 May 1854 letter to Melville the rationale behind the story's rejection: "I am very loth to reject the Two Temples as the article contains some exquisitely fine description, and some pungent satire, but my editorial experience compels me to be very cautious in offending the religious sensibilities of the public, and the moral of the Two Temples would array against us the whole power of the pulpit, to say nothing of Brown, and the congregation of Grace Church" (Jay Leyda, *The Melville Log: A Documentary Life of Herman Melville, 1819–1891*, 2 vols. [1951; New York: Gordian, 1969 with supplement], p. 1: 487).

17. Melville crossed the Atlantic and spent time in Liverpool in both 1839 and 1849. He also had various experiences on board whaling vessels including the *Acushnet* and the *Lucy-Ann* and on the man-of-war *United States* during his time at sea between 1841 and 1844. Since such experiences clearly served as sources of influence for his work, it should be no surprise that his, his family's, and his society's association with alcohol would also play such a prominent role in his writings.

18. The term "American Renaissance" was originated by F. O. Matthiessen in his *American Renaissance: Art and Expression in the Era of Emerson and Whitman* (Oxford: Oxford University Press, 1941). Matthiessen's study covers the period from 1850 to 1855; however, subsequent critics have expanded the years of consideration for the American Renaissance to cover roughly from the 1830s up to the Civil War.

19. Robert S. Levine, "Fiction and Reform I," *The Columbian History of the American Novel*, eds. Emory Elliot et al. (Oxford: Oxford University Press, 1991), p. 138.

20. In addition to the references to drinking from his sent letters and journals, we know that Melville was a frequent drinker with a seemingly high tolerance for alcohol from correspondences that he received. In a 4 January 1861 letter to Melville, for instance, Richard Tobias Greene—with whom Melville abandoned the whaling ship *Acushnet* in 1842—expresses his hope to drink with Melville and that Melville would still be able to imbibe his "'five shares of duff!'" (Herman Melville, *Correspondence*, ed. Lynn Horth [Evanston: Northwestern University Press, 1993], p. 679).

21. Herman Melville, "Bridegroom Dick," *Selected Poems of Herman Melville*, ed. Robert Penn Warren (New York: Barnes and Noble, 1970), line 258.

22. Melville also compares wine drinking to vices in the first of these episodes (Herman Melville, *Moby-Dick*, eds. Hershel Parker and Harrison Hayford [1851; New York: Norton, 2002], pp. 27, 369, 27).

23. Melville makes this damning remark in *Omoo* when he states that the evil "effects of drunkenness" on the islanders "are solely of foreign origin" (Herman Melville, *Omoo* [1847; Minneola: Dover, 2000], p. 179).

24. Drinking is also associated with sinning in Chapter 194 of *Mardi* when Hautia, the queen of Flozella-a-Nina, says: "'Come! let us sin and be merry. Ho! wine, wine, wine!'" (Herman Melville, *Mardi*, eds. Harrison Hayford, Hershel Parker, and G. Thomas Tanselle [1849; Evanston: Northwestern University Press, 1986], p. 650).

25. Herman Melville, *Billy Budd, Sailor (An Inside Narrative)*, eds. Harrison Hayford and Merton M. Sealts, Jr., (1924; Chicago: University of Chicago Press, 1962), p. 76.

26. Stanton Garner et al., "Biographers on Biography: A Panel Discussion," *Melville's Evermoving Dawn: Centennial Essays*, eds. John Bryant and Robert Milder (Kent, OH: Kent State University Press, 1997), p. 244.

27. This argument is in contrast to Paul McCarthy's viewpoint that Melville's characters are only "usually" adversely affected by alcohol (38).

28. One of very few, Brett Zimmerman has previously and accurately noted, albeit with no specific explanation or textual reference as to why, that the narrator's wife from "The Apple-Tree Table" "seems to be a supporter of temperance" (*Edgar Allan Poe: Rhetoric and Style* [Montreal: McGill-Queen's University Press, 2005], p. 363n12).

29. Jay Leyda, Introduction, *The Portable Melville*, ed. Jay Leyda (New York: Viking, 1952), p. xi. Richard Chase has expressed a similar viewpoint, stating that in his writings Melville "is seeking to establish fictional representations of himself, of the differing sides of his own temperament, of the personal situation in which he finds himself" (Introduction, *Herman Melville: Selected Tales and Poems*, ed. Richard Chase [1950; New York: Holt, Rinehart and Winston, 1968], p. v).

Chapter 1

1. Debra Rosenthal and David Reynolds, Introduction, *The Serpent in the Cup: Temperance in American Literature*, eds. Debra Rosenthal and David Reynolds (Amherst: University of Massachusetts Press, 1997), p. 2. See also W. J. Rorabaugh for discussion of the connection between the church and the tavern in early America (28).

2. Kenneth D. Rose, *American Women and the Repeal of Prohibition* (New York: New York University Press, 1996), p. 12. Rose's study contains a graph that show a near seven-gallon average consumption rate during this period, which far exceeds Rosenthal and Reynolds' and Rorabaugh's (by comparison) conservative estimates. This would suggest, as later in the text illustrates, that Americans during the 1830s were consuming more than twice the amount of alcohol than they are in the early twenty-first century.

3. World Health Organization, *Global Status Report on Alcohol and Health* (Geneva: World Health Organization [WHO], 2014), p. 291. The WHO's measurements of America's drinking is measured in litres and found that Americans consumed on average approximately 9 litres of pure alcohol during the period of their study. There are 3.8 litres per gallon, so 9 litres / 3.8 gallons = 2.36 gallons. This means that Americans in the 1830s were possibly drinking nearly three times as much as they are now. Given the social emphasis on club-culture in popular media and on the advertising that glorifies alcohol consumption in the twenty-first century, it is almost impossible to believe the

nonetheless accurate fact that Americans on average currently consume far less than those in the early to mid-nineteenth century.

4. Klaus P. Stich, "Well Tempered Temperance: Hawthorne's Dionysian Aspect," *The New England Quarterly* 68 (1995): 83.

5. Nicholas O. Warner, "God's Wine and Devil's Wine: The Idea of Intoxication in Emerson," *Mosaic* 19 (1986): 56.

6. A Letter to the Mechanics of Boston, Respecting the Formation of a City Temperance Society (Boston: Society for the Suppression of Intemperance, 1831), p. 5.

7. We know that the short story was written during the first half of the 1850s from the 12 May 1854 rejection letter that Melville received for "The Two Temples" from Charles F. Briggs, the editor of *Putnam's Monthly Magazine*. See note 16 to the Introduction for an excerpt from the rejection letter.

8. Herman Melville, *Israel Potter*, eds. Harrison Hayford, Hershel Parker, and G. Thomas Tanselle (1855; Evanston: Northwestern University Press, 1993), p. 15.

9. Carol Mattingly, Introduction, *Water Drops for Women Writers: A Temperance Reader*, ed. Carol Mattingly (Carbondale: Southern Illinois University Press, 2004), p. 1.

10. Andrew J. Furer, "From 'Water Drops' to General Strikes: Nineteenth- and-Early Twentieth-Century Short Fiction and Social Change," *A Companion to the American Short Story*, eds. Alfred Bendixen and James Nagel (Chischester: Wiley-Blackwell, 2010), p. 188.

11. Temperance dramas were also common during this time. At the theatre, plays including William Henry Smith's *The Drunkard; or, The Fallen Saved* did much to promote the cause in the arts beyond the printed word of temperance novels and magazine stories.

12. Although being a work of temperance fiction, *Franklin Evans* has been heavily criticized and scoffed at by critics. F. O. Matthiessen, for instance, describes it as a "hack" novel (600n2). Moreover, it appears that Whitman was more interested in the financial gains that he stood to make as a result of writing temperance fiction as it was "a most popular and profitable subject for writers appealing to a mass audience" (T. J. Matheson, "Poe's 'The Black Cat' as a Critique of Temperance Literature," *Mosaic* 19 [1986]: 72). Money was for some more important than truly spreading the message of temperance (Jennifer Hynes, "Temperance Movement," *The Routledge Encyclopedia of Walt Whitman*, ed. J. R. LeMaster and Donald Kummings [New York: Routledge, 1998], p. 710) as Whitman had purportedly admitted to writing *Franklin Evans* "on the strength of a full bottle of liquor" (Amanda Claybaugh, *The Novel of Purpose: Literature and Social Reform in the Anglo-American World* [Ithaca: Cornell University Press, 2007], p. 49). It has been suggested, however, that he simply made such comments as he himself was not pleased with the quality of his own work.

13. For discussion of these works as temperance fiction, see Debra Rosenthal, "Temperance and Miscegenation in Whitman's *Franklin Evans*," *Race Mixture in Nineteenth-Century U.S. & Spanish American Fiction* (Chapel Hill: North Carolina University Press, 2004), pp. 52–68; Alison Easton, *The Making of the Hawthorne Subject* (Columbia: University of Missouri Press, 1996), pp. 68–69.

14. Joann E. Castanga, "Arthur, Timothy Arthur," *American Masculinities: A Historical Encyclopedia*, ed. Bret Carroll (Thousand Oakes: Sage, 2004), pp. 36–37. Although primarily remembered for his temperance work *Ten Nights in a Barroom*, Arthur also wrote more than 200 novels and shorter works and "uncounted" short pieces in magazines (Castanga 36–37).

15. Walter Issacson, *Benjamin Franklin: An American Life* (New York: Simon & Schuster, 2003), p. 53.

16. Franklin Parks, *William Parks: The Colonial Printer in the Transatlantic World of the Eighteenth Century* (University Park: Pennsylvania State University Press, 2012), p. 52.

17. Franklin's sentiments similarly appear also in *Pierre* when it is stated "hasty words, impulsively returning a blow, fits of domestic petulance selfish enjoyment of a glass of wine while he knows there are those around him who lack a loaf of bread" (Herman Melville, *Pierre*, eds. Harrison Hayford, Hershel Parker, and G. Thomas Tanselle [1852; Evanston: Northwestern University Press, 1971], p. 214).

18. Karen Sanchez-Eppler, "Temperance in the Bed of a Child: Incest and Social Order in Nineteenth-Century America," *American Quarterly* 47 (1995): 3.

19. Although it was published in 1986, Lea Bertani Vozar Newman's *A Reader's Guide to the Short Stories of Herman Melville* (Boston: G. K. Hall, 1986) is still an invaluable resource that gives a plot synopsis and an overview of the critical history of Melville's short fiction. Each of her entries clearly illustrates the countless interpretations that many of Melville's short stories have received.

20. An exception to this claim occurs in Corey Evan Thompson's essay "Melville's 'Cock-A-Doodle-Doo!': A Case Study in Bipolar Disorder," *American Transcendental Quarterly* 17 (2003): 49, where the narrator's bibulousness is discussed briefly in relation to his apparent manic depression.

21. As Arnd Bohm rightfully asks, where precisely will the narrator get this money from in order to buy the rooster ("Wordsworth in Melville's 'Cock-A-Doodle-Doo!," *Leviathan: A Journal of Melville Studies* [9: 2007]: 33)? He is already deeply in debt, as will be discussed in further detail in Chapter 7. In my view, however, Bohm's criticism of Merrymusk for "preposterously" refusing the narrator's offer (33), unrealistic as it is based on his penury, overlooks the spiritual benefits that the rooster has for his family. Merrymusk does not need the money to feed his family because, as we are told by the narrator, "his family never suffered for lack of food. He worked hard and brought it to them" (89).

22. Using characters such as Merrymusk's wife as evidence, it has long been asserted that Melville's writings are misogynistic and that his works contain no significant female characters. In 1926, for instance, the English poet John Freeman called attention to what he perceived as the "rare female presence" in Melville fiction ("The Spiritual Counterpart of *Moby-Dick*," *Critical Essays on Melville's "Pierre*," eds. Brian Higgins and Hershel Parker [Boston: G. K. Hall, 1983], p. 116), while Lewis Mumford, in his 1929 biography of Melville, discredited the female presence in works including *Moby-Dick* altogether (201). Twenty years later and in his own critical biography of Melville, Newton Arvin continued to promote such views, describing most of the women in Melville works as "dimly seen" (*Herman Melville* [New York: Viking, 1950], p. 50). More recently, the women in Melville's writings have been regarded as "virtually absent" (Michael Paul Rogin, *Subversive Genealogy: The Politics and Art of Herman Melville* [1979; New York: Knopf, 1983], p. 48), "often absent" (Caroline Levander, "The Female Subject of *Pierre* and *The Piazza Tales*," *A Companion to Herman Melville*, ed. Wyn Kelley [Oxford: Blackwell, 2006], p. 423), "markedly absent" (Adamson 26), and as "simply not there in any substantial sense" (Rollyson and Paddock 220). Such incorrect views, however, have been largely rectified by Corey Evan Thompson, "Melville's 'The Apple-Tree Table,'" *The Explicator* 64 (2005): 38–41; David Dowling, "'Parlors, Sofas, and Fine Cambrics': Gender Play in Melville's Narrations," *Leviathan: A Journal of Melville Studies* 11 (2009): 37–54; and by the contributors to Haskell Springer and Elizabeth Schultz's edited volume *Melville and Women* (Kent, OH: Kent State University Press, 2006). Each of these critics clearly illustrate not only that women are far more prevalent in Melville's works than previous generations of critics have claimed, but that the female characters also have significant roles in much of his fiction and poetry.

23. William Kerrigan, *Johnny Appleseed and the American Orchard: A Cul-*

tural History (Baltimore: Johns Hopkins University Press, 2012), p. 148.

24. Since the story is set in one of the oldest towns in America, it is highly likely that "The Apple-Tree Table" is set in New England, thereby reinforcing Melville's use of the apple-tree as a symbol of temperance. New England was settled in the early decades of the seventeenth century. The references to Cotton Mather throughout the story also reinforce the New England connection as he lived in and was an influential New England Puritan minister.

25. Barbara Welter, "The Cult of True Womanhood: 1820–1860," *American Quarterly* 18 (1966): 151–174. Stemming from the changing notions of the home that accompanied burgeoning industrial America, there developed a new ideal that was evident in the era's women's magazines and religious journals that provided a new view of women's roles in society. Whereas men were believed to be naturally active, dominant, assertive, and materialistic, women served as their more refined counterparts. They "inherently" possessed such virtues as piety, purity, submissiveness, and domesticity.

26. It could possibly be argued that "The Apple-Tree Table"'s narrator is William Ford, the same narrator of "Jimmy Rose." As countless critics including Richard Harter Fogle have duly noted, "The Apple-Tree Table," "Jimmy Rose," and "I and My Chimney" all contain a narrator (he is named as William Ford only in "Jimmy Rose") who has an unnamed wife, two daughters (Anna and Julia in "The Apple-Tree Table" and "I and My Chimney" but unnamed in "Jimmy Rose"), and a maidservant named Biddy (Richard Harter Fogle, *Melville's Shorter Tales* [Norman: University of Oklahoma Press, 1960], p. 79). See also Rollyson and Paddock (5).

27. Marvin Fisher, *Going Under: Melville's Short Fiction and the American 1850s* (Baton Rouge: Louisiana State University Press, 1977), p. 124.

28. Gothic literature is typically wrought with hyperbolic emotion and irrational fears.

Chapter 2

1. Peter Burne, *The Teetotaller's Companion; Or, A Plea for Temperance* (Ipswich: J. M. Burton, 1847), p. 34.

2. William White, "The Lessons of Language: Historical Perspectives on the Rhetoric of Addiction," *Altering American Consciousness: The History of Alcohol and Drug Use in the United States, 1800–2000*, eds. Sarah W. Tracy and Caroline Jean Acker (Amherst: University of Massachusetts Press, 2004), p. 34.

3. Maria Gifford with Stacey Friedman and Rich Majerus, *Alcoholism* (Westport, CT: Greenwood, 2010), p. 119. See Jellinek's *The Disease Concept of Alcoholism* (New Haven: Hillhouse, 1960). Jellinek's theory of prodromal phase alcoholism has been supported by contributors to an international conference on alcoholism: "An alcoholic's life is consumed with feelings of guilt, shame, anxiety, and remorse, causing him to drink all that much more to attempt an escape of life's problems" (Claudia Black, "Effects of Family Alcoholism," *Alcoholism and the Family*, eds. Satoru Saitho and Marc A. Schuckit [Tokyo: Seiwa Shoten, 1992], p. 277).

4. *Pierre* is "saturated" with Shakespeare's influence (Parker, *Melville* 2: 56). For discussion of the novel's indebtedness to the Bard see Sanford E. Marovitz, "Shakespearean Resonances in *Moby-Dick* and *Pierre*," *Melville Among the Nations: Proceedings of an International Conference, Volos, Greece, July 2–6, 1997*, eds. Sanford E. Marovitz and A. C. Christodoulou (Kent, OH: Kent State University Press, 2001), pp. 267–276. For overall influence, see also and among many others Roma Rosen, *Melville's Use of Shakespeare's Plays* (Evanston: Northwestern University Press, 1962), and, as it relates specifically to Shakespeare and *Moby-Dick*, Julian Markels, *Melville and the Politics of Identity: From "King Lear" to "Moby-Dick"* (Urbana: University of Illinois Press, 1993).

5. Is Melville perhaps suggesting a hereditary connection about alcoholism?

• Notes—Chapter 2 •

Alcoholism possibly ran throughout Melville's family on both sides. His cousins Thomas Wilson Melvill and Guert Gansevoort had issues with alcohol, as possibly did his son Stanwix (Robertson-Lorant, *Melville* 89). For discussion about alcoholism's possible hereditary trait, see Donald Goodwin, *Is Alcoholism Hereditary?* (New York: Ballantine, 1988).

6. Wyn Kelley, Melville's City: Literary and Urban Form in Nineteenth-Century New York (Cambridge: Cambridge University Press, 1996), p. 154.

7. See, among others, Nicholas Knowles Bromwell, *By The Sweat of the Brow: Literature and Labor in Antebellum America* (Chicago: University of Chicago Press, 1993), p. 72; Dan McCall, *The Silence of "Bartleby"* (Ithaca: Cornell University Press, 1989), p. 112; Sharon Talley, *Student Companion to Herman Melville* (Westport, CT: Greenwood, 2007), p. 87; Julie Brown, *Writers on the Spectrum: How Autism and Asperger Syndrome Have Influenced Literary Writing* (Philadelphia: Jessica Kingsley, 2010), p. 85.

8. Critics who have diagnosed Turkey with a condition other than alcoholism include Robert Milder, who believes that Turkey is a manic depressive (*Exiled* 189), and Dieter Meindl, who simply classifies the elderly scrivener as "sanguine" (*Fiction and the Metaphysics of the Grotesque* [Columbia: University of Missouri Press, 1996], p. 90).

9. For an intriguing study of alcoholism and denial, see Joseph L. Kellerman's *Alcoholism: A Merry-go-round Named Denial* (Center City, MN: Hazelden, 1975).

10. J. Hillis Miller, *Versions of Pygmalion* (Cambridge: Cambridge University Press, 1990), pp. 141–178; Rogin (192–201).

11. Thomas Dilworth, "Narrator of 'Bartleby': The Christian-Humanist Acquaintance of John Jacob Astor," *Papers on Language and Literature* 38 (2002): 49. Others who share Dilworth's view include Patrick McGrath, who concedes that viewing Bartleby as the story's focus "is plausible" yet nonetheless believes that the tale is "as much about the narrator, the lawyer, as it is about Bartleby himself" (Foreword, *Herman Melville: "Bartleby, the Scrivener" and "Benito Cereno."* By Herman Melville [London: Hesperus, 2007], p. vii).

12. Leo Marx, "Melville's Parable of the Walls," *Melville's Short Novels*, ed. Dan McCall (New York: Norton, 2002), p. 241.

13. I am not suggesting here that there are only four possible interpretations of Melville's tale. The first three already mentioned are typically the most common, however. Other readings of the story include it being Melville's commentary on "the commodified literary marketplace" or "perhaps a commentary on the lack of originality in commercially popular literature" (Carl Rollyson, Lisa Paddock, and April Gentry, *Critical Companion to Herman Melville: A Literary Reference to his Life and Work* [New York: Facts on File, 2007], p. 24).

14. David Kirby, *Herman Melville* (New York: Continuum, 1993), p. 136.

15. As the narrator himself says, Turkey is "a man with so small an income" (44).

16. Denis Coon, *Psychology: A Modular Approach to Mind and Behavior* (Belmont, CA: Wadsworth, 2006), p. 248.

17. Did the narrator feel in "rare spirits the whole morning" because he was imbibing spirits all morning? The fact that he could "not go down under the circumstances" possibly suggests that he is too drunk to walk down the stairs.

18. The English brewery Barclay and Perkins was founded in 1616 and became known as such in 1781.

19. The "dozen dozen" bottles of alcohol that the narrator refers to is not a typographical error on my part; it truly is what the narrator says. Did he actually buy a "dozen dozen," or 144, bottles of Philadelphia Porter? Or is he so intoxicated and therefore repeated the dozen, or twelve, bottles that he bought? A dozen dozen of anything, let alone bot-

tles of alcohol, does seem like an exorbitant amount to buy at any one time (especially when considering the narrator's financial difficulties) so it is highly likely that it is the latter of the possibilities.

20. Robert Milder, Introduction, *"Billy Budd, Sailor" and Selected Tales*, ed. Robert Milder (Oxford: Oxford University Press, 1997), p. xiii.

21. Even on other ships including whaling vessels during the nineteenth century, alcohol drinking "killed the pain" of lengthy voyages and debilitating work and the sailors on board such ships used liquor "as a form of escape" (David Dowling, *Chasing the White Whale: The Moby-Dick Marathon; or, What Melville Means Today* [Iowa City: University of Iowa Press, 2010)], p. 116).

22. Charles Nordhoff, Man of War Life: A Boy's Experiences in the United States Navy, During a Voyage Around the World, in a Ship of the Line (Cincinnati: Moore, Wilstach, Keys, 1856), p. iii.

23. In the King James version of the Bible Jesus says, "But I say unto you, Love your enemies, bless them that curse you, do good to them that hate you, and pray for them which despitefully use you, and persecute you."

24. As Daniel Paliwoda similarly claims, the sailors "smuggle alcohol onboard, risking flogging, to dull further their dispirited existences" (Daniel Paliwoda, *Melville and the Theme of Boredom* [Jefferson, NC: McFarland, 2010], p. 95).

25. A further example of a character who is unable to perform his regular duty while sober is the Greek translator from the poetic sketch "Under the Rose" (1924; published posthumously). When asked by the Ambassador to translate various verses into "English rhyme" the one-armed Greek translator says he will do so, but only once one request is met. Being an alcoholic, he wants wine: "'My Lord, I will try; but, I pray thee, give me wine,' glancing at the table where remained certain wicker flasks of the choice vintages of both Persia and Cyprus; 'Yes, wine, my Lord,' he repeated" (Herman Melville, "Under the Rose," *Herman Melville: Tales, Poems, and Other Writings*, ed. John Bryant [New York: Modern Library, 2002], p. 444). Without his wine, the translator is either unwilling or unable to do what he has been asked to do. He demonstrates his alcoholism when he quickly drinks five cups of wine in a time when everyone else but the narrator thinks he had only drunk two.

26. See Dwight Vick and Elizabeth Rhoades, *Drugs and Alcohol in the 21st Century: Theory, Behavior, and Policy* (New York: Jones and Bartlett, 2010) for discussion of this unsettling trend.

27. Drunkenness and its effects on characters is not an issue in "The Fiddler"; however, Melville illustrates in this short story that there are alternatives to using alcohol for dealing with the various stresses that one may experience. The damned poet Helmstone, for instance, is frustrated with his life and laments the "Intolerable fate" that his recent poetry review will cause him (195). Instead of relying on alcohol to ease his worries, which he like some of Melville's other characters including the alcoholic sailors on board the *Neversink* in *White-Jacket* could have done while at Taylor's pub by getting drunk on his punch, he finds inspiration in the fiddler Hautboy. This meeting instils in him the confidence to tear up all of his poetry and to begin focussing on other matters and more optimistically on life in general.

Chapter 3

1. Melville traveled to London primarily for the purpose of negotiating and finalizing a publishing contract with his British publisher Richard Bentley for *White-Jacket*. Prior to arriving in England, Melville drank excessively on board the *Southampton* with George Adler (a professor of German philosophy and literature at New York University) and Dr. Frank Taylor (the *Southampton*'s surgeon). At certain times the ship's captain, Robert Griswold, and Theodore McCurdy, the son of the rich merchant

• Notes—Chapter 3 •

Robert McCurdy, would also share in the festivities. The time that these men spent together was both intellectual and, to use Edwin Haviland Miller's description, "alcoholic" (36). For Melville's own detailed descriptions of his drinking on board the *Southampton*, and that of his subsequent imbibing in Europe after his departure from it, see his journal entries that chronicle the trip (Herman Melville, *Journals*, eds. Howard C. Horsford with Lynn Horth [Evanston: Northwestern University Press, 1989], pp. 3–48). Or, see the Afterword for more specific details of Melville's drinking with these men and during this voyage.

2. In early August of 1850, Melville and his wife, Elizabeth, attended a party in Stockbridge, Massachusetts, that was attended by many notable figures in the American literary scene. On 5 August, Melville and the other party-goers ascended Monument Mountain where after taking a break from hiking were given by Holmes much champagne and several silver mugs (Laurie Robertson-Lorant, "Mr. Omoo and the Hawthornes: The Biographical Background," *Hawthorne and Melville: Writing a Relationship*, eds. Jana L. Argersinger and Leland S. Pearson. [Athens: University of Georgia Press, 2008], p. 30). See the Afterword for further discussion of this meeting.

3. See Melville's various correspondences and this study's Afterword for discussion of his various drinking episodes with various people at Arrowhead.

4. Herman Melville, *The Confidence-Man* (1857; Oxford: Oxford University Press, 1989).

5. George Barton Cutton, *The Psychology of Alcoholism* (New York: Scribner's, 1907), pp. 196, 302.

6. Marvin Fisher noted in the mid–1960s that "Jimmy Rose" was critically neglected ("Melville's 'Jimmy Rose': Truly Risen?," *Studies in Short Fiction* 4 [1966]: 1). Especially as it pertains to alcohol's role in the story, not much has changed in the critical landscape surrounding the tale.

7. The narrator's host R. F. C. is based on Robert Francis Cooke, who himself hosted Melville to a dinner when Melville was in London in 1849.

8. After completing a four-year voyage and arriving at the Spouter Inn, the *Grampus*'s crew simply wants to get wasted. This is no different from the bachelor's in Melville's short story; however, the actions of the drunken sailors are not as refined as their alcoholic counterparts: "The liquor soon mounted into their heads, as it generally does even with the arrantest topers newly landed from sea, and they began capering about most obstreperously" (*Moby-Dick* 29). Despite their drunkenness, the bachelors at the Temple Cloisters are not nearly as unruly as are the sailors at the Spouter Inn.

9. David Henry Serlin, "The Dialogue of Gender in Melville's 'The Paradise of Bachelors and the Tartarus of Maids,'" *Modern Language Studies* 25 (1995): 83.

10. Those whose studies maintain such views of genuine friendship include Richard Harter Fogle (46–49) and Alvin Sandberg, "Erotic Patterns in 'The Paradise of Bachelors and the Tartarus of Maids,'" *Literature and Psychology* 18 (1968): 2–8.

11. Robert L. DuPont, *The Selfish Brain: Learning from Addiction* (Center City, MN: Hazelden, 1997), p. 230.

12. Unless it is a total yet unlikely coincidence, Melville's "Jimmy Rose" was a significant influence on F. Scott Fitzgerald's *The Great Gatsby* (1925). Like Rose, Jay (James "Jimmy" Gatz) Gatsby hosted extravagant parties for people with never-ending rivers of alcohol, yet after he was murdered his funeral was attended by only a few people, as is the case with Rose (although Rose was not murdered). Also like Rose, Gatsby had men who showed little-to-no compassion for him. Rose had one gentleman infuriated with him because the man lost $75.75 as a result of Rose's financial demise; one gentleman who was called on to attend Gatsby's funeral—a man who had also drank his fair share of free booze—"implied that [Gatsby]

had got what he deserved" in being murdered (F. Scott Fitzgerald, *The Great Gatsby* [1925; Toronto: Penguin, 1950], p. 161). Interestingly, the word "rose" appears more than a dozen times in Fitzgerald's short novel, with the most notable and suggestive phrase of influence derived from Melville's short story being from consecutive sentences in *The Great Gatsby*'s ninth chapter: "*Jimmy* always liked it better down East. He *rose* up to his position in the East" (159, emphasis added).

13. Paul Deane, "Herman Melville: Four Views of American Commercial Society," *Revue des Langues Vivants* 34 (1968): 504–507; Fogle (61); E. H. Miller (257); James E. Miller, Jr., *A Reader's Guide to Herman Melville* (New York: Noonday, 1962), p. 167.

14. Merton M. Sealts, Jr., "Notes on 'Jimmy Rose,'" *The Piazza Tales and Other Prose Pieces, 1839–1860*, eds. Harrison Hayford, Hershel Parker, and G. Thomas Tanselle (Evanston: Northwestern University Press, 1987), p. 712.

15. Like Rose, who had been forgotten by his "friends" long before his death, Melville was forgotten long before his own death on 28 September 1891. The name "Herman Melville," as Robert Penn Warren writes, "was dead some forty years before the man" (Introduction, *Selected Poems of Herman Melville*, ed. Robert Penn Warren [New York: Barnes and Noble, 1970], p. 3. An obituary from *The Press* states, "Probably, if the truth were known, even his own generation has long thought him dead, so quiet have been the later years of his life" (Leyda, *Log* 2: 836).

Chapter 4

1. In addition to the nine novels that he wrote and had published during this twelve year period, Melville also composed more than a dozen works of short fiction from 1853 to 1856 including the masterpieces "Bartleby, the Scrivener" and "Benito Cereno." After writing *Pierre* he also composed another novel or novella, *The Isle of the Cross*, the manuscript of which was never published and is now lost. For discussion of the circumstances surrounding *The Isle of the Cross*'s genesis, composition, and attempts at its publication, see Hershel Parker, "Herman Melville's *The Isle of the Cross*: A Survey and a Chronology," *American Literature* 62 (1990): 1–16. As it relates to Melville's physical issues, Robert Ryan has suggested that Melville's health problems far exceeded arthritis, back pain, and eye strain. He posits that throughout the late 1850s and for the rest of his life that Melville had possibly experienced several heart attacks: "[Melville], I would bet you, was having heart attacks all along. Literal ones, not figurative ones, not hypochondriacal ones. I'll bet his heart was expanding, as they put it, all the way from at least the 1850s onward" (Garner et al. 227). Melville died just after midnight on 28 September 1891 of heart-related issues. Everett S. Warner signed his death certificate and listed the cause of death as "cardiac dilation, Mitral regurgitation.... Contributory Asthenia," or as his wife Elizabeth wrote in her memoirs, an "enlargement of the heart" (Leyda, *Log* 2: 836).

2. Reviewers of *Pierre* had feared that Melville had gone "clean daft" (Leyda, *Log* 1: 463). One particular review was headlined explicitly with the words "HERMAN MELVILLE CRAZY" (Brian Higgins and Hershel Parker, eds., *Herman Melville: The Contemporary Reviews* [Cambridge: Cambridge University Press, 1995], p. 436). Reviewers had also, seriously or not, questioned whether Melville had been drinking extensively during the novel's composition. The book was regarded as "abominable trash—an emanation from a lunatic rather than the writing of a sober man" (Leyda, *Log* 1: 465). By the mid-to-late 1860s, even Melville's family—his wife most specifically according to Lemuel Shaw—believed that Melville had or was developing mental issues leading toward, possibly like his father during his final illness in 1832, insanity (Parker, *Melville* 2: 585).

• Notes—Chapter 4 •

3. In this letter Melville is detailed about his plans for his trip and expresses his concern for his family while he is away.

4. In discussion of Melville's lack of drinking on the 1856 voyage to Scotland, Horsford says that passengers on board such ships as the *Glasgow* "wouldn't get much" alcohol (Garner et al. 244). The ones to whom Melville refers—the ones who drank "the whole way over"—clearly show that this was not the case. Alcohol must have been plentiful for them to be able to do so.

5. Herman Melville, *Typee*, eds. Harrison Hayford, Hershel Parker, and G. Thomas Tanselle (1846; Evanston: Northwestern University Press, 1973), p. 189.

6. Another example of a person who is hypocritical with his drinking is Wilson (the acting British consul) from *Omoo*. Typee relates an incident prior to the narrative in which Wilson tried to shut down Old Mother Tot's cantina. Wilson made her "abandon her nefarious calling" (137). Shortly thereafter, the old lady sees Wilson himself drunk: "'Ha, ha! my fine *counsellor*,' she shrieked; 'ye persecute a lone old body like me for selling rum—do ye? And here ye are, carried home drunk—Hoot! ye villain, I scorn ye!' And she spat upon him" (138).

7. Herman Melville, *Redburn*, eds. Harrison Hayford, Hershel Parker, and G. Thomas Tanselle (1849; Evanston: Northwestern University Press, 1975), p. 108.

8. Chips and Bungs have such a "devotion to the bottle" (50) that they both risk death for the sake of satisfying their thirst for liquor by secretly siphoning off booze from the ship's hold. As the narrator, Typee, describes the process, "the casks of Pisco were kept down the after-hatchway, which, for this reason, was secured with bar and padlock. The cooper, nevertheless, from time to time, effected a burglarious entry, by descending into the fore-hold; and then, at the risk of being jammed to death, crawling along over a thousand obstructions, to where the casks were stowed. On the first expedition, the only one to be got at lay among others, upon its bilge with the bung-hole well over. With a bit of iron hoop, suitably bent, and a good deal of prying and punching, the bung was forced in; and then the cooper's neck-handkerchief, attached to the end of the hoop, was drawn in and out—the absorbed liquor being deliberately squeezed into a small bucket" (50–51). They are not the only ones from Melville's writings who do this, however. Although it is presented in a more comical manner, the narrator of *Mardi*, Taji, does the same as he explains in Chapter 33. After finding and then drinking the liquor found in the captain's cabin, the narrator comes up with various reasons to keep the stash hidden from Jarl and Samoa. After rationalizing to himself why he should keep it a secret, he says: "So at last, I determined to let it remain where it was: visiting it occasionally, by myself, for inspection" (107). Inspection and, likely, sole consumption.

9. Melville himself had signed such a round robin while on board the *Lucy-Ann* in 1842 (Paul A. Gilje, *Liberty on the Waterfront: American Maritime Culture in the Age of Revolution* [Philadelphia: University of Pennsylvania Press, 2004], p. 253).

10. Calabooza Beretanee means British prison. Their incarceration is a bit of a joke as the sailors are eventually only locked up during the night and during the day they are permitted to roam freely.

11. Milton Meltzer, *Herman Melville: A Biography* (Minneapolis: Lerner, 2006), p. 70.

12. Timothy Shay Arthur's 1854 sketchbook *Ten Nights in a Barroom* in a similar way promotes temperance by pointing to the evil nature of taverns by tracing "the downward course of the tempting vender and his infatuated victims, until both are involved in hopeless ruin" (Bedford, MA: Applewood Books, 1854), p. 3.

13. As Hershel Parker and Harrison Hayford note, the cups that the bartenders use are "doubly deceitful glasses [because they] are tapered rather than

being true cylinders and also sit on false bottoms, so they look deeper than they are" (Hershel Parker and Harrison Hayford, eds., *Moby-Dick*. By Herman Melville [1851; New York: Norton, 2002], p. 27n7).

Chapter 5

1. Gary Lindberg, *The Confidence Man in American Literature* (Oxford: Oxford University Press, 1982), p. 3.

2. Thomas Winter, "Confidence Man," *American Masculinities: A Historical Encyclopedia*, ed. Bret E. Carroll (London: Sage, 2003), p. 103.

3. Sheila Post-Lauria, *Correspondent Colorings: Melville in the Marketplace* (Amherst: University of Massa-chusetts Press, 1996), p. 215.

4. References to Melville's novel are frequent even in non-literary studies or examinations of the confidence man. See, for instance, Stephen Mihm, *A Nation of Counterfeiters: Capitalists, Con Men, and the Making of the United States* (Cambridge: Harvard University Press, 2009); Orville Vernon Burton, *The Age of Lincoln* (New York: Hill and Wang, 2007); Karen Halttunen, *Confidence Men and Painted Women: A Study of Middle-Class Culture in America, 1830–1870* (New Haven: Yale University Press, 1982).

5. By this comment I mean that despite the abundance of con men in Melville's writings, the one(s) from his novel *The Confidence-Man* is/are almost exclusively the only ones who have garnered any commentary from critics. One exception, however, is referenced in note 18 to this chapter and in the text to which the note refers.

6. David Maurer, *The Big Con* (1940; New York: Random House, 2011), p. 1.

7. This allusion to Gansevoort, as critics have mentioned, is a "punning name that alludes to his drinking and his secretiveness regarding the *Somers* affair" (Hennig Cohen and Donald Yannella, *Herman Melville's Malcolm Letter: "Man's Final Lore"* [New York: Fordham University Press, 1992], p. 109n45).

8. For an incredibly thorough overview of Melville's experiences during the Civil War era, see Stanton Garner's *The Civil War World of Herman Melville* (Lawrence: University of Kansas Press, 1993). See also Lee Rust Brown, Introduction, *Battle-Pieces and Aspects of the War: Civil War Poems*. By Herman Melville (1866; New York: Da Capo, 1995), pp. iii-xvi. For Melville's experiences as they relate specifically to "The Scout Toward Aldie," see Jonathan Cook's "History, Legend, and Poetic Tradition in Melville's 'The Scout Toward Aldie,'" *American Transcendental Quarterly* 17 (2003): 61–80.

9. Herman Melville, "The Scout Toward Aldie," *Selected Poems of Herman Melville*, ed. Robert Penn Warren (New York: Barnes and Noble, 1970), lines 372–378.

10. A reviewer from *The Critic* wrote that of all of Melville's works, "readers will find [*The Confidence-Man*] the hardest nut to crack. We are not quite sure whether we have cracked it ourselves—whether there is not another meaning hidden in the depths of the subject other than that which lies near the surface. There is a dry vein of sarcastic humour running throughout which makes us half suspect this" (Leyda, *Log* 2: 572).

11. William B. Dillingham, *Melville's Later Novels* (Athens: University of Georgia Press, 1986), p. 347.

12. Bruat was appointed governor of Tahiti in 1843; he had virtually unlimited power. He left Tahiti in 1847 to become governor of the Antilles (Rollyson and Paddock 22). In the novel, Kitoti is one of four chiefs who is placed in command of one of the four sections of Tahiti into which Bruat divided the island.

13. There is, perhaps, a logical explanation for the critical neglect that in relation to his other novels *Israel Potter* has suffered. As Walter Bezanson notes in his editorial appendix to the Northwestern-Newberry edition of the novel, *Israel Potter* has for the most part been "little known, not widely read, [and] only intermittently in print" (Wal-

ter E. Bezanson, "Editorial Appendix: Historical Note," *Israel Potter*. By Herman Melville. Eds. Harrison Hayford, Hershel Parker, and G. Thomas Tanselle [1855; Evanston: Northwestern University Press, 1982], p. 174).

14. The "sections" of *Israel Potter* are not divisions in the book made by Melville, as is the case in *Pierre*, for instance. Rather, they are thematic divisions into which Rampersad himself divides the book.

15. Arnold Rampersad, *Melville's "Israel Potter": A Pilgrimage and Progress* (Bowling Green, OH: Bowling Green University Popular Press Press, 1969), p. 50.

16. In Chapter 3 Israel had already been kidnapped. He had enlisted on the brigantine *Washington*, which was later captured by the British warship *Foy* and Potter became a prisoner of war. Although he managed to escape, he is later captured as a runaway and brought back to an inn where he is being guarded by two men. In this episode the narrator seems to suggest that Israel has some type of plan to try and escape, and that he is using liquor to assist him with it: "That liquor he drank from the hand of his foe, has perhaps, warmed his heart towards all the rest of his enemies. Yet this may not be wholly so. We shall see" (16). As the narrator says later, this is indeed the case: "At any rate, still he keeps his eye on the main chance—escape. He is cogitating a little plot to himself" (16). Israel is being affable toward the men who are guarding him and offering them the alcohol that is being brought to him so that they will continue drinking with him; Potter hopes that they will get so drunk that they will pass out and make it easier for him to escape to freedom. This is precisely what happens. Although readers are unquestionably rooting for Israel and his plot to escape, Melville nonetheless illustrates that alcohol can be used against those who are not vigilant. Potter's escape to freedom is welcomed by the audience, but his use of liquor to obtain it nevertheless illustrates how easily one can be duped into drinking and then losing something of value; Israel, indeed, deceives them and in this case, the item of value that the drinkers lose is their prisoner, Potter himself. Although having "the gentleness of the dove," Israel is "not wholly without the wisdom of the serpent" (16); he has a plot that will help him escape. He accepts the request that is made for him to entertain the company at the inn by dancing. Yankees, after all, are "extraordinary dancers" (16). He dances for so long and with such enthusiasm that he "danced himself into a perfect sweat, so that the drops fell from his lank and flaxen hair.... Pleased to see the flowing bowl, he congratulated himself that his own state of perspiration prevents it from producing any intoxicating effect on him" (16); he has sweated all of the alcohol from his system all the while everyone else is continuing to drink. Later that night, with the guards passed-out from their excessive drinking, Israel escapes to safety. He has used alcohol against the guards as a confidence man in order to secure his freedom.

17. Melville visited the islands while aboard various ships from this period including the *Acushnet, Charles & Henry*, and the *United States*.

18. John Bryant, "Melville's Comic Debate: Geniality and the Aesthetics of Repose," *On Melville: The Best From American Literature*, eds. Louis J. Budd and Edwin Cady (Durham: Duke University Press, 1988), p. 263.

19. Oberlus has no issue with the sailors using the island for resources such as his potatoes and pumpkins, but he exchanges them "for spirits or dollars" (139), which in part attests to his own alcoholism.

20. William B. Dillingham, *Melville's Short Fiction, 1853–1856* (1977; Athens: University of Georgia Press, 2008), p. 79.

Chapter 6

1. Herman's mother, Maria, added an *e* to *Melvill* after her husband's death. Some have argued that it was merely to

add an aristocratic flourish to the surname (Parker, *Melville* 1: 67), while others have speculated that it was an "attempt to give her first-born son, Gansevoort, a fresh start in the business world by thus distancing himself from the debt and other improprieties associated with his father's business dealing" (Rollyson and Paddock 115). The true reason, naturally, is unknown.

2. On 15 January 1832, Thomas Melvill, Jr., Allan's brother, wrote a letter to Lemuel Shaw that describes just how dire Allan's health was: "[I]n short my dear sir, Hope, is no longer permitted of his recovery, in the opinion of the attending Physicians and indeed,—oh, how hard for a brother to say!—I *ought not* to hope it.—for,—in all human probability—he would live, a *Maniac*" (Leyda, *Log* 1: 52).

3. See William H. Gilman's *Melville's Early Life and "Redburn"* (New York: New York University Press, 1951). Although Melville took inspiration for his work from this trip, the novel is not strictly an autobiographical novel.

4. For the publication history and sales information for Melville's novels, see the respective entries in Rollyson and Paddock or Parker (*Melville* 2: 98–99). Melville's remuneration for his shorter works is more difficult to precisely determine, but see the respective index entries in the second volume to Parker's biography for what information may exist.

5. Despite gaining full-time employment, his position as inspector of customs paid him a salary of a mere $1,200 a year. See the Conclusion of this study for discussion on how the Melvilles were supported financially for the time prior to Herman's acceptance of his job at the custom's house.

6. Stephen Currie, Thar She Blows: American Whaling in the Nineteenth Century (Minneapolis: Lerner, 2001), p. 15.

7. Going to sea, as Milton Meltzer notes, was the "one thing that a man in [Herman's] situation could do" (*Melville* 27).

8. It was shown in the last chapter on Melville's confidence men that Israel Potter while imprisoned and being guarded in Chapter 3 of the novel uses the liquor that he is being given to get his guards heavily intoxicated and to later pass out, allowing him to escape to freedom. Although readers are rooting for Israel and his plot to get away from his captors, a question arises: what will happen to the guards who have, due to their drunkenness, lost a prisoner of war? What will their superiors think when they are told that a prisoner has escaped due to the guards' drunkenness? In *Israel Potter* we are unable to answer this question. In other works, however, Melville is clear about what the consequences will be for those who drink on the job.

9. I qualify *Typee* as Melville's first significant publication as he had published works of juvenilia seven years earlier. Both the two-part "Fragments from a Writing Desk" and the maritime Gothic short story "The Death Craft" were published in Lansingburgh, New York's *Democratic Press* in 1839.

10. There are variant spellings for *Nukuheva* (Nuku Hiva, for example). The one I have chosen to use is the one that Melville uses in his novel. Melville joined the crew of the *Acushnet* in late December 1840, and set sail a few days later on the 3rd of January. Conditions on board the ship and the actions of Captain Valentine Pease caused Melville and Greene to abandon ship in late June 1842. Greene escaped from the island almost immediately, but Melville spent four weeks there before being rescued by the crew of another whaler, the *Lucy Ann*, in August of 1842. That being said, *Typee* is not simply an exciting adventure tale. The narrative is also laced with "critical commentary on a wide range of social, political, moral, and religious issues aimed at stimulating reflections and reassessment of the current politics of imperialistic expansion being conducted by the governments of the United States and Europe" (Emory Elliot, "'Wandering To-and-Fro': Melville and Reli-

• Notes—Chapter 7 •

gion," *A Historical Guide to Herman Melville*, ed. Giles Gunn [Oxford: Oxford University Press, 2005], p. 176).

11. Willard Thorp, "Herman Melville," *Literary History of the United States*, 3rd rev. ed., eds. Robert E. Spiller et al. (London: Macmillan, 1969), p. 442.

12. Edward Said, Introduction, *Moby-Dick*. By Herman Melville (1851; New York: Library of America, 2010), p. xxiii.

13. Although the text is scant with specific detail and therefore why I relegate commentary on it to a note, Captain Crash from *Omoo* seems to have suffered a similar fate as the English harbor pilot. He is an ex-naval officer who, for some unknown reason that he does not want to discuss, refuses to go back to England to report what had happened with his lost ship. Considering his penchant for smuggling and drinking, it is likely that alcohol had some role in his downfall.

14. Despite being an alcoholic, Mad Jack does not drink when the *Neversink* is approaching well-known dangers such as locations including Cape Horn that are renowned for harsh storms (111–112).

15. The only reason that Mad Jack continues to maintain his rank on the *Neversink* is that Captain Claret is arguably a worse drunk who depends on Mad Jack to navigate the ship when he is too intoxicated to do so. As illustrated in Chapter 26 when the ship is caught in a ferocious storm, Captain Claret depends on Mad Jack. In the tempest, Claret orders the ship "Hard *up* the helm," while Mad Jack roars opposite orders of "hard *down*" (206) and ultimately saves the ship from foundering. In the following chapter, White-Jacket attributes Claret's poor decision marking to his inebriation: "[H]ad Captain Claret been an out-and-out temperance man, he would never have given that most imprudent order to *hard up* the helm" (111).

16. Mandeville's epaulets attest to his former rank in the navy. See Royal W. Connell and William M. Mack, *Naval Ceremonies, Customs, and Traditions* (Annapolis: Naval Institute Press, 2004), p. 296.

Chapter 7

1. See James L. Dickerson, *The First Year: Cirrhosis* (New York: Marlowe and Company, 2006).

2. William J. Sonnenstuhl, *Working Sober: The Transformation of an Occupational Drinking Culture* (Ithaca: Cornell University Press, 1996), p. 2.

3. Jack S. Blocker, Jr., David M. Fahay, and Ian R. Tyrrell, *Alcohol and Temperance in Modern History: A Global Encyclopedia* (Santa Barbara: ABC-CLIO, 2003), p. 407. Despite the undeniable negative results of excessive drinking, modern medicine has shown that *moderate* or *occasional* drinking may have certain health benefits. See Gene Ford, *The Science of Healthy Drinking* (New York: Wine Appreciation Guild, 2003).

4. For nineteenth-century works that discuss alcohol avoidance and the various health problems that are caused by drinking, see Peter Burne, *The Teetotaler's Companion; or, A Pleas for Temperance* (Ipswich: J. M. Burton, 1847), p. 215–284; Henry William Blair, *The Temperance Movement; or, The Conflict Between Man and Alcohol* (Boston: William E. Smythe, 1888), pp. 14–31.

5. Stanley Finger, Origins of Neuroscience: A History of Explorations into Brain Function (Oxford: Oxford University Press, 1994), p. 358.

6. Christopher G. White, Unsettled Minds: Psychology and the American Search for Spiritual Assurance, 1830–1940 (Berkeley: University of California Press, 2009), pp. 96–97.

7. There are countless studies that have examined Melville's novella and its commentary on slavery. See among many others, Robert Burkholder's edited collection *Critical Essays on Melville's "Benito Cereno"* (New York: G. K. Hall, 1992), and sections from Carolyn Karcher's *Shadow Over the Promised Land: Slavery, Race, and Violence in Melville's America* (Baton Rouge: Louisiana State University Press, 1980).

179

8. *Cordial* is a type of alcoholic stimulant, or another word for liquor.

9. The cunning and deceitful bartender at the Spouter Inn in *Moby-Dick*, Jonah, also offers sailors alcohol as a cure for their ailments. As Ishmael observes after the *Grampus*'s crew enters the bar, "One complained of a bad cold in his head, upon which Jonah mixed him a pitch-like potion of gin and molasses, which he swore was a sovereign cure for all colds and catarrhs whatsoever, never mind of how long standing, or whether caught off the coast of Labrador, or on the weather side of an ice-island" (29). As will be shown in Chapter 4, however, such actions are in line with his unprincipled nature and he likely claims his drink to be an all-encompassing cure simply to take money from the sailors.

10. Robert L. Gale, Plots and Characters in the Fiction and Narrative Poetry of Herman Melville (Cambridge: MIT Press, 1972), p. 186.

11. Isaac F. Shepard, *Confessions of a Female Inebriate, Drunkards' Progress: Narratives of Addiction, Despair, and Recovery*, ed. John William Crowley (Baltimore: Johns Hopkins University Press, 1999), 69–79. Although presented as the work of a lady, *Confessions*' copyright was issued and therefore authorship attributed to Shepard.

12. Robert L. Gale, *A Herman Melville Encyclopedia* (Westport, CT: Greenwood, 1995), p. 106.

13. Robert Terkeltaub, *Gout and Other Crystal Arthropathies* (Philadelphia: Elsevier Saunders, 2012), p. 138.

14. When the bill collector goes to the narrator's house for the first time, the narrator offers to show him a vast selection of stout superior to Barclay and Perkins (81).

15. Christine Marie Kovic, "Demanding Their Dignity as Daughters of God: Catholic Women and Human Rights," *Women on Chiapas*, eds. Christine Engla Eber and Christine Marie Kovic (New York: Routledge, 2003), p. 139.

16. Jenny Summerfield and Lyn van Oudtshoorn, *Counselling in the Workplace* (Wiltshire: Cromwell Press, 2000), p. 95; Ann M. Manzardo, et al., *Alcoholism*, 4th ed. (Oxford: Oxford University Press, 2008), p. 9.

Chapter 8

1. Many works of temperance fiction, as Carol Mattingly notes, "depict the hardships endured by women when husbands become irresponsible or abusive" (Introduction, *Water Drops*, p. 10). See also Jerome Nadelblaft, "Alcohol and Wife Abuse in Antebellum Male Temperance Literature," *Canadian Review of American Studies* 25 (1995): 15–44. By no means am I suggesting that the narrator should be applauded simply because he does not become abusive toward his wife while intoxicated, just that he does not become violent and is therefore not like many other drunken husbands from works dealing with temperance issues.

2. *Fonoo* means "the girl" (Rollyson and Paddock 56).

3. This phrase could also equally be applied to the prodromal phase alcoholics who use liquor as a way to avoid their life's problems.

4. Melville was familiar with and had read addiction narratives including De Quincey's *Confessions*, which Melville described in one of his journal entries as "a wonderful thing, that book" (*Journals* 46).

5. Carol Margaret Davison, "The Gothic and Addiction: A Mad Tango," *Gothic Studies* 11.2 (2009): 1.

6. Carol Margaret Davison, "'Houses of Voluntary Bondage': Theorizing the Nineteenth-Century Gothic Pharmography," *Gothic Studies* 12.1 (2010): 68–85.

7. For studies that examine these works in the light of addiction, see Nancy Armstrong, "Feminism, Fiction, and the Utopian Promise of *Dracula*," *Differences* 16 (2005): 1–23; Daniel Wright, "'The Prisonhouse of my Disposition': A Study of the Psychology of Addiction in *Dr. Jekyll and Mr. Hyde*," *Studies in the Novel* 26 (1994): 254–267; Susan Zeiger, *Inventing the Addict: Drugs, Race, and Sexuality in Nineteenth-*

Century British and American Literature (Amherst: University of Massachusetts Press, 2009); Barry Milligan, "Morphine Addicted Doctors, The English Opium Eater, and Embattled Medical Authority," *Victorian Literature and Culture* 33 (2005): 541–553. A fascinating study devoted strictly to alcohol in Stevenson's *Jekyll and Hyde* is Thomas L. Reed, Jr.'s *The Transforming Draught: Robert Louis Stevenson, "Jekyll and Hyde," and the Victorian Alcohol Debate* (Jefferson, NC: McFarland, 2006). A comment that Reed makes about Dr. Jekyll's transformation into Mr. Hyde can be equally applied to Melville's characters who will be examined in this chapter: "Henry Jekyll is an addict. Hyde is most simply the persona Jekyll assumes when he pursues an obsessive gratification" (9). Melville's characters are alcoholics and they become evil *others* like Mr. Hyde once they are intoxicated.

8. Mary Ellen Snodgrass, *Encyclopedia of Gothic Literature* (New York: Facts on File, 2005), p. 83.

9. Catherine Spooner, *Fashioning Gothic Bodies* (Manchester: Manchester University Press, 2004), p. 128.

10. When Dr. Jekyll becomes Mr. Hyde, the former man of research and science, he becomes the latter murderous monster responsible for the trampling of an innocent young girl and the death of Danvers Carew. The protagonist of Poe's short story, who is intoxicated throughout the story, commits murder.

11. *Pierre* and "Bartleby" have garnered relatively frequent attention as works of Gothic literature. See, for instance, Robert Miles, "'Tranced Griefs': Herman Melville's *Pierre* and the Origins of the Gothic," *ELH* 66 (1999): 157–177; Ellen Weinauer, "Women, Ownership, and Gothic Manhood in *Pierre*," *Melville and Women*, eds. Elizabeth Schultz and Haskell Springer (Kent, OH: Kent State University Press, 2006), pp. 141–160; Steven Ryan, "The Gothic Formula of 'Bartleby,'" *Arizona Quarterly* 34 (1978): 311–316.

12. Elizabeth Renker notes that the word *drinking* "became a code word for male violence by about 1850" (125).

13. Wendy Stallard Flory, "The Author and the Woman Within in the 'Inside Narrative' of *Pierre*," *Melville and Women*, eds. Elizabeth Schultz and Haskell Springer (Kent, OH: Kent State University Press, 2006), p. 128.

14. Walter E. Bezanson, ed., *Clarel*. By Herman Melville (1876; New York: Hendricks House, 1960), p. 532.

15. A clear example of this occurs early in the story when the narrator is out for a walk (sober) and describes his surroundings with positive and optimistic language: "Ah, here comes the down-train; white cars, flashing through the trees like a vein of silver. How cheerfully the steam-pipe chirps! Gay are the passengers. There waves a handkerchief—going down to the city to eat oysters, and see their friends, and drop in at the circus. Look at the mist yonder; what soft curls and undulations round the hills, and the sun weaving his rays among them.... Well, I feel better for this walk" (80). After he returns home and starts drinking, however, the narrator's emotional status changes drastically: "Come to think of it, that dun may call, though. I'll just visit the woods and cut a club. I'll club him, by jove, if he duns me this day" (80).

16. Yet another example of Dr. Long Ghost's brutal and violent behavior when he is drunk occurs in Chapter 23 of *Omoo* when he tries to convince the crew to set sail on the *Julia* with him as their captain and in the process leaving Captain Guy stranded on the island. The sailors are not entirely convinced that this is a good idea, however, so Long Ghost, who was "by no means yet sober," becomes enraged, an action that is strictly caused by his drinking, or by "the frequency of his potations" (79).

17. In Chapter 71 of *White-Jacket* Melville outlines the history of the Articles of War, which "form the ark and constitutions of the American Navy" (297) and provide the legal justification for flogging. In this chapter, throughout

the entire novel in fact, Melville is highly critical of the harshness of the articles and of the country from which they were adopted: "Whence came they? They cannot be the indigenous growth of those political institutions, which are based on that arch-democrat Thomas Jefferson's Declaration of Independence? No; they are an importation from abroad, even from Britain, whose laws we Americans hurled off as tyrannical, and yet retain the most tyrannical of all" (297).

18. For a comprehensive study of France's involvement in Tahiti and other Pacific islands, see George Pritchard, *The Aggressions of the French at Tahiti and Other Islands in the Pacific* (Auckland: Auckland University Press, 1983).

Chapter 9

1. *Mania-a-potu* is a type of madness that is associated with drinking (McCarthy 46). Davy Jones, or Davy Jones's locker, is an idiom for the state of death for drowned sailors.

2. In some works of dark temperance, the characters' doom is caused by others' addition to alcohol. In Maria Lamas's *The Glass* (Philadelphia: Martin E. Harmstead, 1849), p. 30, a young boy chews off his own arm in an attempt to avoid starvation and later bleeds to death after being locked in a closet by his drunken mother.

3. David Reynolds has previously noted this dark temperance moment to be related from the novel in his work *Beneath the American Renaissance* (146).

4. Although there are no records of anyone jumping overboard during Melville's voyage on the *St. Lawrence* in 1839, a similar incident did occur when he traveled on board the *Southampton* in 1849. A man who "was crazy," as Melville recounts in his journal entry from the trip on 13 October, committed suicide by jumping overboard (*Journals* 5). Whether or not alcohol played a factor in this factual event is naturally unknown.

5. Melville's familiarity with delirium tremens "likely came from sailing experiences, especially aboard the *United States*, which, during Melville's fourteen months, recorded many cases of drunkenness" (McCarthy 38). For medical discussion of delirium tremens, see Kathleen Bucholz, et al., "The Histories of Withdrawal Convulsions and Delirium Tremens in 1,648 Alcohol Dependent Subjects," *Addiction* 90 (1995): 1335–1347.

6. While Ishmael appears to be heralding drunken festivities for certain sailors on board the whaler *Samuel Enderby* in "The Decanter" (Chapter 101), the sailors' intoxication is nonetheless condemned by Melville as it nearly results in the sailors' death. When they are drunk the sailors are forced to go on deck during a storm and are nearly swept overboard (341–342).

7. Charles Brockden Brown, *Wieland; Or, the Transformation*, eds. Philip Barnard and Stephen Shapiro (1798; Indianapolis: Hackett, 2009), p. 18.

8. Again, Reynolds has noted this episode as one of dark temperance (*Beneath* 146).

9. After Ahab gains the trust and control of the crew, Starbuck would have been unable to form any sort of rebellion or mutiny against Ahab. Starbuck sees clearly the insanity of Ahab's quest and clearly voices his opinion to his captain: "'Vengeance on a dumb brute!' cried Starbuck, 'that simply smote thee from blindest instinct! Madness! To be enraged with a dumb thing, Captain Ahab, seems blasphemous'" (139).

10. Translated from Latin, Ahab's words mean "I do not baptize you in the name of the Father, but in the name of the Devil" (Parker and Hayford 372n3).

11. Parker and Hayford note that in this passage Melville "is playing with the sentimental, melodramatic language of Temperance literature" (369n1), which refers back to Chapter 1 in this volume that Melville was aware of and wrote such writings.

12. Richard K. Ries, David. A. Fiellin, Shannon C. Miller, and Richard Saitz, *Principles of Addiction Medicine*, 4th ed.

(Philadelphia: Lippincott Williams, 2009), p. 561. It is not entirely clear whether Perth hears the voices while he is still drinking or only once he has given up the bottle.

13. In reference to Perth's alcoholism, and more specifically the destruction it caused, Ahab says: "Thou should'st go mad, blacksmith; say, why dost thou not go mad? How can'st thou endure without being mad" (370). Earlier in the chapter, Perth describes himself in a manner that perhaps gives an idea to how he is able to endure the constant suffering: "'Because I am scorched all over, Captain Ahab ... I am past scorching; not easily can'st though scorch a scar'" (370). Melville possibly alludes again to suicide at the chapter's conclusion when he writes that "death seems the only desirable sequel" for Perth (369).

Conclusion

1. We know for a fact, as Hershel Parker outlines, that Melville was aware of the Rev. Samuel C. Damon, editor of the Honolulu *Temperance Advocate and Seamen's Friend*, and of various temperance meetings held in Hawaii while Melville was in Lahaina and Honolulu in 1843 (1:240–241).

2. According to Laurie Robertson-Lorant, there is no doubt that Melville had read Hawthorne's temperance work "A Rill from the Town Pump" ("Mr. Omoo" 37). There is no doubt that Melville was familiar with the story even before knowing its author, as Robertson-Lorant rightly notes, as he makes explicit reference to it in *White-Jacket*: "And would that fine countryman, Hawthorne of Salem, had but served on board a man-of-war in his time, that he might give us the reading of a '*rill*' from the scuttle-butt" (283).

3. There are no records, however, of anyone having confronted or discussed Melville's excessive drinking. Edwin Haviland Miller believes that there was a "conspiracy of silence" about Melville's drinking in the family (321), whereas Laurie Robertson-Lorant argues that "some family members blamed Herman's moodiness and poor health on his writing, which was a convenient way of denying his growing dependence on alcohol. Although at this remove and with so little evidence, it's difficult to determine how much Melville drank, it seems certain that during the mid–1850s he came to rely on alcohol for relief of his physical pain and emotional distress.... As Melville's drinking grew worse, his moods became more unpredictable and dangerous, and even if Lizzie and his mother and sisters did not nag him openly, he must have sensed their anxiety" (*Melville* 370–371). If Melville felt his wife's anxiety about his drinking, then it is certainly plausible that "The Apple-Tree Table" is more of an autobiographical work of temperance fiction than the others examined in Chapter 1.

4. E. H. Miller, for one, has claimed that the Melville family maintained a public "conspiracy of silence" about Herman's drinking (321). If his drinking was as out of control as some would suggest, then it would only be natural that someone would have made mention of it to Herman (whether explicit or indirect), or at least made him feel their frustration with it.

5. For detailed discussion of the relationship between Hawthorne and Melville, see Chapters 35–40 of the first volume and the first chapter of the second volume of Hershel Parker's *Herman Melville: A Biography* (1: 729–883; 2: 1–30). For a more succinct overview of the relationship between Melville and Hawthorne, see Laskin (25–94). See also Erik Hage, *The Melville-Hawthorne Connection: A Study of the Literary Friendship* (Jefferson, NC: McFarland, 2014), which is the only extended study to date that examines strictly the Melville-Hawthorne relationship.

6. Edwin Haviland Miller, for instance, posits that Hawthorne left in part due to a sexual advance that Melville made toward him (250), while Andrew Delbanco suggests that Melville "may have

gotten too close to some explosive secret in his friend's private life" (211). Neither Miller nor Delbanco, however, provide any specifics concerning the time, place, or extent of Melville's actions toward or knowledge about Hawthorne. For further discussion by Melville scholars of the exact nature of the Melville-Hawthorne relationship and of how significant it truly was (or was not), see Garner et al. (241–248). For discussion of the possible romantic connection between the two and of the differing meanings of male relationships between the mid-nineteenth and early twenty-first centuries, see Milder (*Exiled* 118–148).

7. "Hawthorne and his Mosses" appeared on the 17th and 24th of August 1850. In addition to "Hawthorne and his Mosses," Melville published in the *Literary World* reviews of Francis Parkman's *The California and Oregon Trail; being Sketches of Prairie and Rocky Mountain Life* (under the review title of "Mr. Parkman's Tour") and J. Ross Brown's *Etchings of a Whaling Cruise* (review title the same).

8. In her biography of Melville, Robertson-Lorant questions why Hawthorne—who clearly disagreed with the *Literary World*'s (Duyckinck) evaluation of *Moby-Dick*—never came to Melville's so-called defence (*Melville* 293). However, the reason for Hawthorne's public silence on the matter seems relatively clear: Melville did not want him to review or provide any other commentary on the book. In his letter to Hawthorne from the middle of November 1851 Melville writes: "Farewell. Don't write a word about the book [*Moby-Dick*]. That would be robbing me of my miserly delight. I am heartily sorry I ever wrote anything about you—it was paltry" (*Correspondence* 213). Moreover, how would it look had Hawthorne—the man to whom the book is dedicated—written a glowing review? How seriously or reliably would such a review be taken by the literary public had they read a review that was written by the man to whom the book was inscribed? Despite not reviewing *Moby-Dick* publicly, he nonetheless expressed his disagreement with the *Literary World*'s review when he wrote to Duyckinck on 1 December 1851: "What a book Melville has written! It gives me an idea of much greater power than his preceding ones. It hardly seemed to me that the review of it, in the Literary World, did justice to its best points" (Leyda, *Log* 1: 438).

9. Wilson Heflin, *Herman Melville's Whaling Years*, eds. Mary K. Bercaw Edwards and Thomas Ferel Heffernan (Nashville: Vanderbilt University Press, 2004), p. 7–8.

10. Hershel Parker speculates on what this type of money would represent in the early twenty-first century's economy: "Now, no one has done a good job with equivalents, even the U.S. government with its inflation charts, which would suggest that $2,000 in 1847 would equal $50-some thousand. But in terms of comparable New York City property values, $2,000 in 1847 would buy something roughly like $2,000,000 now: you have to multiply not by twenty-five or thirty but by a thousand. Everyone acknowledges that a million dollars is not what it used to be, and $2,000 now certainly isn't anything like it used to be. This was very serious money—two or three years' income for an average urban family, perhaps" ("Damned by Dollars: *Moby-Dick* and the Price of Genius," *Moby-Dick*. By Herman Melville, eds. Harrison Hayford and Hershel Parker [New York: Norton, 2002], p. 715).

11. Melville was aware of his dire financial situation during the mid-nineteenth century and, in an attempt to get money, took the initiative to reluctantly write two novels that he hoped would earn him much-needed income: *Redburn* and *White-Jacket*. As he writes to his father-in-law Lemuel Shaw on 6 October 1849, "For Redburn I anticipate no particular reception of any kind. It may be deemed a book of tolerable entertainment;—& may be accounted dull.—As for the other book [*White-Jacket*], it will be sure to be attacked in some quarters. But no reputation that is

gratifying to me, can possibly be achieved by either of these books. They are two *jobs*, which I have done for money—being forced to it, as other men are to sawing wood" (*Correspondence* 138).

12. Melville published many of his short stories including "Cock-A-Doodle-Doo!," "Jimmy Rose," and "The Apple-Tree Table" in *Harper's*. Others including "Bartleby, the Scrivener," "Benito Cereno," and "The Bell-Tower" appeared in *Putnam's Monthly Magazine*.

13. Daniel Shepherd was Melville's brother Allan's lawyer and a man who Melville had previously met in Lake George, New York, in August of 1856. In his letter to Shepherd, Melville poetically invites him to come to Arrowhead and drink:
Come, Shepherd, come visit me:
Come, we'll make it Arcady; ...
Of Bourbon that is rather new
I brag a fat black bottle or two
[Melville, *Correspondence* 337–339].

It is uncertain whether Shepherd accepted Melville's invitation or that Melville's letter was ever sent at all. Nonetheless, such a letter demonstrates Melville's desire to drink excessively with others at Arrowhead.

14. See note 22 to Chapter 1 for an overview of the discussions that critics since the 1920s have had concerning Melville's so-called misogynistic and womanless fiction.

15. Hardwick insinuates that Melville had been abusive toward Elizabeth and an alcoholic right from the beginning of their marriage (51–52). An extended period of abuse (or at least maltreatment in some capacity) is also suggested by Elizabeth's half-brother, Samuel. See note 17 to the Conclusion for further discussion.

16. John Bryant describes the "charge of wife-beating" as "unlikely" ("Writer" xxxix). Robert Milder "do[es] not believe that Melville was guilty of frequent or deliberate physical abuse" toward Elizabeth (*Exiled* 188). Hershel Parker also goes to great lengths to demonstrate how much of the abuse theory is based on circumstantial and, in certain cases, utterly false information that has been presented, passed down, and in the process accepted as truth and again propagated by subsequent generations of critics (*Melville* 2: 628–635).

17. In a letter to the Rev. Bellows dated 6 May 1867, Elizabeth's half-brother Samuel S. Shaw suggests that Melville's mistreatment of Elizabeth had been going on long before the mid–1860s: "I thank you much for the interest which you have taken in my sisters [*sic*] case and am very glad to have your opinion and advice in the matter, which has been a cause of anxiety to all of us for years past. She will tell you that all the reasons set forth in your letter have been urged over and over again by me as a ground for a separation that we have offered to assist her to the best of our ability and that the Melvilles also, though not till quite recently, have expressed a willingness to lend their assistance" (Melville, *Correspondence* 858). See the full letters concerning this situation in Melville's *Correspondence* (857–860). See also Walter D. Kring and Jonathan S. Carey, "Two Discoveries Concerning Herman Melville," *Proceedings of the Massachusetts Historical Society*," 87 (1975): 137–141. Although her essay on the whole delves into much circumstantial or possible and unsubstantiated evidence on the matter, the early parts of Elizabeth Renker's "Herman Melville, Wife Beating, and the Written Page" provides a fairly thorough overview of the factual documents concerning this rough time in Elizabeth's life and of the proposed kidnapping plot suggested by Bellows.

18. Had Elizabeth gone through with the legal separation then she would have lost everything: "Given the laws of the time, Elizabeth Melville would forfeit everything—children, home, and all property—if she should leave her husband" (Rollyson and Paddock xx).

19. In her biography of Melville, Robertson-Lorant offers a variety of scenarios that could possibly explain

Melville's tardiness: "If he was much later than usual, was it because he stopped off at a tavern to fortify himself before confronting Malcolm, or did he stop off to see Evert Duyckinck, either to procrastinate, or to ask his old friend for advice about how to handle his rebellious son? Was he unconsciously mirroring his son's irresponsible behavior and causing Lizzie worry, or was he simply stuck at the office, having to work late" (666n42)?

20. In the end of her letter to Henry, Catherine states that Elizabeth cannot feel in any way guilty for Malcolm's death because she was not harsh with him upon his return home: "So she cannot blame herself for having induced him from despair at her fault-finding, to put an end to his life" (Leyda, *Log* 2: 691).

21. "In the twenty-first century," Hershel Parker writes, "one of Melville's great-grandchildren remembers being told fiercely by Melville's grand-daughter Frances Thomas Osborne *never* to allow anyone to refer to Malcolm's death as suicide: it was an accident" (*Melville* 2: 644).

22. For those who regard Malcolm's death as an unquestionable suicide, see, among many others, Joseph Adamson (20), John Bryant ("Writer" xxxix), Robert Milder (*Exiled* 186), Edwin Haviland Miller (316), Carl Rollyson and Lisa Paddock (121), and Michael Paul Rogin (289).

23. Edwin. S. Shniedman, "Some Psychological Reflections on the Death of Malcolm Melville," *Suicide and Life-Threatening Behavior* 6 (1976): 233.

24. The date of this famous letter to Hawthorne was long believed to be around June 1, 1851; however, in the first volume of his biography on Melville, which was published in 1996, Hershel Parker uncovers evidence that re-dates the letter a month earlier to early May of 1851 (*Melville* 1: 841–844; Parker and Hayford 538n2). Despite Parker's findings, however, authors and editors of post–1996 Melville-related publications continue to cite what is now the incorrect date of 1 June 1851 (see, for instance, Delbanco 134, 349n4; John Bryant, ed., *Herman Melville: Tales, Poems, and Other Writings* [New York: Modern Library, 2002], p. 38).

Afterword

1. Robert Ryan has presented a similar view as Garner about Melville's drinking, claiming that he is unsure whether "we can say anything for sure about his drinking" (Garner et al. 244).

2. The second reason I offered for its frequency in his writing is its overwhelming presence in his society at large.

3. Thomas Gradgrind is the headmaster at the school in Dickens's fictional city Coketown who is solely interested in the students' learning of facts. As he describes his philosophy in the novel's opening paragraph, "'Now, what I want is, Facts. Teach these boys and girls nothing but Facts. Facts alone are wanted in life. Plant nothing else, and root out everything else. You can only form the minds of reasoning animals upon Facts: nothing else will ever be of any service to them. This is the principle on which I bring up my own children, and this is the principle on which I bring up these children. Stick to Facts, sir!" (Charles Dickens, *Hard Times* [1854; New York: Penguin, 1995], p. 9).

4. Melville likely drank heavily while on board the various ships and while docked in places including Hawaii from 1841–1843, but there are no explicit or factual references to such drinking excursions in any known documents so is exempt from any significant commentary.

5. Melville and Greene somewhat resurrected their friendship after they parted ways in 1842, but merely through correspondence. Therefore, Greene's reference to Melville's drinking in his letter must have been based on whatever experiences they had together imbibing up to July of 1842. Hershel Parker states that Greene knew Melville "as a phenomenal eater and an enthusiastic drinker" (*Melville* 2: 456). Although Greene dates this letter 4 July 1860, the editorial committee of Melville's *Corre-*

• Notes—Afterword •

spondence note that due to Greene's reference to "Old Abe" (Lincoln) taking the oath of the Presidency, the date must have been 1861 and that the date that Greene specifies was simply an error, albeit perplexing, on Greene's part (editorial note in *Correspondence* 178–179).

6. The checklist is from Melville's *Journals* (138):
Oct. 15 small bottle of stout (Dinner)
One bottle   "
two bottles (one at night)
one bottle (one at night)
  "   "   afternoon
  "   "   "

7. Melville's entry for this drinking event is listed as the 6th of November, yet it was actually for the 5th. See note 12.16 to his *Journals* on page 269 for discussion of the incorrect date that Melville wrote in his journal.

8. Melville was clearly ecstatic with the deal that he had negotiated with Richard Bentley for *White-Jacket*: "6 O'clock P.M. Hurrah & three cheers! I have just returned from Mr. Bentley's, & have concluded an arrangement with him that gives me tomorrow his note for £200.... This takes a load off my heart" (*Journals* 40).

9. Field was an American lawyer and law reformer, not to be confused with his father of the same name.

10. Melville makes this admission in an 1863 letter to Sophia Van Matre. She had written Melville to request an autograph to be sold at the Great Western Sanitary Fair in Cincinnati. As Melville writes in response, "I should be very happy indeed to comply with your request to furnish you with my autographs from old letters, were it not that it is a vile habit of mine to destroy nearly all my letters" (*Correspondence* 387).

11. As discussed in the final note to the Conclusion, this letter had long been believed to be from early June 1850. I date it here as from May due to Parker's findings. See note 24 to the Conclusion. See Parker (*Melville*, 1: 841–844) or Parker and Hayford (538n2) for discussion of the letter's altered date.

12. This trip to Nantucket that Melville took with Shaw would be—or perhaps could have been—of great importance to Melville's literary career. It was during this trip that Melville met the lawyer John Clifford, who would relate to Melville the story of Agatha Hatch: a heroic woman who would be betrayed by the very man whose life she saved. On 13 August 1852, only four weeks after this meeting, Melville wrote to Hawthorne a detailed letter about his visit to Nantucket and enclosed a document pertaining to the Agatha story that he was told (*Correspondence* 232–237). As Clifford related to Melville and as Melville later relayed to Hawthorne, Agatha Hatch was the daughter of a lighthouse keeper from Falmouth, Massachusetts. She married a sailor named James Robertson, whom Agatha had saved from drowning, and shortly after their wedding they moved to Nantucket. After Agatha became pregnant, Robertson left for sea and she did not hear from him for 17 years. Upon his return he saw his child, a daughter, for the first time. Shortly thereafter, Robertson would again disappear, only to return on the eve of his daughter's wedding to give her a wedding gift. After Robertson died, Agatha learned that he had married two other women. His second wife died, but the third, like Agatha, survived her husband. Although suspecting bigamy while her husband was alive, "Agatha had done nothing, not wanting to make his second family unhappy and not wanting to drive him away from their own daughter" (Parker, *Melville* 2: 114–115). In essence, Agatha was the exception to the famous yet frequently misquoted line from William Congreve's seventeenth-century play *The Mourning Bride*, "hell hath no fury like a woman scorned" (the actual line is spoken by Zara in Act III, Scene VIII, and goes "Heav'n has no rage, like love to hatred turn'd, Nor hell a fury, like a woman scorn'd"). Hawthorne apparently declined Melville's invitation to write the story, so Melville decided to do it himself; some have argued that Melville unconsciously always wanted to write the story himself,

187

anyway (Hans Bergmann, *God in the Street: New York Writing from Penny Press to Melville* [Philadelphia: Temple University Press, 1995], p. 173). Either way, the story was written and the result, as Hershel Parker believes, was the now-lost novel or novella *The Isle of the Cross* (Parker, "*Isle*" 1–16).

13. Samuel Savage was the nephew of Hope Savage Shaw, Elizabeth Melville's step-mother. Elizabeth's biological mother died in 1822 and Lemuel Shaw subsequently remarried.

14. I say "at least" two novels as there is the great possibility that he also wrote *The Isle of the Cross* after he had finished *Pierre* in 1852. See note 1 from Chapter 4 for discussion of the details surrounding the history behind and composition of the now-lost novel or novella.

15. Melville had intended to see Hawthorne on the 9th yet went to the house that Hawthorne had moved from a year and a half prior so he had to wait until the 10th (*Journals* 50).

16. Not only is Melville's language in his journal entry significantly different (less poetic and profound) than that of his letters to Hawthorne, but Hawthorne noticed physical and emotional differences in Melville's countenance. As Hawthorne recounts in his own journal, "A week ago last Monday, Herman Melville came to see me at the Consulate, looking much as he used to (a little paler, and perhaps a little sadder" (Leyda, *Log* 2: 528–529). Hawthorne would make another solemn observation about Melville in his journal entry from 17 November (coincidently the five-year anniversary of Melville's "farewell" letter to Hawthorne): "I saw him again on Monday, however. He said that he already felt much better than in America; but observed that he did not anticipate much pleasure in his rambles, for that the spirit of adventure is gone out of him. He certainly is much overshadowed since I saw him last; but I hope he will brighten as he goes onward" (Leyda, *Log* 2: 531).

17. Howard C. Horsford with Lynn Horth, "Textual Record," *Journals*. By Herman Melville, ed. Howard C. Horsford with Lynn Horth (Evanston: Northwestern University Press, 1989), p. 388.

18. As Melville relates in his journal, he was supposed to sail on the 17th, but much to his dissatisfaction the voyage was "put off till tomorrow. Great disappointment. Tired of Liverpool" (51).

19. Madeira is an archipelago off the coast of Portugal whose wine-making history dates back to the sixteenth century (Rodney Bolt, *Madeira and Port Santo* [New York: Cadogan Guides, 2007], p. 38).

Bibliography

Adamson, Joseph. *Melville, Shame, and the Evil Eye*. Albany: State University of New York Press, 1997.

Armstrong, Nancy. "Feminism, Fiction, and the Utopian Promise of *Dracula*." *Differences* 16 (2005): 1–23.

Arvin, Newton. *Herman Melville*. New York: Viking, 1950.

Bergmann, Hans. *God in the Street: New York Writing from Penny Press to Melville*. Philadelphia: Temple University Press, 1995.

Bezanson, Walter E., ed. *Clarel*. By Herman Melville. 1876. New York: Hendricks House, 1960.

———. "Editorial Appendix: Historical Note." *Israel Potter*. By Herman Melville. Eds. Harrison Hayford, Hershel Parker, and G. Thomas Tanselle. 1855. Evanston: Northwestern University Press, 1982. 173–235.

Black, Claudia. "Effects of Family Alcoholism." *Alcoholism and the Family*. Eds. Satoru Saitho and Marc A. Schuckit. Tokyo: Seiwa Shoten, 1992. 272–281.

Blair, Henry William. *The Temperance Movement; or, The Conflict Between Man and Alcohol*. Boston: William E. Smythe, 1888.

Blocker, Jack J., David M. Fahay, and Ian R. Tyrell. *Alcohol and Temperance in Modern History: A Global Encyclopedia*. Santa Barbara: ABC-CLIO, 2003.

Bohm, Arnd. "Wordsworth in Melville's 'Cock-A-Doodle-Doo!'" *Leviathan: A Journal of Melville Studies* 9 (2007): 25–41.

Bolt, Rodney. *Madeira and Porto Santo*. New York: Cadogan Guides, 2007.

Bromwell, Nicholas Knowles. *By the Sweat of the Brown: Literature and Labour in Antebellum America*. Chicago: University of Chicago Press, 1993.

Brown, Charles Brockden. *Wieland; or, The Transformation*. 1798. Eds. Philip Barnard and Stephen Shapiro. Indianapolis: Hackett, 2009.

Brown, Gillian. *Domestic Individualism: Imagining Self in Nineteenth-Century America*. Berkeley: University of California Press, 1990.

Brown, Julie. *Writers on the Spectrum: How Autism and Asperger Syndrome Have Influenced Literary Writing*. Philadelphia: Jessica Kingsley, 2010.

Brown, Lee Rust. Introduction. *Battle Pieces and Aspects of the War: Civil War Poems*. 1866. By Herman Melville. New York: Da Capo. 1995. iii-xvi

Bryant, John, ed. *Herman Melville: Tales, Poems, and Other Writings*. New York: Modern Library, 2002.

———. "Herman Melville: A Writer in Process." *Herman Melville: Tales, Poems, and Other Writings*. Ed. John

Bryant. New York: Modern Library, 2002. xvii-l.

———. "Melville's Comic Debate: Geniality and the Aesthetics of Repose." *On Melville: The Best from American Literature*. Eds. Louis J. Budd and Edwin Cady. Durham: Duke University Press, 1988. 254–276.

Bucholz, Kathleen, et al. "The Histories of Withdrawal Convulsions and Delirium Tremens in 1,648 Alcohol Dependent Subjects." *Addiction* 90 (1995): 1335–1347.

Burkholder, Robert. *Critical Essays on Herman Melville's "Benito Cereno."* New York: G. K. Hall, 1992.

Burne, Peter. *The Teetotaller's Companion; Or, A Plea for Temperance*. Ipswich: J. M. Burton, 1847.

Burton, Orville Vernon. *The Age of Lincoln*. 2007. New York: Hill and Wang, 2008.

Carrie. Dir. Brian De Palma. Perf. Sissy Spacek, John Travolta, and Piper Laurie. United Artists, 1976.

Castanga, Joann E. "Arthur, Timothy Shay." *American Masculinities: A Historical Encyclopedia*. Ed. Bret Carroll. Thousand Oaks: Sage, 2004. 35–36.

Chase, Richard. Introduction. *Herman Melville: Selected Tales and Poems*. 1950. New York: Holt, Rinehart and Winston, 1968. v-xix.

Clark, Tom. *Jack Kerouac: A Biography*. New York: Da Capo, 2001.

Claybaugh, Amanda. *The Novel of Purpose: Literature and Social Reform in the Anglo-American World*. Ithaca: Cornell University Press, 2007.

Cohen, Hennig, ed. *Selected Poems of Herman Melville*. New York: Fordham University Press, 1992.

Cohen, Hennig, and Donald Yannella. *Herman Melville's Malcolm Letter: "Man's Final Lore."* New York: Fordham University Press, 1992.

Connell, Royal W., and William P. Mack. *Naval Ceremonies, Customs, and Traditions*. Annapolis: Naval Institute Press, 2004.

Cook, Jonathan. "History, Legend, and Poetic Tradition in Melville's 'The Scout Toward Aldie.'" *American Transcendental Quarterly* 17 (2003): 61–80.

Coon, Dennis. *Psychology: A Modular Approach to Mind and Behavior*. Belmont, CA: Wadsworth, 2006.

Cordell, Ryan. "'Enslaving You Body and Soul': The Uses of Temperance in *Uncle Tom's Cabin* and 'Anti-Tom' Fiction." *Studies in American Fiction* 36 (2008): 3–26.

Currie, Stephen. *Thar She Blows: American Whaling in the Nineteenth Century*. Minneapolis: Lerner, 2001.

Cutton, George Barton. *The Psychology of Alcoholism*. New York: Scribener's, 1907.

Davison, Carol Margaret. "The Gothic and Addiction: A Mad Tango." *Gothic Studies* 11.2 (2009): 1–8.

———. "'Houses of Voluntary Bondage': Theorizing Nineteenth-Century Gothic Pharmography." *Gothic Studies* 12.1 (2010): 68–85.

Deane, Paul. "Herman Melville: Four Views of American Commercial Society." *Revue des Langues Vivants* 34 (1968): 504–507.

Delbanco, Andrew. *Herman Melville: His World and Work*. New York: Knopf, 2005.

Dickerson, James L. *The First Year: Cirrhosis*. New York: Marlowe and Company, 2006.

Dillingham, William B. *Melville's Later Novels*. Athens: University of Georgia Press, 1986.

———. *Melville's Short Fiction*. 1977. Athens: University of Georgia Press, 2008.

Dilworth, Thomas. "Narrator of 'Bartleby': The Christian-Humanist Acquaintance of John Jacob Astor." *Papers on Language and Literature* 38 (2002): 49–75.

Dowling, David. *Chasing the White Whale: The "Moby-Dick" Marathon; or, What Melville Means Today*. Iowa City: University of Iowa Press, 2010.

———. "'Parlors, Sofas, and Fine Cambrics': Gender Play in Melville's Narrations." *Leviathan: A Journal of Melville Studies* 11 (2009): 37–54.

DuPont, Robert L. *The Selfish Brain:*

Learning from Addiction. Center City, MN: Hazelden, 1997.

Easton, Alison. *The Making of the Hawthorne Subject*. Columbia: University of Missouri Press, 1996.

Elliot, Emory. "'Wandering To-and-Fro': Melville and Religion." *A Historical Guide to Herman Melville*. Ed. Giles Gunn. Oxford: Oxford University Press, 2005. 167–204.

Emerson, Ralph Waldo. "The Poet." *Emerson's Essays: First and Second Series*. New York: Gramercy, 1995. 195–217.

Finger, Stanley. *Origins of Neuroscience: A History of Explorations into Brain Function*. Oxford: Oxford University Press, 1994.

Fisher, Marvin. *Going Under: Melville's Short Fiction and the American 1850s*. Baton Rouge: Louisiana State University Press, 1977.

____. "Melville's 'Jimmy Rose': Truly Risen?" *Studies in Short Fiction* 4 (1966): 1–11.

Fitzgerald, F. Scott. *The Great Gatsby*. 1925. Toronto: Penguin, 1950.

Flory, Wendy Stallard. "The Author and the Woman Within in the 'Inside Narrative' of *Pierre*." *Melville and Women*. Eds. Elizabeth Schultz and Haskell Springer. Kent, OH: Kent State University Press, 2006. 121–140.

Fogle, Richard Harter. *Melville's Shorter Tales*. Norman: University of Oklahoma Press, 1960.

Ford, Gene. *The Science of Healthy Drinking*. New York: Wine Appreciation Guild, 2003.

Freeman, John. "The Spiritual Counterpart of *Moby-Dick*." *Critical Essays on Melville's "Pierre."* Eds. Brian Higgins and Hershel Parker. Boston: G. K. Hall, 1983. 113–116.

Furer, Andrew J. "From 'Water Drops' to General Strikes: Nineteenth-and-Early Twentieth-Century Short Fiction and Social Change." *A Companion to the American Short Story*. Eds. Alfred Bendixen and James Nagel. Chischester: Wiley-Blackwell, 2010. 187–214.

Gale, Robert L. *A Herman Melville Encyclopedia*. Westport, CT: Greenwood, 1995.

____. *Plots and Characters in the Fiction and Narrative Poetry of Herman Melville*. Cambridge: MIT Press, 1972.

Garner, Stanton. *The Civil War World of Herman Melville*. Lawrence: University of Kansas Press, 1993.

Garner, Stanton, et al. "Biographers on Biography: A Panel Discussion." *Melville's Evermoving Dawn: Centennial Essays*. Eds. John Bryant and Robert Milder. Kent, OH: Kent State University Press, 1997. 225–258.

Gifford, Maria, Stacey Friedman, and Rich Majerus. *Alcoholism*. Westport, CT: Greenwood, 2010.

Gilje, Paul A. *Liberty on the Waterfront: American Maritime Culture in the Age of Revolution*. Philadelphia: University of Pennsylvania Press, 2004.

Gilman, William H. *Melville's Early Life and "Redburn."* New York: New York University Press, 1951.

Goodwin, Donald. *Is Alcoholism Hereditary?* New York: Ballantine, 1988.

Gunn, Giles B., ed. *A Historical Guide to Herman Melville*. Oxford: Oxford University Press, 2005.

Hage, Erik. *The Melville-Hawthorne Connection: A Study of the Literary Friendship*. Jefferson, NC: McFarland, 2014.

Halttunen, Karen. *Confidence Men and Painted Women: A Study of Middle-Class Culture in America, 1830–1870*. New Haven: Yale University Press, 1982.

Hardwick, Elizabeth. *Herman Melville*. New York: Viking, 2000.

Heflin, Wilson. *Herman Melville's Whaling Years*. Eds. Mary K Bercaw Edwards and Thomas Ferel Heffernan. Nashville: Vanderbilt University Press, 2004.

Horsford, Howard, with Lynn Horth. "Textual Record." *Journals*. By Herman Melville. Evanston: Northwestern University Press, 1989. 211–585.

Hynes, Jennifer. "Temperance Movement." *The Routledge Encyclopedia of Walt Whitman*. Eds. J. R. LeMaster and Donald Kummings. New York: Routledge, 1998. 709–710.

Isaacson, Walter. *Benjamin Franklin: An American Life*. New York: Simon & Schuster, 2003.

Jellineck, E. M. *The Disease Concept of Alcoholism*. New Haven: Hillhouse, 1960.

Johnson, Bradley A. *The Characteristic Theology of Herman Melville: Aesthetics, Politics, Duplicity*. Eugene: Pickwick Publications, 2012.

Karcher, Carolyn. *Shadow Over the Promised Land: Slavery, Race, and Violence in Melville's America*. Baton Rouge: Louisiana State University Press, 1980.

Kellerman, Joseph L. *Alcoholism: A Merry-go-round Named Denial*. Center City, MN: Hazelden, 1975.

Kelley, Wyn. *Melville's City: Literary and Urban Form in Nineteenth-Century New York*. Cambridge: Cambridge University Press, 1996.

Kerrigan, William. *Johnny Appleseed and the American Orchard: A Cultural History*. Baltimore: Johns Hopkins University Press, 2012.

Kirby, David. *Herman Melville*. New York: Continuum, 1993.

Kovic, Christine Marie. "Demanding Their Dignity as Daughters of God: Catholic Women and Human Rights." *Women on Chiapas*. Eds. Christine Engla and Christine Marie Kovic. New York: Routledge, 2003.

Kring, Walter D., and Jonathan S. Carey. "Two Discoveries Concerning Herman Melville." *Proceedings of the Massachusetts Historical Society* 87 (1975): 137–141.

Laing, Olivia. *The Trip to Echo Spring: Why Writers Drink*. Edinburgh: Canongate Books, 2013.

Lamas, Maria. *The Glass*. Philadelphia: Martin E. Harmstead, 1849.

Laskin, David. *A Common Life: Four Generations of American Literary Friendship and Influence*. New York: Simon & Schuster, 1994.

A Letter to the Mechanics of Boston, Respecting the Formation of a City Temperance Society. Boston: Society for the Suppression of Intemperance, 1831.

Levander, Caroline. "The Female Subject of *Pierre* and *The Piazza Tales*." *A Companion to Herman Melville*. Ed. Wyn Kelley. Oxford: Blackwell, 2006.

Levine, Robert S. "Fiction and Reform I." *The Columbia History of the American Novel*. Ed. Emory Elliot et al. Oxford: Oxford University Press, 1991. 130–154.

Leyda, Jay. Introduction. *The Portable Melville*. Ed. Jay Leyda. New York: Viking, 1951. xi-xxii.

———. *The Melville Log: A Documentary Life of Herman Melville, 1819–1891*. 1951. 2 vols. New York: Gordian, 1969 (with supplement).

Lindberg, Gary. *The Confidence Man in American Literature*. Oxford: Oxford University Press, 1982.

Manzardo, Ann M., et al. *Alcoholism*, 4th ed. Oxford: Oxford University Press, 2008.

Markels, Julian. *Melville and the Politics of Identity: From "King Lear" to "Moby-Dick."* Urbana: University of Illinois Press, 1993.

Marovitz, Sanford E. "Shakespearean Resonances in *Moby-Dick* and *Pierre*." *Melville Among the Nations: Proceedings of an International Conference, Volos, Greece, July 2–6, 1997*. Eds. Sanford E. Marovitz and A. C. Christodoulou. Kent, OH: Kent State University Press, 2001. 267–276.

Marx, Leo. "Melville's Parable of the Walls." *Melville's Short Novels*. Ed. Dan McCall. New York: Norton, 2002. 239–256.

Matheson, T. J. "Poe's 'The Black Cat' as a Critique of Temperance Literature." *Mosaic* 19 (1986): 69–81.

Mathiessen, F. O. *American Renaissance*. 1941. Oxford: Oxford University Press, 1968.

Mattingly, Carol. Introduction. *Water Drops for Women: A Temperance Reader*. Ed. Carol Mattingly. Carbondale: Southern Illinois University Press, 2004. 1–18.

Maurer, David. *The Big Con*. 1940. New York: Random House, 2011.

McCall, Dan. *The Silence of "Bartleby."* Ithaca: Cornell University Press, 1989.

Bibliography

McCarthy, Paul. *"The Twisted Mind": Madness in Herman Melville's Fiction.* Iowa City: University of Iowa Press, 1990.

McGrath, Patrick. Foreword. *Herman Melville: "Bartleby, the Scrivener" and "Benito Cereno."* By Herman Melville. London: Hesperus, 2007. vii-ix.

Meade, Marion. *Dorothy Parker: What Fresh Hell is This?* New York: Penguin, 1989.

Meltzer, Milton. *Edgar Allan Poe: A Biography.* Minneapolis: Lerner, 2003.

———. *Herman Melville: A Biography.* Minneapolis: Lerner, 2006.

Melville, Herman. "The Apple-Tree Table." 1856. *Great Short Works of Herman Melville.* 1969. Ed. and intro. Warner Berthoff. New York: Perennial Classics, 2004. 362–382.

———. "Bartleby, the Scrivener." 1853. *Great Short Works of Herman Melville.* 1969. Ed. and intro. Warner Berthoff. New York: Perennial Classics, 2004. 39–74.

———. *Billy Budd, Sailor (An Inside Narrative).* 1924. Eds. Harrison Hayford and Merton M. Sealts, Jr. Chicago: University of Chicago Press, 1962.

———. "Bridegroom Dick." 1888. *Selected Poems of Herman Melville.* Ed. and intro. Robert Penn Warren. New York: Barnes and Noble, 1970. 285–304.

———. *Clarel.* 1876. Ed. Walter E. Bezanson. New York: Hendricks House, 1960.

———. "Cock-A-Doodle-Doo!" 1853. *Great Short Works of Herman Melville.* 1969. Ed. and intro. Warner Berthoff. New York: Perennial Classics, 2004. 75–97.

———. *The Confidence-Man.* 1857. Oxford: Oxford University Press, 1989.

———. *Correspondence.* Ed. Lynn Horth. Evanston: Northwestern University Press, 1993.

———. "The Encantadas." 1854. *Great Short Works of Herman Melville.* 1969. Ed. and intro. Warner Berthoff. New York: Perennial Classics, 2004. 98–150.

———. "The Fiddler." 1854. *Great Short Works of Herman Melville.* 1969. Ed. and intro. Warner Berthoff. New York: Perennial Classics, 2004. 195–201.

———. "I and My Chimney." 1856. *Great Short Works of Herman Melville.* Ed. and intro. Warner Berthoff. 1969. New York: Perennial Classics, 2004. 327–354.

———. *Israel Potter.* 1855. Eds. Harrison Hayford, Hershel Parker, and G. Thomas Tanselle. Evanston: Northwestern University Press, 1982.

———. "Jimmy Rose." 1855. *Great Short Works of Herman Melville.* 1969. Ed. and intro. Warner Berthoff. New York: Perennial Classics, 2004. 316–326.

———. *Journals.* Ed. Howard C. Horsford with Lynn Horth. Evanston: Northwestern University Press, 1989.

———. *Mardi.* 1849. Eds. Harrison Hayford, Hershel Parker, and G. Thomas Tanselle. Evanston: Northwestern University Press, 1986.

———. *Moby-Dick.* 1851. Eds. Hershel Parker and Harrison Hayford, 2d ed. New York: Norton, 2002.

———. *Omoo.* 1847. Mineola: Dover, 2000.

———. "The Paradise of Bachelors and the Tartarus of Maids." 1855. *Great Short Works of Herman Melville.* 1969. Ed. and intro. Warner Berthoff. New York: Perennial Classics, 2004. 202–222.

———. *Pierre.* 1852. Eds. Harrison Hayford, Hershel Parker, and G. Thomas Tanselle. Evanston: Northwestern University Press, 1971.

———. "Poor Man's Pudding and Rich Man's Crumbs." 1854. *Great Short Works of Herman Melville.* 1969. Ed. and intro. Warner Berthoff. New York: Perennial Classics, 2004. 165–178.

———. *Redburn.* 1849. Eds. Harrison Hayford and G. Thomas Tanselle. Evanston: Northwestern University Press, 1975.

———. "The Scout Toward Aldie." *Selected Poems of Herman Melville.* Ed. Robert Penn Warren. New York: Barnes & Noble, 1970. 285–301.

———. "The Two Temples." 1924. *Great*

Short Works of Herman Melville. 1969. Ed. and intro. Warner Berthoff. New York: Perennial Classics, 2004. 151–164.

———. *Typee.* 1846. Eds. Harrison Hayford, Hershel Parker, and G. Thomas Tanselle. Evanston: Northwestern University Press, 1973.

———. "Under the Rose." 1924. *Herman Melville: Tales, Poems, and Other Writings.* Ed. John Bryant. New York: Modern Library, 2002. 441–446.

———. *White-Jacket.* 1850. Eds. Harrison Hayford, Hershel Parker, and G. Thomas Tanselle. Evanston: Northwestern University Press, 1970.

Meindl, Dieter. *Fiction and the Metaphysics of the Grotesque.* Columbia: University of Missouri Press, 1996.

Metcalf, Eleanor Melville. *Herman Melville: Cycle and Epicycle.* Cambridge: Cambridge University Press, 1953.

Metcalf, Paul, ed. *Enter Isabel: The Herman Melville Correspondence of Clare Spark and Paul Metcalf.* Albuquerque: University of New Mexico Press, 1991.

Meyers, Jeffrey. *Hemingway: A Biography.* New York: Da Capo, 1986.

Michelsohn, Lynn. Afterword. *In the Galapagos with Herman Melville: "The Encantadas; or Enchanted Isles."* By Herman Melville. Roswell: Cleanan Press, 2011. 139.

Milder, Robert. *Exiled Royalties: Melville and the Life We Imagine.* Oxford: Oxford University Press, 2006.

———. Introduction. *"Billy Budd, Sailor" and Selected Tales.* Ed. Robert Milder. Oxford: Oxford University Press, 1997. vii-xxxix.

Mihm, Stephen. *A Nation of Counterfeiters: Capitalists, Con Men, and the Making of and the United States.* Cambridge: Harvard University Press, 2009.

Miles, Robert. "'Tranced Griefs': Herman Melville's *Pierre* and the Origins of the Gothic." *ELH* 66 (1999): 157–177.

Miller, Brett C. *Elizabeth Bishop: Life and the Memory of It.* Berkeley: University of California Press, 1993.

Miller, Edwin Haviland. *Melville.* New York: George Braziller, 1975.

Miller, J. Hillis. *Versions of Pygmalion.* Cambridge: Cambridge University Press, 1990.

Miller, James E., Jr. *A Reader's Guide to Herman Melville.* New York: Noonday, 1962.

Milligan, Barry. "Morphine Addicted Doctors, The English Opium Eater, and Embattled Medical Authority." *Victorian Literature and Culture* 33 (2005): 541–553.

Minter, David. *William Faulkner: His Life and Work.* Baltimore: Johns Hopkins University Press, 1997.

Mumford, Lewis. *Herman Melville.* New York: Harcourt, Brace, 1929.

Nadelblaft, Jerome. "Alcohol and Wife Abuse in Antebellum Male Temperance Literature." *Canadian Review of American Studies* 25 (1995): 15–44.

Newman, Lea Bertani Vozar. *A Reader's Guide to the Short Stories of Herman Melville.* Boston: G. K. Hall, 1986.

Nordhoff, Charles. *Man of War Life: A Boy's Experiencing in the United States Navy, During a Voyage Around the World, in a Ship of the Line.* Cincinnati: Moore, Wilstach, Keys, 1856.

Olson, Charles. *Call Me Ishmael.* 1947. Baltimore: Johns Hopkins University Press, 1997.

O'Reilly, Edward. *F. Scott Fitzgerald: A Biography.* Westport, CT: Greenwood, 2005.

Paliwoda, Daniel. *Melville and the Theme of Boredom.* Jefferson, NC: McFarland, 2010.

Parker, Hershel. "Damned by Dollars: *Moby-Dick* and the Price of Genius." *Moby-Dick.* By Herman Melville. 1851. Eds. Hershel Parker and Harrison Hayford, 2d ed. New York: Norton, 2002. 713–724.

———. *Herman Melville: A Biography*, 2 vols. Baltimore: Johns Hopkins University Press, 1996–2002.

———. "Herman Melville's *The Isle of the Cross*: A Survey and a Chronology." *American Literature* 62 (1990): 1–16.

Parker, Hershel, and Harrison Hayford,

eds. *Moby-Dick*. By Herman Melville. 1851. 2d ed. New York: Norton, 2002.

Parks, Franklin. *William Parks: An American Life: The Colonial Printer in the Transatlantic World of the Eighteenth Century*. University Park: Pennsylvania State University Press, 2012.

Post-Lauria, Shelia. *Correspondent Colorings: Melville in the Market Place*. Amherst: University of Massachusetts Press, 1996.

Pritchard, George. *The Aggressions of the French at Tahiti and Other Islands in the Pacific*. Auckland: Auckland University Press, 1983.

Rampersad, Arnold. *Melville's "Israel Potter": A Pilgrimage and Progress*. Bowling Green, OH: Bowling Green University Popular Press, 1969.

Reed, Thomas L., Jr. *The Transforming Draught: "Jekyll and Hyde," Robert Louis Stevenson, and the Victorian Alcohol Debate*. Jefferson, NC: McFarland, 2006.

Reiff, Raychel Haugrud. *Herman Melville: "Moby-Dick" and Other Works*. Tarrytown: Marshall Cavendish, 2008.

Renker, Elizabeth. "Herman Melville, Wife Beating, and the Written Page." *American Literature* 66 (1994): 123–150.

Reynolds, David S. *Beneath the American Renaissance: The Subversive Imagination in the Age Emerson and Melville*. Oxford: Oxford University Press, 1988.

_____. "Black Cats and Delirium Tremens: Temperance and the American Renaissance." *The Serpent in the Cup: Temperance in American Literature*. Eds. Debra Rosenthal and David S. Reynolds. Amherst: University of Massachusetts Press, 1997. 22–59.

Ries, Richard K., David A. Fiellin, Shannon C. Miller, and Richard Saitz. *Principles of Addiction Medicine*, 4th ed. Philadelphia: Lippincott Williams, 2009.

Robertson-Lorant, Laurie. *Melville: A Biography*. New York: Clarkson Potter, 1996.

_____. "Melville and the Women in his Life." *Melville and Women*. Eds. Elizabeth Schultz and Haskell Springer. Kent: Kent State University Press, 2006. 15–37.

_____. "Mr. Omoo and the Hawthornes: The Biographical Background." *Hawthorne and Melville: Writing a Relationship*. Eds. Jana L. Argersinger and Leland S. Pearson. Athens: University of Georgia Press, 2008. 27–49.

Rogin, Michael Paul. *Subversive Genealogy: The Politics and Art of Herman Melville*. 1979. New York: Knopf, 1983.

Rollyson, Carl, and Lisa Paddock. *Herman Melville A to Z: The Essential Reference to His Life and Work*. New York: Facts on File, 2001.

Rollyson, Carl, Lisa Paddock, and April Gentry. *Critical Companion to Herman Melville: A Literary Reference to His Life and Work*. New York: Facts on File, 2007.

Rorabaugh, W. J. *The Alcoholic Republic: An American Tradition*. Oxford: Oxford University Press, 1979.

Rose, Kenneth D. *American Women and the Repeal of Prohibition*. New York: New York University Press, 1996.

Rosen, Roma. *Melville's Use of Shakespeare's Plays*. Evanston: Northwestern University Press, 1962.

Rosenthal, Debra. "Temperance and Miscegenation in Whitman's *Franklin Evans*." *Race and Mixture in Nineteenth-Century U.S. & Spanish American Fiction*. Chapel Hill: North Carolina University Press, 2004. 52–68.

Rosenthal, Debra, and David S. Reynolds. Introduction. *The Serpent in the Cup: Temperance in American Literature*. Eds. Debra Rosenthal and David S. Reynolds. Amherst: University of Massachusetts Press, 1997. 1–9.

Ross, John J. "The Many Ailments of Herman Melville." *Journal of Medical Biography* 16 (2008): 21–29.

Ryan, Steven. "The Gothic Formula of 'Bartleby.'" *Arizona Quarterly* 34 (1978): 311–316.

Said, Edward. Introduction. *Moby-Dick*. By Herman Melville. 1851. New York: Library of America, 2010. xiii-xxix.

Sallinger, Sharon V. *Taverns and Drinking in Early America.* Baltimore: Johns Hopkins University Press, 2002.

Sanchez-Eppler, Karen. "Temperance in the Bed of a Child: Incest and Social Order in Nineteenth-Century America." *American Quarterly* 47 (1995): 1–33.

Sandberg, Alvin, "Erotic Patterns in 'The Paradise of Bachelors and the Tartarus of Maids.'" *Literature and Psychology* 18 (1968): 2–8.

Schultz, Elizabeth, and Haskell Springer, eds. *Melville and Women.* Kent, OH: Kent State University Press, 2006.

Sealts, Merton M., Jr. "Notes on 'Jimmy Rose.'" *The Piazza Tales and Other Prose Pieces, 1839–1860.* Eds. Harrison Hayford, Hershel Parker, and G. Thomas Tanselle. Evanston: Northwestern University Press, 1987. 712–713.

Serlin, Henry David. "The Dialogue of Gender in Melville's 'The Paradise of Bachelors and the Tartarus of Maids.'" *Modern Language Studies* 25 (1995): 80–87.

Shniedman, Edwin. S. "Some Psychological Reflections on the Death of Malcolm Melville." *Suicide and Life-Threatening Behavior* 6 (1976): 231–242.

Snodgrass, Mary Ellen. *Encyclopedia of Gothic Literature.* New York: Facts on File, 2008.

Sonnenstuhl, William J. *Working Sober: The Transformation of an Occupational Drinking Culture.* Ithaca: Cornell University Press, 1996.

Spooner, Catherine. *Fashioning Gothic Bodies.* Manchester: Manchester University Press, 2004.

Stich, Klaus P. "Well Tempered Temperance Hawthorne's Dionysian Aspect." *The New England Quarterly* 68 (1995): 83–105.

Summerfield, Jenny, and Lyn van Oudtshoom. *Counselling in the Workplace.* Wiltshire: Cromwell Press, 2000.

Talley, Sharon. *Student Companion to Herman Melville.* Westport, CT: Greenwood, 2007.

Terkeltaub, Robert. *Gout and Other Crystal Arthropathies.* Philadelphia: Elsevier Saunders, 2012.

Thompson, Corey Evan. "Herman Melville's 'The Apple-Tree Table' as Temperance Fiction." *The Explicator* 71 (2013): 135–139.

____. "The Locale of Melville's Gothicism." *Papers on Language and Literature* 43 (2007): 190–204.

____. "Melville's 'Cock-A-Doodle-Doo!': A Case Study in Bipolar Disorder." *American Transcendental Quarterly* 17 (2003): 43–53.

____. "Melville's 'The Apple-Tree Table.'" *The Explicator* 64 (2005): 38–41.

____. "The Prodromal Phase of Alcoholism in Herman Melville's 'Bartleby, the Scrivener' and 'Cock-A-Doodle-Doo!'" *The Explicator* 71 (2013): 275–280.

Thorp, Willard. "Herman Melville." *Literary History of the United States,* 3d rev ed. Eds. Robert E. Spiller et al. London: Macmillan, 1969. 441–471.

Vick, Dwight, and Elizabeth Rhoades. *Drugs and Alcohol in the 21st-Century: Theory, Behavior, and Policy.* New York: Jones and Bartlett, 2010.

Warner, Nicholas O. "God's Wine and Devil's Wine: The Idea of Intoxication in Emerson." *Mosaic* 19 (1986): 55–68.

Warren, Robert Penn. Introduction. *Selected Poems of Herman Melville.* Ed. Robert Penn Warren. New York: Barnes and Noble, 1970. 3–88.

Weinauer, Ellen. "Women, Ownership, and Gothic Manhood in *Pierre.*" *Melville and Women.* Eds. Elizabeth Schultz and Haskell Springer. Kent, OH: Kent State University Press, 2006. 141–160.

Welter, Barbara. "The Cult of True Womanhood: 1820–1860." *American Quarterly* 18 (1966): 151–174.

White, Christopher G. *Unsettled Minds: Psychology and the American Search for Spiritual Assurance.* Berkeley: University of California Press, 2009.

White, William. "The Lessons of Language: Historical Perspectives on the Rhetoric of Addiction." *Altering American Consciousness: The History* of *Drug and Alcohol Use in the United States, 1800–2000*. Eds. Sarah W. Tracy and Caroline Jean Acker. Amherst: University of Massachusetts Press, 2004. 33–60.

Winter, Thomas. "Confidence Man." *American Masculinities: A Historical Encyclopedia*. Ed. Bret E. Carroll. London: Sage, 2003.

World Health Organization. *Global Status Report on Alcohol and Health*. Geneva: World Health Organization, 2014.

Worth, Richard. *Teetotallers and Saloon Smashers: The Temperance Movement and Prohibition*. New York: Enslow, 2009.

Wright, Daniel. "'The Prisonhouse of my Disposition': A Study of the Psychology of Addiction in *Dr. Jekyll and Mr. Hyde*." *Studies in the Novel* 26 (1994): 254–267.

Zeiger, Susan. *Inventing the Addict: Drugs, Race, and Sexuality in Nineteenth-Century British and American Literature*. Amherst: University of Massachusetts Press, 2009.

Zimmerman, Brett. *Edgar Allan Poe: Rhetoric and Style*. Montreal: McGill-Queen's University Press, 2005.

Index

addiction narratives 102–110; *see also* Gothic pharmographies
Adler, George 44, 53, 138–140
alcohol(ism): in America 1, 17–20; death caused by 111–119; defined by 30; as disease 30–31; drunken American stereotype 18–19; for escape 30–42, 170*n*3; and health 88–96; and Melville 5–6, 136–150; and Melville's relatives 121, 125–128; and poverty 96–100, 129; and professional reputations 79–87, 125–128; and selfishness/trustworthiness 43–63, 100; transformative effects of 101–110, 130–132
Alcott, Louisa May 20
"The Apple-Tree Table" 8, 10–11, 20, 22, 24–29, 101, 121; narrator 24–29, 101–102, 117, 151; narrator's wife 24–29, 101, 151
Arthur, Timothy Shay 20, 62, 168*n*14

"Bartleby, the Scrivener" 7, 11, 13, 34–37, 92, 103, 106; Bartleby 34–36; narrator 34–36, 106, 152; Turkey 34–37, 42, 73, 106, 121, 130, 152, 171*n*8
"The Bell Tower" 7; 165*n*13
Bellows, the Rev. Henry Whitney 131–132, 185*n*17
"Benito Cereno" 7, 13, 36, 89–90; Babo 90; Captain Amasa Delano 90, 152; Captain Don Benito Cereno 90

Billy Budd, Sailor 7, 11–12, 51, 54, 57–58, 63, 86–87; Billy Budd 58; Captain Graveling 58, 152; Captain Vere 58; John Claggart 57–58, 87; Lieutenant Ratcliffe 58, 152
Bishop, Elizabeth 164*n*2
"The Black Cat" 103, 105
Blair, Sen. Henry William 89
Bleak House 114
Boston Society for the Suppression of Intemperance 18
"Bridegroom Dick" 8, 12–13, 65–66, 107–109; Captain Turret 107–109, 130, 152; the Finn 107–108; Lieutenant Tom Tight 66–67, 152
Brown, Charles Brockden 114
Burne, Peter 30

Carrie (film and novel) 114
"The Cask of Amontillado" 65
Clarel 8, 13, 31, 105, 166*n*15; the Arnaut 105, 153; the Cypriote 31, 166*n*15; the Cypriote's lady 153, 166*n*15; Derwent 105; the Lesbian 105
Coan, Titus Munson 130, 148–149
"Cock-A-Doodle-Doo!" 7, 10–11, 13, 20, 22–24, 29, 37–39, 92, 96–97, 105–106, 121, 129; bill collector (dun) 38, 106, 153; Jake 38, 106, 153; Merrymusk 22–24, 37, 39, 153; Merrymusk's wife 23–24, 39, 153; narra-

· INDEX ·

tor 22–24, 37–39, 42, 73, 96–97, 105–106, 117, 121, 130, 153
Confessions of a Female Inebriate 92–93
The Confidence-Man 7, 12–13, 44, 52, 65, 68–70, 89, 91–93, 118; Charles Arnold Noble 44, 68–70, 153; Francis Goodman 44, 68–70, 154; old lady of Goshen 91–93, 118, 128, 154; old lady of Goshen's doctor 93, 154; old lady of Goshen's husband (the deacon) 93, 154
confidence men 12, 64–78, 116

dark temperance literature 111–119, 132
Darwin, Charles 77
"The Death Craft" 178*n*9
De Palma, Brian 114
De Quincey, Thomas 102, 180*n*4
Dickens, Charles 114, 137; *Bleak House* 114; *Hard Times* 137, 186*n*3
Doppelgänger 13, 103–104, 107–110
Duyckinck, Evert A. 44, 124–125, 138, 143, 149

Easton, Virgil 102
Emerson, Ralph Waldo 5, 147
"The Encantadas" 7, 12, 71, 75–78; Oberlus 75–78, 154
"Etchings of a Whaling Cruise" 184*n*7

Faulkner, William 5
"The Fiddler" 7, 166*n*14, 172*n*27
Fitzgerald, F. Scott 5, 48; *The Great Gatsby* 48, 173*n*12
"Fragments from a Writing Desk" 178*n*9

Gansevoort, Guert (cousin) 126–127
Gansevoort, Henry (cousin) 148
Gothic literature 24, 27, 103–104, 170*n*28, 181*n*11;
Gothic pharmographies 103–104; *see also* addiction narratives
The Great Gatsby 48, 173*n*12
Greene, Richard Tobias 81, 137, 166*n*20, 178*n*10, 186*n*5
Griswold, Captain Robert 138–140
Gulick, John Thomas 130, 148–149

"The Happy Failure" 7
Hard Times 137, 186*n*3
Hawthorne, Nathaniel 5, 44, 122–125, 129–130, 135, 142–147, 149; *The House of the Seven Gables* 20; "A Rill from the Town Pump" 20, 183*n*2; *The Scarlet Letter* 20; *Twice Told Tales* 20
"Hawthorne and His Mosses" 82–83, 124, 184*n*7
Hemingway, Ernest 5
Hoffman, E. T. A. 103–104
The House of the Seven Gables 20
Huss, Dr. Magnus 30

"I and My Chimney" 7, 170*n*26
The Isle of the Cross 174*n*1, 187*n*12, 188*n*14
Israel Potter 7, 10–12, 18, 20–22, 29, 71–74, 121; Benjamin Franklin (fictional) 21–22, 72, 74, 154; Benjamin Franklin (historical) 21; Horne Tooke 72–73; inn's landlord 18, 154; Israel Potter 18, 21–22, 71–74, 78, 154; Israel Potter's kidnappers 73–74, 154; James Bridges 72–73; Squire John Woodcock 21, 72–73

Jackson, Dr. James 89
Jellinek, Dr. E.M. 11, 31
"Jimmy Rose" 8, 11, 45, 48–51, 54, 122; Jimmy Rose 48–51, 155; partygoers 48–51, 155; William Ford 48–51, 170*n*26

Kerouac, Jack 5
King, Stephen 114

Lamas, Maria 182*n*2

Mardi 7, 13, 89, 95–96, 102; Borabolla (King of Mondoldo) 95–96, 155; Hautia 155, 167*n*24; King Donjalolo (Fonoo) 102; Taji (narrator) 102, 155, 175*n*8
Mather, Cotton 26, 28
McCurdy, Theodore 138–140
Melvill, Allan (father) 79
Melvill, Priscilla (aunt) 121
Melvill, Thomas Wilson (cousin) 125–126
Melville, Allan (brother) 53, 125, 127, 149
Melville, Elizabeth (daughter) 6, 53
Melville, Elizabeth (wife) 6, 53, 131–134, 142, 150

Index

Melville, Frances (daughter) 6, 53
Melville, Herman: drinking by 5–6, 136–150; and finances 12, 79–80, 129–130, 184*n*11; and Hawthorne 122–124, 142–147, 187*n*12; and health 6, 52–53, 128–129; and lecturing 147–148; and Malcolm's death 132–134; purportedly abusive nature of 6, 130–132, 185*n*16, 185*n*17; and teaching 79–80; and travels 80, 122, 137–149, 182*n*4; and women 131, 169*n*22; works by *see individual titles*
Melville, Malcolm (son) 6, 53, 132–134
Melville, Stanwix (son) 6, 53
"Mr. Parkman's Tour" 184*n*7
Moby-Dick 7–8, 10, 12, 13, 20, 22, 32, 36, 45, 51, 54, 62–63, 102, 116–118, 124, 129; Aunt Charity 20, 155; Captain Ahab 116–118, 155, 183*n*13; Dr. Jack Bunger 54, 155; Dough-Boy 20; *Grampus*'s crew 45–46, 62–63, 155, 180*n*9; Ishmael 102; Jonah 62–63, 155–156, 180*n*9; *Pequod*'s crew 116–117, 156; Perth 117–118, 156, 183*n*13; Perth's wife and children 117–118, 156; Queequeg 102; Starbuck 116, 182*n*9

Nordhoff, Charles 39

Omoo 7, 11–13, 15, 54–59, 63, 70, 80–81, 85–86, 89, 98–99, 107–110; Armand-Joseph Bruat 70, 156; Bungs 55–57, 125, 156; Captain Crash 58–59, 156, 179*n*13; Captain Guy 57, 85–86, 99, 107, 156; Chips 55–56, 125, 157; Dr. Long Ghost 85–86, 94–95, 98–99, 107–108, 128, 130, 157; fourteen-year-old girl 59, 157; French soldiers 109–110, 157; John Jermin 81, 108–109, 130, 157; Kitoti 70, 157; Old Mother Tot 157, 175*n*6; Tahitian islanders 70, 109–110, 157; Varvy 94–95, 99, 157; Wilson 57, 157, 175*n*6

"The Paradise of Bachelors" 8, 11, 45–48, 51, 54, 122; narrator 45–48; nine bachelors 45–48, 158; R.F.C. 45, 158
Parker, Dorothy 164*n*2
"The Piazza" 7

Pierre 7, 11, 13, 31–33, 52, 103–105, 148; Isabel Banford 32–33, 104–105, 158; Isabel Banford's foster parents 104–105, 158; Mary Glendinning 31–32, 37, 158; Pierre Glendinning 31–33, 37, 73, 104, 158
Poe, Edgar Allan 5, 65, 103–104; "The Black Cat" 103, 105; "The Cask of Amontillado" 65
"Poor Man's Pudding and Rich Man's Crumbs" 166*n*15

Redburn 7–8, 11, 13, 15, 51, 54–55, 62–63, 89–91, 97–100, 112–116, 129; Captain Riga 99–100, 158; the Greenlander 54–55, 91, 158; Harry Bolton 99; Liverpool's bartenders 62, 158; Liverpool's destitute 97–98, 158–159; Miguel Saveda 114–116, 159; passed out drinker on tomb 113–114, 159; shrieking suicidal drunken sailor 112–113, 159; stuttering passenger 54–55, 159; Tobias Drinker 113–114, 159; Wellingborough Redburn 90–91, 97, 99–100, 115, 159
"A Rill from the Town Pump" 20, 183*n*2

Savage, Samuel 145–146
The Scarlet Letter 20
"The Scout Toward Aldie" 8, 12, 66–67; the Colonel 67, 159; Reb 67, 159
Shakespeare, William 32
Shaw, Lemuel (father-in-law) 52–53, 121, 129, 145
Shaw, Samuel 185*n*17
Shepard, Isaac 92; *Confessions of a Female Inebriate* 92–93
Shepherd, Daniel 130, 149, 185*n*13
Sigourney, Lydia Howard Huntley 20
Smith, William Henry 168*n*11
Stanton, Elizabeth Cady 20
Stevenson, Robert Louis 103–104; *The Strange Case of Dr. Jekyll and Mr. Hyde* 103, 105
Stoker, Bram 103
Stowe, Harriet Beecher 20
The Strange Case of Dr. Jekyll and Mr. Hyde 103, 105

Taylor, Dr. Frank 44, 53, 138–140
temperance literature 10–11, 17–29, 121

Index

temperance movement 10–11, 18–20
Thompson, William 64–65
Thoreau, Henry David 147
Tolstoy, Leo 102
Twice Told Tales 20
"The Two Temples" 8, 18, 166n16, 168n7; narrator 18, 159; young English boy bartender 18, 159
Typee 7, 12, 54, 80–83; English harbor pilot 81–83, 87, 160; King Mehevi 54, 160

"Under the Rose" 8, 172n25; the Ambassador 172n25; Greek translator 160, 172n25

Washingtonians 19
White-Jacket 2–3, 7–8, 11–13, 15, 25, 39–42, 51, 54, 59–63, 80–81, 83–85, 91, 94–95, 112, 142; Bland 61–62, 160; Captain Claret 61–62, 160, 179n15; Cockswain 60, 160; Landless (Happy Jack) 40, 160; Lieutenant Bridewell 84–85; Mad Jack 83, 85, 160–161, 179n14, 179n15, Mandeville 83–85, 87, 94–95, 128, 161; old toper of a top-man 161; Pills 91; Scriggs 61–62, 161; sheet-anchor man 40, 161; Yarn 60, 161
Whitman, Walt 20
Woman Question 1, 25, 131–132, 170n25
World Health Organization 17

www.ingramcontent.com/pod-product-compliance
Lightning Source LLC
Chambersburg PA
CBHW061348300426
44116CB00011B/2037